W9-CZM-366

John F. Kennedy
and the
Business
Community

John F. Kennedy and the Business Community

Jim F. Heath

37825

THE UNIVERSITY OF CHICAGO PRESS

CHICAGO AND LONDON

To Carole

Standard Book Number: 226–32231–9
Library of Congress Catalog Card Number: 75–82114

THE UNIVERSITY OF CHICAGO PRESS, CHICAGO 60637
THE UNIVERSITY OF CHICAGO PRESS, LTD., LONDON W.C. 1

Contents

Preface

As one of the powerful forces in American society, business is intimately involved in nearly all parts of contemporary life. Private enterprise significantly influences, and is influenced by, the policies and actions of the federal establishment. Interest in traditional domestic issues—taxes, economic growth, inflation, industrial relations, antitrust, and the freedom of the marketplace—commingles with concern for international problems—foreign aid, world trade, the cold war, and the balance of payments. This book is an early look at Kennedy's relations with the business community, or more precisely, the nonmonolithic business communities. It is essentially an economic history of the New Frontier years with the focus on the relationship between free enterprise and government rather than on economic theory.

The tragic assassination of a respected and popular leader makes his admirers more ardent in their defense of his deeds while substantially muting the attacks of all but his most insensitive critics. For this reason November 22, 1963, was a watershed for students of the career of John Fitzgerald Kennedy. It is likely that many years will pass before responsible adversaries of the late president will express their antagonism in the same fashion that they did while he was alive. Even so, observations, pro and con, made after his death cannot avoid being influenced at least to some degree by his martyrdom.

Early in the genesis of this study, I approached a number of prominent business leaders, posing specific questions about the relationship between the New Frontier and the private sector. In some instances, answers to my questions were restricted to use without source. The responses that I received reinforced my initial belief that I could more correctly appraise my subject by concentrating on public expressions made about the president, his administration, and his policies before his assassination. The writings, speeches, and comments before congressional hearings by businessmen, coupled with editorial opinion in business publications, were a treasury of information. On the government side, the public papers of Kennedy, the memoirs and letters of his advisers, and a wide variety of government documents provided the basis of my research.

As new information becomes available, this topic will be reexamined many times. But as the historian Allan Nevins said of his studies of Franklin D. Roosevelt, it is never too soon to evaluate the place of such a leader in the stream of American and world events. Every generation makes its own estimate of the past; appraisals of Kennedy made today will be reassessed many times in the future with the benefit of longer perspective and fuller knowledge.

Few if any books are the author's alone. I received assistance and encouragement from many people. This project was begun at the suggestion of Thomas A. Bailey, Byrne Professor of American History at Stanford University. The debt I owe to him for his patient counsel can be fully appreciated only by those who have had the opportunity to work with this distinguished scholar. For probing questions and respected advice, I am also especially grateful to Stanford Professor Barton J. Bernstein.

My study was also read by Professors Otis Pease of the University of Washington, Jesse Gilmore of Portland State College, Mark Mancall of Stanford, A. B. Rollins, Jr., of the University of Vermont, and Walter W. Heller, the chairman of Kennedy's Council of Economic Advisers—now of the University of Minnesota. Dr. Heller's comments were particularly valuable, but each reader helped to make the book better than it otherwise would have been. Any errors that remain are mine alone.

A generous fellowship from Stanford University made the writing of my doctoral dissertation on this subject immeasurably more pleasant. The assistance provided by Professor Gilmore and the Department of History at Portland State College eased the chore of revising a dissertation into a book. As one who types by the laborious hunt-and-peck method, I have nothing but admiration for the four fine typists—Maria Devendorf, Kathy Hansen, Carolyn Wilton, and Sherrie Axtell—who worked on my manuscript at various stages. Thanks are due also to William Lenon, a graduate student at Portland State, who prepared much of the index.

I owe my greatest debt to my wife, Carole, for her prodding criticism, indispensable encouragement, and love; and to my daughters, Nancy and Ann, for their patience with a writing father who all too often was "bearish" rather than attentive.

1

The New Frontier: Campaign and Interregnum

For many, the story of John F. Kennedy and the business community revolves around the widely publicized and dramatic steel crisis of April 1962. While this was the most famous confrontation between the president and business, it was only one of many areas of friction and potential friction. The experience of the Kennedy administration added a new link to the long chain of contention between private enterprise and government. Populism, Progressivism, the New Deal, and the Fair Deal are familiar landmarks in American history. In each the dialogue between the public and private sectors was frequently discordant.

Such disagreement is not necessarily unhealthy. It may be reasonably argued that the proper relationship between business and government is one of tempered antagonism, with neither the captive of the other.[1]

This does not imply that cooperation between these two giant forces is undesirable. Nor was cooperation nonexistent during the Kennedy years. Coming upon the heels of eight years of Republican control of the executive branch, however, the Kennedy administration was subject to natural suspicion by businessmen. A common assessment of the election of Eisenhower in 1952 was that America was ready for a breathing spell: a time to rest, to regroup, and to enjoy the fruits of the remarkable technological advancement stimulated by World War

II. It was a time of celebrated affluent living for a majority of Americans. Critical problems, both international and domestic, were not forgotten, but most citizens seemed content to see them shunted from the headlines.

John F. Kennedy recognized this phenomenon in his campaign for the presidency in 1960. Early in his drive for election he began to emphasize repeatedly a grand theme: "get America moving." He pointed to shrinking United States prestige abroad, a gnawing recession at home, a missile gap (later proved nonexistent), and the need for energetic action to remove social and economic sores from the public body.[2]

KENNEDY'S APPEAL FOR BUSINESS SUPPORT

As a candidate Kennedy recognized, and a variety of polls affirmed, that business traditionally regards the Republican party as "its" party.[3] He sensed too that the Democratic platform, in the words of Theodore C. Sorensen, "promised . . . too many antagonistic specifics that could not be fulfilled, raising too many unwarranted hopes and unnecessary fears."[4] The liberal 1960 platform seemed unlikely to encourage business support for the Democratic ticket.

Nevertheless, Kennedy hoped to woo votes from businessmen. In his speeches he emphasized the importance of a prosperous and expanding economy to free enterprise and to the maintenance of America's position as the leader of the free world.[5] In his first radio-television debate with Richard M. Nixon, Kennedy stressed the value of productive power in the struggle with world communism and voiced his dissatisfaction with the progress the nation was making in this direction. Throughout the debate, he reiterated his belief that the United States could and should grow faster economically, tying "growthmanship" to his grand theme of moving America forward.[6] Both continued as leitmotivs during his years as president.

The question of sufficient economic growth became increasingly significant because of the deepening recession. With unemployment expanding rapidly, the public was acutely interested in this issue, despite Republican efforts to minimize its importance. Business too was feeling the effects of the economic slump. Profits, which had recovered dramatically in 1959 after the painful 1958 recession, slid downward again in 1960.[7]

On October 12, 1960, Kennedy aired in detail his views about business and the economy in a speech and question-and-answer session before the Associated Business Publications Conference in New York City. Labeling the idea of an inevitable conflict between the business community and the Democratic party "one of the great political myths of our time," he frankly asked the support and help of businessmen.[8] The presidential candidate assured his listeners that his administration would be oriented neither to business, to labor, nor to agriculture. More specifically, he amplified what he termed the "conservative" economic policy that he would follow if elected: more flexible monetary policies to stimulate growth and the use of other tools if necessary to control extravagant booms; the budget utilized as an instrument of economic stabilization, but balanced over the course of the business cycle; close government relations with labor and management to develop wage and price policies consistent with stability; proper encouragement of plant modernization; equal attention to the men who operate the plant; and government-encouraged research to achieve the proper development of natural resources. Kennedy warned that capitalism could be perpetuated only by making it work and "by serving it as well as it has served us."[9]

As the campaign drew to its close, he spoke directly to critics skeptical of his ardor for free enterprise: "I believe in an America where the free enterprise system flourishes for all other systems to see and admire." No monopoly, no racketeer, and no government bureaucracy, he stressed, should be able to put a man out of a business that he has built with his own initiative.[10] Senator Kennedy also assured the nation that he advocated no changes in the constitution of the Federal Reserve System; and most businessmen regarded an independent Federal Reserve as essential to stable and conservative government fiscal policies.[11]

A little over a week later, the voters chose John Fitzgerald Kennedy —liberal son of a millionaire businessman—as president in an election marked by its tantalizing closeness. It is impossible to know precisely how many businessmen eventually voted for him, but no available information suggested that the Democratic candidate had reversed the traditional Republican orientation of the business community. Certainly the new president himself had no illusion about being the first choice of the business world, as he confessed in a speech to the United States Chamber of Commerce.[12]

THE UNRUFFLED BUSINESSMEN

Surveys of business reaction to the Kennedy victory, conducted informally by direct interview or telephone conversation immediately after election day, revealed a general absence of any deep concern. *Business Week* reported the prevailing attitude to be, "Sure, I voted for Nixon, but I don't believe Kennedy's administration can bring us any real harm." Only a small handful of businessmen reported voting for Kennedy, but emotionalism approaching alarm was rare. Some even foresaw a positive boom for business, at least in the short run. While fear of inflation was common, most spokesmen indicated a belief that it would have occurred even if Nixon had been elected.[13]

Business leaders expressed hope that the new governmental team would formulate its program with prudence and avoid going on a spending spree.[14] But an executive who had campaigned for the Democratic ticket predicted, "people are really going to be surprised how conservative Jack Kennedy will be."[15] Industrial concerns engaged in defense and space contracting reflected optimism about the election of Kennedy, who had urged a buildup in these areas. Dan A. Kimball, president of Aerojet-General Corporation and secretary of the navy under Truman, pointed out that America must move ahead in defense and space exploration in order to meet "the dual challenge of Soviet aggressiveness and the pressing demands of man's persistent quest for knowledge and understanding of his universe."[16]

A *Wall Street Journal* survey of over one hundred executives reported a common belief that the lack of a mandate, obvious from the narrowness of the election, would curb whatever liberal economic tendencies the new president might have. Editorially, the *Journal,* along with many other business publications, found relief in the lack of a mandate and the absence of sectional unanimity. The margin of victory was interpreted as the people's refusing to issue a blank check to Mr. Kennedy and the Democratic party to pursue the liberal platform written at the Los Angeles convention.[17]

For the businessman interested enough to dig into the Kennedy career before 1960, there was the reassuring fact that the president-elect, too, could read election returns. His past performance in the House and Senate and his election campaign statements provided no basis for deep alarm about the future. His record indicated that, while liberal in many of his views, he was keenly aware of the give-and-take compromise so essential in democratic government. Above all he yearned to make a distinguished record as a successful chief executive. Kennedy, cognizant that politics, like diplomacy, is the art of the possible, was unlikely to try to reshape and remold the prevailing American system.[18]

In addition, the conservative coalition in Congress could be expected to continue its role of blunting excessive executive spending programs. Congressmen, always sensitive to the currents of public feeling, needed no news commentators or editorials to point to the indecisive nature of the thin Kennedy victory. A Gallup poll, taken in January 1961, confirmed the middle-of-the-road mood of the American voter. Forty-two percent preferred Kennedy's policies to be in the center, while 24 percent favored a move toward a more conservative position and 23 percent hoped he might take a more liberal stance.[19]

SELECTING THE CABINET

If the business community in general viewed the president himself with something approaching equanimity, the same could not be said about their feelings toward his campaign advisers. The thought of such brain trusters as "statist-economist John Kenneth Galbraith, New-Dealing historian Arthur Schlesinger, Jr., utopian Adlai Stevenson, the fuzzy do-gooder Chester Bowles, the socialist-inclined Walter Reuther" being influential in the new administration was not something the *Wall Street Journal* relished with any pleasure, though the *Journal* drew solace from the belief that Kennedy's traditionalist, conservative sense of history showed his true instincts.[20]

As the process of cabinet formation unfolded, business began to breathe easier. Galbraith and the liberal G. Mennen Williams, former governor of Michigan, were shunted to overseas diplomatic posts; Stevenson was called upon to use his matchless wit and rhetoric as ambassador to the United Nations; Reuther stayed out of government altogether; and Bowles went to the State Department not as Secretary of State, but as a subordinate to middle-of-the-road Dean Rusk. Schlesinger joined the White House staff, where, as presidential aide and confidant Theodore Sorensen observed, he functioned effectively both as contact man with the liberal intellectual community and "as a lightning rod to attract Republican attacks away from the rest of us."[21]

The appointment of Douglas Dillon, Eisenhower's undersecretary of state, as secretary of the treasury pleased business. To a private visitor, presumably a Democrat, Kennedy allegedly defended his choice of Dillon, a Republican and a former Wall Street banker, as a gesture made necessary by the narrow margin of his victory over Nixon. This brought a polite rejoinder from the guest, who wondered if a victorious Nixon would have picked Leon Keyserling to be secretary of the treasury as a favor to the liberals.[22]

The remainder of the cabinet appointments also served to woo business. Secretary of Defense Robert McNamara was president of the Ford Motor Company and a Republican, while Secretary of State Dean Rusk was a foundation executive. Neither had been active politically. Stewart Udall, Orville Freeman, Luther Hodges, and Abraham Ribicoff at the Departments of Interior, Agriculture, Commerce, and Health, Education, and Welfare, respectively, were active Democratic politicans, progressive but scarcely calculated to frighten free-enterprise-minded Americans. Hodges, whose position would place him in closest contact with business, was himself a former successful businessman. Secretary of Labor Arthur Goldberg was a distinguished labor lawyer so widely respected by management officials for his integrity and fairness that he breezed through the Senate Labor Committee hearing on his nomination with accolades.[23] While the appointment of the president's brother, Robert F. Kennedy, as attorney general incurred considerable hostility, largely on the grounds of nepotism, the criticism was hardly confined to the business community.

Although the cabinet selections attracted the greatest public attention, they totaled only a fraction of the personnel needed to staff the multitude of government posts. Robert Kennedy and the president's brother-in-law, Sargent Shriver, led the drive to recruit members of the new administration team. Under them, Lawrence O'Brien, Richard Donahue, and Ralph Dungan worked mainly through the political network developed during the campaign. Shriver, Adam Yarmolinsky, and Harris Wofford concentrated their talent hunt on the business, professional, and university worlds. At the same time, twenty-nine task forces staffed by experts studied problems facing the incoming administration.[24]

Inevitably, the Kennedy appointees evoked comparison with the New Deal team of Franklin D. Roosevelt. The *American Banker* reflected on the similarity between the two, particularly the use of intellectuals, but noted that the Kennedy cabinet was more conservative. Officials who would affect fiscal policy and spending were viewed especially favorably. Joseph P. Kennedy, the president's father and a man of proved fiscal responsibility, was seen as likely to have a big influence in the new administration. Business circles were pleased that the more radical elements were not given the most critical positions.[25]

INTELLECTUALS IN GOVERNMENT

Frequent criticism of appointees and advisers continued throughout the Kennedy years, particularly criticism of the use of intellectuals in large numbers. The new administration had barely settled into office before Schlesinger drew heavy fire from critics because of his remarks in a debate with the conservative William F. Buckley, Jr. Schlesinger, defining a welfare state as one that provided citizens with the basic elements of life, such as food, clothing, shelter, education, and opportunity, called it the best defense against communism. Senator Strom Thurmond (Democrat, South Carolina) attacked the historian's statements sharply, charging that communism and welfare statism were in essence the same; an annoyed Republican congressman implored "God save the President and the nation from some of his socialist friends."[26]

The legislators' criticism mirrored business distrust of intellectuals. A major oil company president lamented the appointment of persons known to be hostile to the free enterprise system to high government positions exercising vast power over business. He cautioned, "We in the business world must not abdicate our authority to the ivory-towered socialists or fuzzy-minded theorists."[27]

While this view of intellectuals was perhaps more extreme than the opinion of most business leaders, there seems little reason to doubt that the two groups regarded each other with considerable suspicion. In 1962 the Opinion Research Corporation surveyed 114 corporation executives and 132 writers, thinkers, and teachers about their own and each other's roles in society. An overwhelming number in each category claimed to place a high value upon the individual, but seven of ten intellectuals and six of ten executives did not believe that the other group would feel the same.

Both groups saw intellectuals as critics of the established order, primarily oriented toward ideas, valuing creativity more than technical skill, having difficulty with practical problems, and generally underpaid. Executives were viewed by both as primarily interested in raising the nation's productivity, wary of governmental solutions, respected in the community, preferring gradual social change, and relying on intuition and experience in decision making. Each group was suspicious of the motives of the other, but surprisingly, majorities of each liked people in the other. However, about half of each did not believe that members of the other group liked them.[28]

Businessmen especially questioned the intellectuals' contempt for the profit motive, although ironically the marketplace itself has become apologetic of its pursuit of profit maximization in recent years.[29] Since President Kennedy remained popular with the general public throughout his administration, intellectual officeholders and presidential advisers proved to be convenient and logical targets for criticism.[30]

This hostility actually proved a useful safety valve for attacks on government policy, leaving the president above much of the rancor and in a receptive mood to keep lines of communication open and to cooperate with his critics.

BUSINESSMEN IN GOVERNMENT

The business world disagreed at times with the policies of the Eisenhower administration but generally felt more comfortable with the Republican appointees than with the Kennedy team. Eisenhower chose men of integrity and achievement for important government positions, but basically he repeated the Hoover pattern of a government of big business manned by personnel with close ties to the major corporations.[31] Kennedy changed this standard. Seymour Harris has noted that the New Frontier drew much more heavily from the ranks of government, academic, and nonprofit institutions for high-level appointments than did the previous administration.[32] To staff the upper-echelon positions in the executive departments which most critically influenced business decisions—Defense, State, Treasury, and Commerce—Eisenhower initially appointed almost twice as many businessmen as did Kennedy.[33]

Less important, but equally symbolic of the diminished rapport between business and the chief executive, were the White House social guest lists. Whereas Eisenhower preferred to surround himself socially with leaders from the business world, Kennedy made headlines with his invitations to a wide variety of people, including men and women of the arts, scientists, intellectuals, and sports figures. He and Mrs. Kennedy, with her broad interest in the arts, used social occasions to encourage a cultural and intellectual revival in America.[34] It was not that businessmen were no longer welcome at the White House; they were, but with the change in administrations, there was a shift in emphasis. Kennedy prided himself on being an intellectual, and he enjoyed being with practical intellectuals.

While the business community naturally feels more at home with an administration staffed heavily with businessmen, a valid question for students of public administration and leadership is how good a job businessmen do in government. A survey by the American Foundation for Continuing Education addressed itself in part to this question, interviewing fifty-two leading Americans from various occupations who were then or previously had been active in government. Many of the businessmen interviewed had served in the Eisenhower administration.

Surprisingly, they gave a relatively low assessment of businessmen in Washington, with few exceptions. They readily conceded the superiority of other occupational groups for government service, particularly lawyers, educators, and journalists, and pointed to the drawbacks for the businessman in public service, notably the salary differential, the reluctance to be in a "goldfish bowl" environment, and the basically unsympathetic attitude of businessmen toward government itself.[35]

While it is not possible to say with certainty that the businessmen involved in this survey were representative of the business community as a whole, the findings do raise the possibility that businessmen were not greatly concerned about their relatively lessened role in the Kennedy administration. It is probable that business is much less interested in having businessmen as such in government appointive and advisory positions than in having persons in these jobs who are simply sympathetic, or at least not prejudiced, toward private enterprise.

Logically, management officials did not expect the New Frontier to be oriented toward business. But Kennedy's preinaugural actions, like his congressional career and his campaign statements, gave little reason to believe that he would be a menace to the free enterprise system. If they were not warmly enthusiastic about his election, businessmen could at least join with the corporation executive who declared, "Let's wish them well and hope they can do something. If they can't, they have no alibis."[36]

2

The Business Community and Government

What is the Business Community?

In his classic "cross of gold" speech in 1896, William Jennings Bryan complained to the Gold Democrats, "you have made the definition of a business man too limited in its application." For Bryan and his followers, the man employed for wages, the attorney in the country town, the crossroads merchant, the miner, and the farmer were all businessmen.[1]

Few in America today would agree with Bryan's broad definition of businessmen. In 1960 there were 28,750,000 white-collar employed citizens in the United States. Included in this number were over 7,000,000 nonfarm managers, officials, and proprietors who could be safely called businessmen.[2] In addition, an indeterminate number of the remaining 21,000,000 nonunion white-collar personnel sympathized with the business viewpoint and considered themselves to be members of the business class. Clearly, consensus is rare as to what, or who, constitutes the business community. It is more accurate to speak of business *communities,* though in both business and general statements the singular term is far more commonly used, perhaps for simplicity of expression.

Since the differences which divide the millions of American businessmen are so numerous, no responsible scholar attempts today to argue that business is a monolithic force. Despite this fact, a predominant business mood develops on many major issues affecting the group as a whole. What must always be remembered is that unanimity does *not* occur in every case involving business interest. It is the frequency of exception that makes "the" business view so fascinating, and yet so difficult to define.[3]

A striking feature of American political life is the extent to which political parties are supplemented by private associations organized to influence public policy. Such pressure groups, business or otherwise, are by nature minority interests which seek to gain some special minority benefit. Individual proprietors or companies seek the strength of numbers offered by association to apply more effective pressure, either positive or negative, on government to secure goals broadly beneficial to the group. There are more than two thousand national business organizations, largely trade associations. State, regional, and local trade associations number more than eleven thousand, in addition to over five thousand local chambers of commerce.[4] Varying widely in size, resources, and objectives, most associations focus on the restricted interests of a particular industry. A few organizations, such as the United States Chamber of Commerce, attempt to speak for the nation's business as a whole.[5]

National and regional business groups rely heavily upon their printed publications to educate and guide members. Better known as business "opinion makers" are periodicals such as *Business Week, Fortune,* and the *Wall Street Journal.* At least as influential on business opinion, and possibly more so, are the financial sections and editorial comments of the nation's daily newspapers.

Raymond A. Bauer and others in *American Business and Public Policy: The Politics of Foreign Trade* provided useful information on the reading habits of businessmen. Three separate surveys made in the 1950s agreed that the local daily was read most frequently by business people, followed by the *Wall Street Journal,* the *New York Times,* and the *New York Herald Tribune.* Among news magazines, *Time, United States News and World Report,* and *Newsweek* were preferred, in that order. About half of the executives reported reading two or more general business magazines regularly, with *Business Week* most popular and *Fortune* second. The *Harvard Business Review* and the *Kiplinger Letter* were also frequently mentioned. *Life* and *Saturday Evening Post* were cited as the most-read general magazines, while the *Reader's Digest* rated high among small-business readers but low with executives of larger concerns.[6]

Business publications purport to represent business thought and to analyze national issues from a business perspective, but, more realistically, they represent the opinions of their editors and publishers. John F. Kennedy read widely in newspapers and periodicals to ascertain what Congress and the public were reading. As an alert politician, he recognized the ability of the media editorial offices to shape opinion. Conversely, the news media also recognize the ability of government to "manage news" by concealment and distortion. While the so-called credibility gap became peculiarly associated with the Johnson administration, newsmen also castigated the New Frontier for attempting to "manage news," particularly during the Cuban missile crisis in 1962.[7]

Some business publications are diligent in trying to reflect the underlying current of business sentiment in their editorial position. Media which have far-flung reporting staffs, which keep in touch with national and regional trade associations, and which present controversial articles and issues in conflict with stereotyped business positions obviously offer their readers better-balanced information. Others operate editorially from inflexible positions. A few seem never to have recovered from the horror of the New Deal and their fear of the growing acceptance of modern economic ideas.[8]

In general, editorials in business publications, with few exceptions, appear to be more conservative in tone and more firmly rooted in traditional business ideology than speeches and statements by management, especially the executives of the large corporations. By their restraint, business leaders evidence a much greater awareness of the need for business-government rapport than do their editorial colleagues. Nevertheless, for the vast majority of businessmen, especially small proprietors, with little free time to read widely or probe deeply into complex issues, business publications, along with the financial and editorial pages of local newspapers, are likely to be important molders of opinion.

Trade associations function both to reflect industry opinion and to form the opinions of members. Association officials, devoting themselves full time to the problems facing the industry and often drawing upon the help of research and administrative staffs, are in a powerful position to shape the thinking of busy members of the organization. In many cases the views of a few strong industry leaders, transmitted through trade association staffs, dominate the policies of the whole industry. President Kennedy turned to trade and industry associations in the 1960 campaign for ideas on matters of business interest. Aware of the importance of trade associations, he used this maneuver as a tactic to woo business support.[9]

THE ESTABLISHMENT

The locus of power within the business community may rest with an amorphous group of big businessmen who are part of the power elite or establishment, which exerts great influence on government policies. The power elite theme was developed in some detail, but without naming specific individuals, by the late sociologist C. Wright Mills. According to Mills, the power elite is composed of political, economic, and military leaders "chosen not by meritorious ability, but by means of power, sources of wealth, and mechanics of celebrity and being."[10] Further, he wrote, even the political elite is clearly dominated and controlled by big businessmen and ascendant military men.[11]

Mills's thesis has not gone without serious challenge. *The Power Structure* by Arnold Rose, published in 1967, carefully examined the Power Elite concept and synthesized recent studies of the political power structure in the United States. Rose concluded that while the United States is not completely democratic, the power structure is highly complex and diversified rather than unitary and monolithic. Rose also argued that "the political elite influences or controls the economic elite at least as much as the economic elite controls the political elite."[12]

Despite sharp criticism, a modification of the power elite theme—the idea of an establishment—has seemingly become entrenched in American political thought. President Eisenhower gave credence to this belief in his farewell address to the nation. Noting that the conjunction of an immense military establishment and a large arms industry was a new American experience, Eisenhower somberly warned that, "In the councils of government, we must guard against the acquisition of unwarranted influence, whether sought or unsought, by the military-industrial complex. The potential for the disastrous rise of misplaced power exists and will persist." The retiring president, while acknowledging the importance of scientific research, also pointed to the danger of public policy's becoming the captive of a scientific-technical elite.[13]

During the 1960s groups as disparate as archconservatives and the New Left movement have articulated versions of the establishment thesis. Both pointed to a shadowy elitist structure, wielding awesome power and frustrating genuine democracy, as a prime cause of America's ills.

Supporters of conservative Barry Goldwater charged that opposition to his nomination as Republican candidate for president in 1964 was directed and financed by the eastern establishment. Allegedly, this was the same group which had thwarted efforts of genuine conservatives, like Robert Taft, to win the nomination in the past. Flexible and non-monolithic, the establishment centered on the east coast, with New York City as headquarters. Members of the establishment, both Democrats and Republicans, were united by a loose community of interest, including attendance at Ivy League prep schools and colleges, ties with Wall Street and international finance, and family and social relationships. A key goal of this elite was to make sure that the presidential nominees and platforms of both parties were favorable to establishment policies, especially liberal domestic programs, foreign aid, and concessions to the Communists.[14]

As viewed by today's New Left, the establishment is much broader. It is composed of the various irresponsible elites who conspire to control all parts of society. Big businessmen are leaders of the economic elite, while most small entrepreneurs are willing accomplices in perpetuating capitalism—a system which denies to millions of citizens their rightful share of material goods and, in many instances, their real freedom.[15]

BUSINESSMEN IN POLITICS

John F. Kennedy became president during a period when business was showing signs of discarding its policy of noninvolvement in political elections. Traditionally, business groups exerted their influence outside the election arena, but following the example of organized labor, in the 1950s business increasingly began to seek majority support at the polls.

Some individual companies, such as Johnson and Johnson, Gulf Oil, and General Electric, initiated their own nonpartisan political education programs for employees on company time. However, a rash of businesswide political education programs, backed enthusiastically by trade associations, reached many more businessmen. The Effective Citizens Organization, founded in 1954, was perhaps the first nonprofit, nationwide organization to enter the field. In 1957 the Manufacturers Association of Syracuse, New York, gained national recognition for its efforts in upper New York. The National Association of Manufacturers became involved in 1958, but the plan, because of its conservative format, proved too inflexible and restrictive for wide appeal, and it was dropped in 1962.[16]

Democratic gains of thirteen Senate seats and forty-eight House positions in the 1958 congressional elections shocked businessmen into increasing their political activity, as many business leaders feared New Deal policies' being revitalized.[17] Easily the most successful political education endeavor was developed the following year by the United States Chamber of Commerce. This program was offered by an estimated 1,100 local chambers in its initial year, though the number declined in subsequent years.[18]

Despite such efforts, the average businessman, possessed by exaggerated fears of the effect of political activity upon his business operations, remained remarkably naïve politically. All too often, when a businessman did become active in politics, his motive was overtly to offset the power of labor or to try to lower taxes. Such single-minded emphasis did little to endear the businessman to political party professionals. James C. Worthy, a top Sears, Roebuck executive, admonished his colleagues for doing so little to match labor in showing loyalty to the political parties. Worthy noted that trade associations are more frequently negative than positive in their political positions, citing, as an example, the attacks of powerful business groups on Eisenhower's record peacetime budget in 1957. The criticism weakened the position of a president generally considered favorable to business.[19]

While Kennedy's election was greeted by business without significant alarm, spokesmen did not cease urging businessmen to pursue their burgeoning interest in practical politics.[20] Conservative business elements reiterated the theme of government intervention in the lives and rights of citizens as the reason why businessmen should exert their influence at the ballot box.[21]

INCREASED POLITICAL ACTIVISM

The presidency of John F. Kennedy coincided with the rise to national prominence of the extreme right-wing John Birch Society, which drew heavy backing from businessmen. Significantly, however, the society did not attract support from large, publicly owned, executive-managed corporations such as Standard Oil or General Motors.[22] But the blue-chip firms did draw heavily from radical-right material for use in community and employee seminars that they sponsored, though there were also many examples of intelligent, balanced corporate anti-communist programs.[23] The activities of extremist groups, the promotion of anticommunist seminars, and the election of a Democrat to the White House combined to stimulate increased interest in the business world for political activism.

One survey of businessmen, taken shortly after Kennedy's use of government power to pressure the steel industry to rescind price increases in April 1962, revealed that 96 percent of the respondents favored businessmen's playing a more active role in politics; although, ironically, only 60 percent indicated that they personally planned to do more. Over 80 percent indicated their belief that the president, along with federal officials and legislators, did not understand the needs and problems of business.[24] More companies also began to develop written or informal policies to deal with employee political candidates.[25]

If businessmen hoped their efforts would result in important Republican gains in the 1962 congressional elections, they were doomed to disappointment. The Democrats suffered milder interim election losses in the House than usual, only three seats, and managed a net addition of two senators. Business, while having a marked effect and influence on administrative policy and legislation, simply did not have the votes to swing most elections. Business messages to the public on politics and economics too often dealt with generalities and failed to identify business objectives with the advancement of public, rather than special, interest. In addition, individual businessmen and businesses were prone to leave political matters to their trade associations.[26]

In August 1963, thirteen executives collaborated to form the Business-Industry Political Action Committee (BIPAC) with a stated goal of backing congressional candidates who shared business views.[27] Kenton R. Cravens, chairman of the Mercantile Trust Company of Saint Louis and first chairman of BIPAC, explained that the new organization represented the competitive, free enterprise view of the great majority of the American business community. Bipartisan, independent, and voluntary, BIPAC aimed to offset organized labor's Committee on Political Education and the Americans for Democratic Action by concentrating financial support in districts where a close race was anticipated.[28]

In 1964, a survey of *Harvard Business Review* subscribers provided some measure of management's growing concern with its role in public affairs. A large majority expressed belief that the influence of business on political issues and elected officials had increased since 1960. But the executives stressed that much more had to be done to improve the political climate for business. The survey also indicated that more companies were actively participating in shaping the policies of trade associations and other organizations seeking to tell the "free enterprise story."[29]

THE BUSINESS ADVISORY COUNCIL

Beginning in 1933, the business community extended its advice and assistance to the government through the Business Advisory Council (BAC), an exclusive and self-perpetuating organization of blue-ribbon corporation executives. With a total membership of 150 men, including 60 active members who actually set policy, the BAC met at least twice annually with government officials in closed-door sessions, normally at elite resort hotels. As secretary of commerce, Luther H. Hodges, supposedly "business's man in the Kennedy cabinet," was the administration's liaison man with the council. The courtly Hodges, perhaps trying to prove that he was the "man" of no one except the president, moved to revise the BAC almost before the new administration settled into office. The former North Carolina governor suggested that the BAC open its ranks to representatives of small business and allow the press to attend all its meetings involving participation by government officials. The proposed innovations were not received with favor by the council.[30]

At the same time, another delicate problem plagued Hodges in his relations with the BAC. Price-fixing convictions of twenty-nine major electrical companies, including General Electric, were handed down in late January, and Ralph Cordiner, board chairman of GE, was chairman of the BAC. It was Hodges's opinion that Cordiner, because of the firm's conviction, should resign as council chairman. However, the secretary of commerce was reluctant to add to his existing friction with the council by actually demanding the resignation. Hodges told a press conference on February 14 that Cordiner and the BAC would have to make the decision.[31]

Although Cordiner did resign as BAC chairman shortly thereafter, giving the pressure of private business as the reason, Hodges had apparently already decided to reduce the influence of the council. Although publicly he referred to the BAC as valuable, privately he was reported to feel that the group had done little in recent years and was too big-business-oriented.[32] Roger Blough, chief executive officer of United States Steel, succeeded Cordiner as top official of the BAC, and on April 4 the business group agreed to Hodges's desired changes. Five small businessmen were to be added to the sixty active members, with Hodges nominating ten and the council selecting half; the secretary of commerce was to be general chairman of the BAC, with power to call meetings and arrange agenda; all meetings involving government personnel were to be open to the press; and minutes of the meetings were to be kept.[33]

Hodges attended the regular spring meeting of the BAC at Hot Springs, Virginia. His comments at a press conference, three days after the conclusion of the affair, were coolly gracious but reflected his feelings that there was too little discussion of subjects useful to the Department of Commerce.[34]

The controversy between the council and the secretary of commerce simmered for almost two months and then culminated in the BAC's withdrawing from its quasi-official status in government. With Hodges on vacation, President Kennedy invited the council's executive committee to the White House on July 6 to discuss mutual grievances. Blough, to the president's surprise, revealed the council's intention to become independent. The BAC delegation tempered the abruptness of the break by assuring Kennedy of its desire to broaden the base of the council's advisory services to other government agencies besides the Commerce Department. The meeting ended in apparent harmony, with the president issuing a statement of his satisfaction with the new arrangement and Blough relaying Kennedy's agreement to waiting newsmen.[35]

Two days later Undersecretary of Commerce Edward Gudeman wrote Blough to warn that the council would be replaced if it went through with its announced intention to end its government ties.[36] The die was cast, however, for on July 10 eighty-two members of the BAC, meeting in New York City, formally voted to go independent. The business group, as Gudeman suggested in his letter, adopted a new name, the Business Council, and affirmed its desire to assist any government agency that desired help.[37]

The Kennedy administration did not follow through with its threat to form a new quasi-official BAC, although Hodges mentioned the possibility at a press conference as late as September.[38] Instead, the administration made pointed overtures to heal the rift with the old organization. By the end of the summer, international problems in

Berlin, Laos, Vietnam, and Cuba forced the president to increase spending, resulting in a deficit. With the nation's economic prospects still uncertain from the recent recession, Kennedy needed all the business support he could muster. In marked contrast to the spring meeting of the BAC, when Hodges was the lone major administration official to attend, the president dispatched some of his top economic specialists to the Business Council's October meeting. Dillon, Treasury Undersecretary Henry Fowler, Deputy Secretary of Defense Roswell Gilpatric, and Chairman Walter Heller of the Council of Economic Advisers addressed the business leaders. The Kennedy gestures of friendship were not lost on Business Council members. Though still skeptical of the President's motives, as well as some of his recent actions, the executives were gratified at the prospects of improved relations with the government.[39]

Significantly, the autumn meeting of the council followed the traditional pattern of closed meetings. If businessmen were annoyed and dismayed by the efforts of Secretary Hodges to establish more government control over the BAC, they could find satisfaction in the cordial manner with which the president accepted the July decision of the organization and in his subsequent endeavor to better relations with the new Business Council. Corporate leaders, including steel executives, doubtless made a mental note of Kennedy's response. It is not inconceivable that this chain of events helped convince the steel industry that the administration was susceptible to pressure and to a fait accompli.[40]

The Business Council continued its generally cordial, but unofficial, ties with the government throughout the New Frontier years. Heller responded to the invitation of Roger Blough to establish a liaison committee of about eight top business executives and the members of the CEA, and this group met regularly.[41] Not even the steel crisis in 1962 shattered the relationship, and the Business Council proved a useful vehicle for Kennedy's use in reestablishing business confidence in his administration.[42]

BUSINESS ETHICS

The electrical industry price-fixing case initiated another early administration-business episode in which Secretary Hodges played a prominent role. In his 1961 State of the Union message, President Kennedy warned, "Morality in private business has not been sufficiently spurred by morality in public business."[43] A few days later he told a press conference of his hope that executive agencies and Congress would concern themselves with the problems of conflict of interest, monopoly, and "even more illicit practices conducted in the American business community." Kennedy endorsed as beneficial the establishment by business groups of codes of ethical practices.[44]

Hodges, shocked by the electrical industry scandals and genuinely concerned about the image of free enterprise in the world, suggested the formation of a Business Ethics Advisory Council (BEAC) to grapple with the problem of business ethics and to write a workable code. Kennedy gave the idea enthusiastic support, and twenty-six leading businessmen, educators, clergymen, and publishers were subsequently named to the committee.[45]

The BEAC, with William C. Decker of the Corning Glass Works as chairman, met for the first time on May 17 to develop a plan of operation. On November 11, the council convened to receive a draft of the code prepared by its steering committee and to review an illuminating questionnaire study of ethics in business, prepared by Father Raymond C. Baumhart for the *Harvard Business Review*. This survey, based upon 1,700 responses from persons in a variety of industries, underlined the need of business to improve its ethical standards. An alarming 68 percent of the respondents admitted knowledge of at least a few unethical practices being committed in their industries, and 71 percent affirmed their belief that a code would raise the ethical level of business.[46]

On January 16 ,1962, the BEAC met with President Kennedy and issued "A Statement on Business Ethics and a Call for Action." As Chairman Decker explained, the Council deliberately avoided drafting a code for the whole business community, because it would have been so generalized as to be merely platitudinous. Instead, the BEAC chose to suggest guideposts, stressing the social responsibilities of business, to aid individual companies and industries in writing specific, detailed codes.[47] The chief executive expressed delight with the report, adding his confidence that "American business will respond."[48]

In his book, *The Business Conscience,* Hodges contrasted the president's obvious interest in the work of the BEAC with the frigid reception that Chairman Decker and the secretary of commerce received when they met with the Business Council to explain the nature and purpose of the "Call to Action." Several of the Business Council members actually spoke against making the work of the Ethics Council public, with one industrialist charging it would make people feel that all business is unethical. Not a single person stood up to endorse the proposed code. As Hodges acknowledged, it was the wrong day and the wrong crowd; or perhaps the business representatives simply had other things on their minds.[49]

The *Wall Street Journal* sounded a similar discordant note. Reminding its readers that "a climate of morality cannot be legislated," the newspaper reproached the government for sponsoring an attempt to deluge the country with confusing laws and regulations that even the most ethical might unwittingly be led to break.[50]

Certainly, not all big-business leaders were so loath to recognize ethical failings. Henry Ford II bluntly declared that management must accept the responsibility for occasional misdeeds and take swift and sure corrective action. Ford chided business commentators who pointed to the administration's call for improved ethics as an attack on business.[51] Clarence Randall, retired chairman of Inland Steel, applauded Kennedy for putting the responsibility on industry to improve ethics by appointing distinguished businessmen to the Ethics Council. He urged business groups to seize the initiative in denouncing business misconduct.[52]

Kennedy and Hodges deserved better cooperation from business than they received in their drive to raise ethical standards in America. Like motherhood, high ethics is not a topic normally subjected to criticism. The frosty reception given the Ethics Council statement by big-business leaders in the Business Council suggested that the wounds caused by the skirmish with the government the previous year were far from healed.

3

Recession and Recovery

The recession which gripped America in 1960 contributed to John F. Kennedy's election as president.[1] In areas with mounting unemployment dissatisfaction with the economy was keen, and the more than four million jobless Americans and their families were potentially a great source of support for the Democratic candidate. But as a campaign issue the recession generated more heat than light.

During the early fall, Kennedy addressed himself to the recession only tangentially, usually when emphasizing the need for economic growth or when speaking in localities where large numbers were unemployed. Not wanting to be accused of using scare tactics, he even specifically denied the appropriateness of calling the economic slowdown by "the official name of recession."[2] Near the end of the campaign, however, he did warn that a recession was likely in the winter of 1961 unless a new administration took charge of the national government.[3]

The Republican party and its candidate, Richard M. Nixon, naturally emphasized the record level of output, jobs, incomes, savings, and spending in America.[4] Raymond J. Saulnier, the chairman of Eisenhower's Council of Economic Advisers, repeatedly rebuked those who talked of a recession. He explained that the economy was undergoing a period of readjustment and freely predicted an upswing in the near future.[5] President Eisenhower, too, continued until the end of his term to emphasize the favorable features in the economic outlook.[6]

Businessmen and economists were far less restrained than the Democratic presidential candidate—and much less confident than the administration—in enunciating their concern about the American economy during 1960. In the spring, a succession of falling economic indicators made businessmen somber about the future. By summer, management and labor were uneasy and waiting apprehensively for signs of encouragement. Despite the optimistic pronouncements by government spokesmen in the weeks before the election, bad news far outweighed the good, and business leaders showed growing pessimism.[7] *Business Week* noted that despite official denials of a recession, the Eisenhower administration was quietly making decisions which, although not a crash program, were clearly designed to stimulate business.[8] The economy continued to slump in the months following the election, and purchasing agents, viewing the decline of new orders for goods, gloomily predicted the year's ending in a recession.[9]

The perspective of time confirmed the judgment of those businessmen and economists who correctly described the economic downturn in 1960 and early 1961 as a recession, not merely a readjustment. In retrospect it is also possible to see why the situation was not immediately recognized by others. A prolonged steel strike, lasting over much of the last half of 1959, punished the national economy. When the steel mills resumed production, the replenishment of stocks caused a temporary spurt in inventory investment. The subsequent slump in investment in the second quarter of 1960 was initially viewed as normal after the heavy first-quarter demand.[10] But the trend of falling corporation profits and slumping industrial production rates which began at this time continued until the spring of 1961.[11]

While political considerations played a part in the Eisenhower administration's refusal to publicly acknowledge serious concern about the economy in 1960, it is true that it may be almost impossible to precisely identify a recession in its initial stages. The longer recognition is delayed, the more difficult effective remedial action by government becomes. And, particularly when congressional legislation is required, discretionary efforts by government can be painfully slow. More immediate success in stemming an economic slump comes from built-in stabilizers, such as social security, which function automatically. In each of the four post–World War II recessions, including that of

1960–61, built-in stabilizers moderated the fall in private income when the gross national product declined.[12]

President Kennedy appreciated the value of these automatic stabilizers. In 1962, he suggested to Congress than the chief executive be given standby authority, subject to congressional veto, to adjust personal income-tax rates downward and to accelerate federal capital improvement programs when there was a rise in unemployment. The legislators, jealous of their power over taxes and spending, failed to act on the recommendations.[13]

THE DEMOCRATS AND THE RECESSION

Despite Kennedy's reluctance during the campaign to state boldly that America was in a recession, after the election he moved with vigor to determine how to reverse the business slump and reduce the growing number of unemployed. The president-elect named Paul Samuelson, a distinguished economist who was reportedly his first choice for chairman of the Council of Economic Advisers, to head a task force on the economy.[14] The Samuelson report, delivered to Kennedy two weeks before the inauguration, flatly declared that America was in the midst of its fourth postwar recession. Picking up the principal Kennedy campaign theme of moving America forward, the task force warned that the economy had not grown since 1956 at the same dramatic rate as Western Europe or Japan. The report specified high employment as the proper first goal of the new administration, coupled with measures to stimulate an expansion that would not quickly falter and cause a subsequent recession. Increased government expenditures, both for defense requirements and for social and welfare services, were projected as the main strategy, with a temporary tax cut proposed as a second line of action if the spending policy failed to achieve the desired results.[15]

More directly concerned with the plight of the unemployed was the report on area redevelopment prepared by a task force under Senator Paul Douglas (Democrat, Illinois), the author of two area redevelopment measures vetoed by President Eisenhower. The Douglas report, which urged a variety of federal measures to stimulate economic activity in labor surplus and low income areas, provided the blueprint for the administration's area redevelopment bill, submitted in late January.[16]

Once inaugurated, Kennedy wasted little time in pressing for action on recession problems. In his first executive action, he ordered the secretary of agriculture to expedite and improve the program of government-surplus food distribution to needy persons in areas of chronic unemployment.[17] Five days after taking office, he dramatized the urgency of conditions by making the area redevelopment bill his first request for legislation. Referring to substantial and persistent unemployment as a serious handicap to our national health, the president declared that neither private initiative nor state or local governments could carry the burden alone. The only alternative was federal aid to supplement other efforts.[18]

President Kennedy delivered a candid appraisal of economic conditions in his first State of the Union message. "The present state of our economy is disturbing," he asserted. "We take office in the wake of seven months of recession, three and one-half years of slack, seven years of diminished growth, and nine years of falling farm income." After supplying additional unpleasant details, the chief executive promised to send to Congress within fourteen days measures designed to improve the dismal picture.[19]

While the president's technique of acknowledging the hard economic facts appealed to businessmen, they generally believed that the speech suggested "unnecessary gloom and the danger of inflation, if all administration proposals are carried out." Sensitive to threats to "confidence," many business leaders agreed with the executive of a major watch manufacturer who worried that the somber tone of the speech might "scare the consumer to death."[20]

Fully aware that legislative remedies are a slow solution at best, Kennedy hunted for administrative procedures that could alleviate the effects of recession. In rapid succession he ordered five pilot projects for food-stamp distribution in areas of chronic unemployment, instructed the Veterans Administration to accelerate the payment of National Insurance dividends, and directed government agencies concerned with construction projects to lower interest rates and hasten approval of work wherever possible.[21]

The president also sought to manipulate interest rates to hold down the costs of the long-term borrowing necessary to investment in plant and equipment, while raising short-term rates to lessen the outflow of volatile funds to other countries. This unnatural monetary "twist" was essential on two counts: to stimulate the investment needed for recovery and to combat the loss of dollars which was contributing to the worsening American balance-of-payments difficulty.[22] This maneuver required the cooperation of the Federal Reserve Board and its respected chairman, William McChesney Martin, Jr., who was considered by business to be the most reliable check on any wild Democratic monetary tactics. Although the board never officially admitted to a sustained effort to reduce long-term rates, the Federal Reserve's policies clearly harmonized with "operation twist."[23] Some members of the business community were shocked at the action of the FRB, but most agreed that the plan was both desirable and sensible in the prevailing circumstances.[24]

On February 2, 1961, President Kennedy sent a special message to Congress detailing his program for economic growth and recovery. The chief executive announced his intention to ask for legislation to add a temporary thirteen-week supplement to state unemployment benefits, to increase social security payments and privileges, and to raise the minimum wage and broaden its coverage.[25]

Republican leaders were quick to censure the presidential proposals as high in cost and low in economic impact.[26] For most business leaders, however, Kennedy's economic message was a distinct relief. His proposals were essentially modest and were clearly distinct from any suggestion of a "hundred days" of frenetic economic activity by government paralleling Franklin D. Roosevelt's New Deal. "Caution" was the term most business journals used to describe the Kennedy program, though uneasiness was reflected over what might come next if the economy did not improve.[27] Businessmen were by no means unconcerned about the soaring unemployment rate; but, although they were anxious to see the problem corrected, they feared that a Democratic president, with campaign obligations to trade unions, might acquiesce to excessive demands by labor. Heavy cost pressure was viewed by nearly all business elements as a serious detriment to the private investment needed to create jobs.[28]

The president realized that traditional ideology in America restricted his flexibility in moving the economy forward. Early in January he urged Walter Heller to "use the White House as a pulpit for public education in economics, especially on the desirable effects of a Federal deficit in a recession."[29]

Administration proposals for recovery were preceded and followed by intense debate between presidential advisers. Supporters of two currents of economic thought, the structural and the fiscal, struggled for ascendancy. Proponents of the former, notably officials of the Federal Reserve Board and the departments of Commerce, Treasury, Labor, and Health, Education, and Welfare, argued that increased technological developments in industry made it impossible to reduce unemployment below an indeterminate rate (4 percent was commonly specified) by fiscal and monetary tools alone. Only by improving the social structure by better schooling, vocational training, and area redevelopment could hard-core unemployment be trimmed. The strongly fiscalist Council of Economic Advisers viewed deficient aggregate demand as the chief reason for the shortage of jobs. Heller termed the problem "fiscal drag," which he described as high tax levels draining needed purchasing power and thereby causing expansion to stop short of full employment.[30]

Kennedy, although impressed with the Heller argument, was aware that to suggest a tax cut so soon after calling for sacrifice in his inaugural address would be a political mistake. Conscious of his campaign pledges of fiscal responsibility, the president initially demanded that the recession be fought within the bounds of a balanced budget. To the relief of the White House economists, he did leave loopholes for essential deficit spending in his 1961 State of the Union and economic messages.[31] During the New Frontier, the ideas of the structuralists were used extensively in an attempt to solve the unemployment dilemma. But Kennedy's eventual decision to seek growth-stimulating tax reductions revealed his acceptance of the fiscalists' contention that structural remedies alone could not provide a sufficient number of new jobs.

By the first of February 1961, no one was denying the applicability of "recession" to America's economic situation. In January unemployment reached 7.7 percent of the labor force (6.6 percent seasonally adjusted), and it climbed even higher the next month.[32] On February 10, Kennedy dispatched Secretary of Labor Arthur Goldberg on a politically useful three-day tour of depressed areas in the Middle West. Goldberg declared that the United States was in a "full-fledged recession" and urged prompt action to forestall a "real depression."[33]

After dramatizing the need for immediate action, the president attempted to bring the business community into full partnership with the government in the drive for economic recovery. In a speech to the National Industrial Conference Board, Kennedy expressed confidence in the high purposes of the American business community and emphatically denied that he and his cabinet associates were opposed to business. Noting that the drop in corporate profits in 1960 cost the federal government over three billion dollars in tax revenue, he stressed that "far from being natural enemies, Government and business are necessary allies." Referring to the recession, the chief executive reminded his audience that the economic program before Congress was essentially a program for recovery, not growth. "But," he added, "it is an essential first step. Only by putting millions of people back to work can we expand purchasing power and markets."[34]

The day after speaking to the business executives, President Kennedy conferred with Democratic congressional leaders in an effort to spur them to action on his program. After briefings by cabinet officials, Speaker of the House Sam Rayburn soberly referred to the economic situation as "the most serious since the 1930s."[35] Yet despite attempts to emphasize the seriousness of the economic downturn, particularly in terms of human suffering, Congress remained surprisingly lethargic.

Businessmen may have been flattered by Kennedy's frank bid for an alliance, but he did not closely reflect the attitudes and philosophies of America's big-business leaders, and few rallied to the support of his legislative proposals.[36] Opposition to the extension of temporary unemployment compensation focused on the threat to state control of the unemployment-compensation systems.[37] Critics of the area redevelopment plan depicted federal help to particular industries or companies as unfair and as likely to lead to the pirating of businesses from one area to another. The National Association of Manufacturers and the national Chamber of Commerce countered the government program with suggestions for state and local development credit corporations on a nonpreference basis. Small businessmen, however, approved of the government plan and worried that it might not go far enough.[38]

RECOVERY BEGINS

During early February 1961, administration officials continued to depict economic gloom. Labor officials, as sensitive to the unemployment rate as businessmen were to the profit rate, made no effort to conceal their feeling that Kennedy was not doing enough to end the plight of the jobless.[39] Then, on February 18, Secretary of Commerce Luther Hodges expressed his "hunch" that the business slump would reverse itself by April.[40] The announcement, made without flourish and given scant attention by most news media, subsequently made Hodges appear prescient. When all the statistics became available, economists generally agreed that the recession reached its low point in February and that the economy began a slow upward movement in March.[41] The Kennedy "boom," which started so unspectacularly in the spring of 1961, developed into the longest peacetime cycle of prosperity in modern American history.

With economic indicators reflecting the improving conditions, Kennedy and his advisers adroitly revised their tactics to call for measures to prevent *future* recessions, a shift that did not go without notice by businessmen or Congress.[42] Theodore Sorensen, on seeing the Council of Economic Advisers in a solemn huddle during the period when signs of recovery were becoming more definite, called out, "There they are, contemplating the dangers of an upturn."[43] By the middle of March the public sensed the improvement in the economy, and 73 percent reported that they were not noticeably affected by the recession.[44]

The upward trend of business became apparent while the Senate and House committees were holding hearings on the proposal to raise the minimum wage to $1.25 per hour and extend coverage to millions of retail and service employees. Of all the president's early legislative measures, this bill aroused the most bitter opposition from business. With various national retail trade associations leading the fight, the proposal was attacked on grounds ranging from unconstitutionality to the threat of inflation. The most telling argument presented was that a higher minimum wage would force many small businesses to lay off marginally productive workers, especially the very young and the old, thus actually adding to the national unemployment total. The president's original bill proposed extending the minimum wage to 4.3 million additional workers, but Congress exempted more than 700,000 employees—mainly employees of laundries and intrastate enterprises with small annual sales volume.[45] By not extending coverage to large numbers of the lowest-paid workers—those who needed help the most —the 1961 act repeated the failures of many previous amendments to the minimum wage law.

By the end of June, a time Sorensen refers to with pride as concluding "161 days of action," the president's initial legislative requests to combat recession were law. In addition to minimum wage extension, Congress also enacted measures to supplement unemployment compensation, give aid to children of unemployed workers, stimulate area redevelopment, increase social security benefits, provide emergency relief for feed-grain farmers, and federally finance home building and slum clearance.[46]

Combined with the president's early use of executive programs, the congressional actions underscored the administration's determination to use government power vigorously to relieve human suffering. But recovery actually began before the new legislative programs could take effect. As Wilfred Lewis noted in his perceptive study of federal fiscal policy during recessions, the Kennedy antirecession measures contributed to the speed of recovery but not to the turning point.[47]

In his economic message in early February, Kennedy promised that if the measures he proposed were insufficient to put America on the road to full recovery and sustained growth, he would submit further proposals to Congress within seventy-five days.[48] This was an unmistakable reference to the second line of defense recommended by the Samuelson task force—a temporary tax cut—coupled with a massive spending program. Throughout the early spring, the president's economic advisers, the liberal Americans for Democratic Action, a sizeable portion of the business community, and the AFL-CIO found themselves in unaccustomed agreement in urging a tax cut, although they were far from harmonious about the type of reduction or the qualifications attached to it.[49]

By mid-April, the scheduled time for deciding on additional antirecession legislative proposals, Kennedy was convinced that recovery would continue and that Congress would pass neither a tax cut nor a major spending program.[50] In August, when the Berlin crisis dictated a costly rise in defense spending, the president even tentatively planned to request a tax increase. Only the energetic efforts of Sorensen and Heller, plus a persuasive last-minute appeal by economist Samuelson, convinced the chief executive that such a course would seriously cripple the growing momentum of recovery.[51]

Not all economic indicators during the summer of 1961 were favorable. The continuing high unemployment rate worried administration officials and reinforced arguments by economists that additional government fiscal programs were needed to invigorate the economy.[52] With both a tax cut and effective public welfare spending ruled out by political considerations, defense outlays, necessitated by the Berlin situation, served a double purpose. Kennedy asked Congress for over three billion dollars in new defense appropriations.[53] Although it was somewhat sluggish in its effect on the economy, spending for national security, with its remarkable sanctity from attack by pressure groups, including business, thus took the place of massive public works.

4

Fiscal Responsibility: Myth or Reality?

MODERN ECONOMIC POLICY

The surge of prosperity which followed the 1960–61 recession gained its momentum from many sources. The inherent vitality of the American economy itself, including the efficiency and initiative of American business, was one major cause. Also important were the policies fostered by the Kennedy administration.

In his first State of the Union address, President Kennedy described his economic objectives: to reduce unemployment, to put unused capacity to work, to stimulate new productivity, to promote greater economic growth within a range of sound fiscal policies and relative price stability, and to eliminate the knotty balance of payments deficit.[1] In less than three years, he planted the seeds for new and exciting possibilities to cope with modern economic challenges. The rate of growth increased significantly, while inflationary pressures were held in check.[2] But despite these impressive accomplishments, unemployment and the balance of payments remained unsolved and serious problems. Since both vitally influenced the nation's economic health, the president's lack of success in solving these dilemmas caused him continuing distress and played an imposing role in shaping administration policies.

Economists Seymour Harris and Walter W. Heller described Kennedy as the first modern economist in the American presidency, although neither claimed that he was a Keynesian when he became chief executive. Rather, both emphasized his remarkable ability to learn while in office.[3] Before coming to the White House, Kennedy had a limited background in economics. His formal education in the subject consisted of a basic course at Harvard; a brief session, interrupted by illness, with Harold J. Laski at the London School of Economics; and six months at the Graduate School of Business at Stanford.[4] During his fourteen years in Congress, Kennedy showed little more zest for economic matters than he had in his college years. His chief interest was foreign affairs.[5] But as the representative of a state with declining industries, he did become well acquainted with the sticky problems of unemployment, area redevelopment, labor, and trade protection.[6]

Edward S. Flash, in his study of the Council of Economic Advisers, depicted the CEA, principally Chairman Heller, as encouraging the president to develop a sophisticated economic philosophy, thus transforming his instinctive conservatism into a cautious liberalism.[7] However, Kennedy's extensive early reliance upon professed Keynesian advisers like Paul Samuelson, Harris, and Heller indicated that the president's conservatism was tempered from the start by a receptiveness toward the ideas and methods of Keynesian economics. The presidency was not only Kennedy's initial opportunity to exercise executive responsibilities, but also the first position challenging him to master the intricacies and possibilities of the new economics.

During the election campaign of 1960 and in his early presidential messages, Kennedy emphasized growth as the key to both recovery and continuing prosperity. Speaking directly to businessmen, he cited the need to put millions of men back to work as a requirement for the expanded purchasing power essential to reducing the slack in industrial capacity operation.[8] Business leaders enthusiastically agreed with the president, but they were equally concerned that growth take place in a climate of economic freedom and individual initiative. Growth required investment, and investment came largely out of profits. The business community named rising labor costs, inflation, high tax rates, and excessive government rules and regulations as the chief adversaries in the battle against declining profits.[9]

Businessmen continually worry about fiscal responsibility in Washington, especially when a Democrat is president. Whereas Kennedy's economic advisers urged increased government expenditures as a means to end recession and trigger growth, business favored reduced federal spending and a balanced budget as the first step in stimulating growth and brightening the economic picture.[10] Shortly after his inauguration, the president warned that not only was the current fiscal year almost certain to show a budget deficit, but the budget for fiscal 1962, submitted by Eisenhower, would remain in balance only if business conditions improved rapidly and if Congress enacted all revenue measures requested. Kennedy emphasized that he intended to seek no additional nondefense expenditures which would of themselves unbalance the budget.[11]

Reviewing the budget outlook in detail two months later, Kennedy criticized the Eisenhower budget for fiscal 1961 for overestimating revenue and underestimating expenditures. These miscalculations, combined with essential antirecession spending, resulted in Eisenhower's estimated $4.2 billion surplus turning into a deficit in excess of $2 billion. The president stressed his intention to seek a balanced budget and to be a "prudent caretaker of the public funds," but he avowed his belief in the contracyclical approach to budgeting. This concept envisioned the budget in balance over the years of the business cycle, with a deficit in years of recession, when revenues decline and the economy requires stimulation, and a surplus in times of prosperity.[12]

The contracyclical theory was neither new nor startling to most of the business community.[13] Since the days of the Great Depression, the public has become increasingly conscious of business cycles and more aware of the possible necessity of government action to smooth out economic fluctuations.[14] The Council of Economic Advisers was not pleased by the president's endorsement of the contracyclical approach. As Heller explained the Council's views, "In 1961, once recession had turned into recovery, nothing was more urgent than to raise the sights of economic policy and to shift its focus from the ups and downs of the cycle to the continuous rise in the economy's potential."[15]

Based heavily upon the ideas of Keynes, the so-called new economics of the president's advisers stressed the use of government fiscal and monetary powers to achieve full employment, steady growth, and stable prices. Intrinsic to their thinking was the belief that if business activity is to continue advancing steadily, total purchasing power must advance at somewhat the same rate. The CEA rejected the traditional concept that business can be stimulated by reducing wage costs, because lower wages would only mean less aggregate demand.

THE CONVERSION OF A PRESIDENT

Kennedy's eventual acceptance of the dynamics of growth as a positive good instead of merely as a corrective device geared to the performance of the cycle symbolized his willingness to make extensive use of Keynesian economics. The president's conversion did not come overnight, and it was not achieved in 1961. Throughout the 1960 presidential campaign, he had stressed his commitment to a balanced budget over the period of the cycle, unless there was a serious recession or a major national emergency. And during his first year in the White House, he continued to affirm his intention to balance the budget. As previously noted, he even considered a tax raise to finance the additional defense outlays required by the Berlin crisis in the summer of 1961, which destroyed hopes for a balanced budget in fiscal 1962.[16]

The president's budget for fiscal 1963, submitted to Congress in January 1962, was a blend of the policies recommended by his economic advisers and his instinctive sensitivity to political possibility. Cautiously forecasting a half-billion-dollar surplus, he warned that in view of the business upturn a deficit would swell inflationary pressures but that too large a surplus would risk prematurely stifling the momentum of recovery. To improve the administration's ability to cope with fluctuating economic conditions, he asked Congress for new discretionary weapons. His request, which went unheeded by the legislators, would have given the chief executive standby authority, subject to a congressional veto, to reduce personal income tax rates and initiate federal public-works programs whenever unemployment rose sharply.[17]

Not unexpectedly, the business community responded without enthusiasm to the record $92.5 billion budget for fiscal 1963. Kennedy's prediction of a small surplus was regarded as wishful thinking at best, or, more probably, fiscal "slight of hand" for political reasons.[18] While some criticism of the budget undoubtedly stemmed from the prevailing business suspicion of the New Frontier, a more fundamental objection was the intense and genuine fear that budget deficits spawned inflation. Not even assurances to the contrary by the respected secretary of the treasury, C. Douglas Dillon, succeeded in soothing the anxieties of private entrepreneurs.[19]

By early 1962, it was obvious that the recovery was beginning to lose its momentum. Even the improved performance of the economy in 1961 proved too weak to reduce the level of unemployment much below an intolerably high 6 percent.[20] Although the majority of Americans were prosperous in the early 1960s, Kennedy did not forget the jobless and the poor. Measures to improve their plight were sprinkled liberally among his legislative requests. But improving economic conditions lessened the sense of imperative in Congress to enact these proposals.[21]

His determination to lower unemployment significantly was critical in convincing the president to reorient his economic strategy during 1962. The annual rate of growth in America, as measured by the gross national product (the sum total of the nation's goods and services), measured less than 3 percent for the eight years of the Eisenhower administration and was only 3.5 percent in mid-1961.[22] Projections by the Council of Economic Advisers indicated that this growth rate was too low to cut unemployment to an acceptable level. In addition, Kennedy believed that this low rate of growth was inadequate to maintain America's position of dominance in its economic rivalry with the Soviet Union.[23] Motivated by the Council's estimates, the president began in 1962 to focus on "gap-closing and growth." The economic goal of the New Frontier would be budget balance at full employment, rather than balance each year or over the business cycle.[24]

Although welcoming economic expansion, many in business circles remained skeptical about the use of the gross national product as a measuring tool. So much of the GNP was tied to government expenditures, argued the *Wall Street Journal,* that federal spending action actually made the GNP go up or down, thus creating only an illusion of growth.[25]

In pursuing a goal of full employment, the CEA worried that increasing prosperity, feeding on its own momentum, might trigger a built-in cutoff before the production gap was closed or maximum employment was reached. The flexible federal tax schedule, designed to curtail automatically the growth of private income in time of economic boom, was a particular threat. By siphoning billions of dollars out of the private economy, the tax system was becoming a "fiscal drag" and was choking expansion. To offset this adverse effect, the council prescribed "fiscal dividends" in the form of tax cuts or larger federal spending programs. The tax reduction requested in 1963 was just such a corrective action.[26]

The End of Vacillation

The characterization of Kennedy as a reckless spender, so prevalent in some business publications, was irresponsible and inaccurate.[27] He strongly believed that public funds must be handled prudently, and he personally scrutinized every agency request for funds and encouraged his budget director to kill expendable programs.[28]

But by late spring 1962 the chief executive was convinced that deficit spending would be required to achieve the desired rates of growth and unemployment. On June 11, 1962, in a speech at Yale University, he made a major effort to educate the public in the usefulness of new economic ideas. In this address, described by Walter W. Heller as "the most literate and sophisticated dissertation on economics ever delivered by a president," Kennedy directly confronted the economic myths that threatened to prevent effective action in domestic affairs.[29]

Government, he noted, had indeed grown bigger, but it had grown less rapidly than the economy as a whole. The size of the national debt, a matter of unending concern to fiscal conservatives, had increased only 8 percent since World War II, compared with a 305 percent jump in private debt and a 378 percent growth in state and local government debt. The president particularly challenged the idea of the administrative budget as a measure of fiscal integrity. While admitting that this conventional budget had uses, he criticized its omission of special trust funds and changes in assets and inventories. He especially condemned its failure to distinguish between operating expenditures and long-term investments. Kennedy also assailed the cliché that federal deficits automatically create inflation and budget surpluses prevent it.[30]

The president's attack on economic myths appeared to be aimed directly at the business community. It came at a time when relations between business and the Kennedy administration, aggravated by the April crisis with the steel industry and by a steep decline of stock prices, were at their worst. Business spokesmen countered that the Kennedy speech was in essence big-government mythology and demanded that the president listen to opinions of businessmen if he really wanted their help. Business agreed to the chief executive's call for a new economic dialogue, but not strictly on his terms.[31] One executive, summarizing business sentiments, declared, "businessmen are not hobbled by out-of-date myths, but are standing up realistically to basic economic facts of life."[32]

Surprisingly, two weeks after the president's myth speech, the United States Chamber of Commerce dropped its insistence on a balanced budget as the first aim of government and urged an immediate $7.5 to 10 billion tax cut, even at the risk of a budget deficit.[33] This paralleled the recommendations of Heller and the CEA. The Chamber's willingness to accept a temporary deficit was a significant shift in policy, but business groups, including the Chamber, continued to demand reductions in government spending.[34]

Heller and the economic advisers felt confident that the Yale speech "marked a new era in American policy."[35] Kennedy's public statements during the remainder of his administration did reflect his growing reliance upon the new economics. Yet the president also promised not to let federal spending become excessive and referred frequently to the savings being achieved by government departments.[36] In speeches to business audiences, he continued to speak against unquestioning adherence to the stereotypes of fiscal policy while at the same time pledging his undiminished support of the competitive free enterprise system.[37]

Budget and fiscal policy in 1963 concentrated on the president's proposed tax cut (examined in detail in chapter 13), which was designed to generate sufficient economic growth to produce future budget surpluses.[38] The administration reasoned that an immediate deficit, caused by loss of tax revenues, would be far better than the chronic deficits certain in a stagnant economy.[39] Kennedy, keenly aware of the political obstacles to passage of his tax bill, sought to woo congressional support by coupling tax reduction with allusions to the danger of renewed recession. This temporary detour to the short-run anticycle context was contrary to the recommendations of his economic advisers, who preferred to emphasize the tax cut as the key to long-run expansion.[40]

The renewed upward surge of the economy in 1963, which increased business profits, made it harder to secure support for the president's fiscal policy. As the *Wall Street Journal* observed, "if the budget can't be balanced in high prosperity, when will it be?"[41] Businessmen feared that the benefits of growth induced by deliberate deficit financing would be seriously diluted by inflation. Instead the business community offered an alternate proposal: match tax cuts with reduced federal spending.[42] Ironically, the use of credit by government was taboo to executives who would never think of paying cash for long-term investment outlays by their own companies.[43]

Kennedy had no intention of eliminating social services by reducing federal spending. Liberal chastisement of his administration for not doing more to help the jobless and the poor deeply disturbed the president.[44] He decided to seek a general tax cut as much in the hope of striking at the unyielding unemployment rate as for any other reason, and before his assassination he was developing strategy for a broad campaign to attack degrading poverty.[45] Although unemployment and poverty were not identical, they frequently overlapped. Closely related, too, were the need for better education and for medical care. Since minority groups contributed a sizeable portion of the sufferers from both poverty and unemployment, civil rights also found a place in a program to erase the causes and effects of substandard living conditions.

BUSINESS AND THE NEW ECONOMICS

Without abandoning their belief that nonessential government outlays should be vigorously curtailed, sophisticated corporation executives, to a remarkable degree, have agreed with Kennedy's argument that the new economics would stimulate growth.[46] James Tobin, one of the president's able economic advisers, termed this transformation of thinking by men of affairs—businessmen, bankers, congressmen, financial journalists, editorial writers—nothing less than a revolution.[47]

Unquestionably, the key reason for free enterprise approval has been the spectacular economic boom which began in America under Kennedy in 1961. As prosperity and high profits accelerated during the administration of President Johnson, business acceptance of the new economics became even more pronounced, in part because businessmen felt more comfortable with Johnson; his style suited them far better than did Kennedy's intellectual manner.[48] But Kennedy laid the groundwork for his successor's extensive execution of the new policies.

Not all of the nonmonolithic business community would agree with Tobin. For many entrepreneurs, the new economics suggested more intrusion from Washington, unrealistic social experiments, and occult mysteries.[49] Wall Street has appreciated the value of an increased government role in economic management far more than Main Street, although both have welcomed the attempt to level the fluctuations of the business cycle.

By the mid-1960s, even skeptics were willing to admit at least temporary success for the modernized Keynesian ideas. But as Maurice Stans, Eisenhower's director of the budget, warned, there was no proof that the new methods could produce results in the long run.[50] In particular, greater government planning and the fear that insufficient attention was being given to the risk of inflation has disturbed conservatives.[51] Many economists, both in and out of business, have also maintained that Washington can affect purchasing power and economic activity only by changing the rate of growth of the total monetary supply, not by "fine tuning" fiscal policy.[52] Among both friends and opponents of the new economics, doubt has persisted about the accuracy of tools available for forecasting economic trends. Obviously, failure to appraise the future correctly could result in costly policy errors.[53]

Since 1966, serious inflation has somewhat blunted enthusiasm for the new economics among businessmen. For the government to manage demand effectively through fiscal and monetary policy, congressional cooperation is essential. And in 1967 and 1968, the legislators proved reluctant to act on the administration's request for a tax increase. The delay underlined a crucial question about the Kennedy-Johnson economics: It worked successfully to stimulate expansion, but can it also cool an overheated economy?[54]

The final verdict on the ability of the new economics to conquer the business cycle is not yet in. It may be hoped that refinements in economics and public administration will significantly improve forecasting tools and government's ability to respond rapidly to changing conditions. Meanwhile, business is unlikely to disregard the role of the new economics in the longest expansion in American history. And the enlightened managers of major corporations appear to depend too heavily upon federal policies and spending to return to classical economic ideas.

THE BALANCE OF PAYMENTS CRISIS

The Kennedy administration's efforts to stimulate economic growth were undertaken while watching the chronic balance of payments deficit, which threatened to restrict flexibility in fiscal policy. Simply stated, the payments problem resulted when more dollars flowed out— via business investment, tourist spending, import purchases, and foreign and military aid—than came in. Beginning in 1958, foreign holders of dollars began to convert their surplus American currency into gold, reducing reserves in the United States. This action coincided with a sharp increase in the size of American payments deficits and created concern about the stability of the dollar. Actually, the dilemma of a gold drain has recurred throughout American history.[55] After World War II, the nation's cash gold reserves were high and small annual deficits in most years were useful because they raised gold and dollar reserves in the rest of the free world. Not until 1958 did it become necessary to check the loss of gold.[56]

Possible cures for the dilemma fell into three general areas: (1)

rigid government controls, including limitations on foreign economic and military aid; (2) new approaches in the international monetary system, involving the ending of America's position as world banker; (3) increased trade surpluses. The first was highly undesirable in the light of traditional freedoms and America's worldwide commitments to defend the free world, and the difficulty of reaching agreement among a multitude of nations made the second doubtful. The third solution was the most appealing but required a sizeable advance in the already favorable American trade balance in the face of growing world competition.[57]

The reluctance of foreigners to continue accumulating dollars implied a lack of confidence in the strength of the United States economy and offered the business community a potent weapon to use against federal deficit spending. Businessmen agreed that expanded exports would help; some argued for higher interest rates to attract investors.[58] But they placed greatest emphasis on the need for maintaining the soundness and integrity of the dollar. To achieve this goal, Kennedy was urged to make a determined effort to balance the budget through vigorous pruning of nonessential, usually meaning nondefense, government programs.[59]

As president, Kennedy moved swiftly in an attempt to correct the gold outflow by a variety of methods, including mild controls, higher short-term interest rates, efforts to improve international monetary institutions, attraction of foreign tourists and investments, export promotion, and bargaining for lower tariffs.[60] His firm and repeated declaration that he would not devalue the dollar drew strong support from private enterprise.[61]

Most businessmen, however, criticized an administration plan to eliminate tax-deferral privileges on income earned by American enterprises operating in *developed* countries. Between 1957 and 1960, capital investment by United States companies in Western Europe and Canada exceeded dividends remitted home by $655 million. Business spokesmen stressed the net excess of funds accruing to the United States from investments in both developed *and* less-developed nations, and they argued that the White House proposal would diminish private incentive and hinder the growth of domestic firms. More than seventy representatives of individual businesses, trade and industry associations, and chambers of commerce testified against this measure before the House Ways and Means Committee. Only the National Retail Merchants Association appeared in support.[62]

Despite some improvement during the first two years of the Kennedy administration, serious concern over the American balance of payments position continued into 1963. Outlining more drastic measures to correct the loss of gold, Kennedy explained to Congress, "continued confidence at home and cooperation abroad require further administrative and legislative inroads into the hard core of our continuing payments deficit." He disclosed that the United States had asked for and received a $500 million standby credit from the International Monetary Fund, promised that defense and other government expenditures overseas would be trimmed from the 1962 level by $900 million, and asked Congress to enact an interest equalization tax to raise the cost of interest by approximately 1 percent for foreigners obtaining capital in the United States.[63] Simultaneously, the Federal Reserve increased its discount rate from 3 percent to 3.5 percent in an attempt to minimize short-term capital outflows.[64] Businessmen at home and bankers abroad expressed disapproval with the equalization tax as a device that would simply force borrowers to seek money elsewhere.[65] For American lenders, the tax would mean diminished profits.

Although the majority of businessmen maintained their support of foreign aid in principle, they increasingly questioned the wisdom of heavy overseas economic grants in the face of continuing payments difficulties. In defending mutual assistance as vital to the free world's security, Kennedy liked to remind business that large international investments by domestic firms played a major role in aggravating the loss of gold.[66] The president favored such investments as important to the growth of American industry, however, and he steadfastly opposed direct capital controls as "contrary to our basic precept of free markets."[67]

President Kennedy was not expected to end the baffling balance of payments problem miraculously. Only a relative handful of economists, government officials, and business leaders understood its complexities, and few of the experts could agree on a solution. The New Frontier's, principal contribution to eliminating the payments deficit was the Trade Expansion Act of 1962. And like the president's blueprint for "gap-closing and growth," this measure was designed to produce long-range, enduring benefits.

5

Incentive but not Reform: Business and Taxes, 1961–62

THE INVESTMENT TAX CREDIT

Shortly after his inauguration as president, Kennedy disclosed his intention to seek special tax incentives for the expansion and modernization of industrial plant and equipment.[1] Not even the Eisenhower administration, widely regarded as friendly to business, had dared to offer such a plum to industry. Democratic majorities in Congress during Eisenhower's last six years in the White House—consistent with the dictum that "only the Democrats can pass a sales tax, and only the Republicans can recognize Red China"—would probably have defeated such a proposal by a Republican president.[2]

Kennedy was aware that the business community greeted his election without enthusiasm. But his tax-credit plan, which marked a historic new commitment for the Democratic party, was more than a gesture to woo the political support of businessmen. He firmly believed that expansion and modernization were essential to growth and that business cooperation was vital if his goals were to be reached. As Walter W. Heller, of the Council of Economic Advisers, explained later, "The clear answer, though un-Democratic in tradition, was to offer special tax incentives for investment in machinery and equipment."[3]

The administration's investment incentive plan, revealed in detail on April 20, 1961, featured a tax credit for new investment, rather than accelerated depreciation allowances. To avoid unbalancing the budget by the loss of an estimated $1.7 billion in federal revenues that would result from the credit, the president asked Congress for a variety of tax reforms as a first step toward a projected broad revision of the income-tax laws. A majority of the changes suggested by Kennedy directly affected the interests of business.[4]

The House Committee on Ways and Means, heeding the president's call for immediate action, conducted hearings on the proposed tax bill the following month. However, the conjunction of economic recovery and stubborn opposition by interest groups delayed further action on the measure during 1961. Not until October 1962 did an investment tax credit and substantially modified tax reforms become law.[5]

In attempting to provide the largest possible inducement to new investment, which would not otherwise be made, the president shunned an across-the-board tax credit in favor of a sliding-scale formula, tying a variable tax credit to the size of the investment. Kennedy chose to separate the question of depreciation from investment incentive but promised that the Treasury Department would review existing depreciation schedules to determine if changes were appropriate.[6]

The business community was not united in its attitude toward the tax credit. Manufacturers were almost universally disappointed with the president's proposal. They welcomed incentive for modernization and expansion as a step in the right direction, but the majority viewed the sliding-scale formula as "gimmick-ridden," excessively complex, and far less effective than a simple acceleration of depreciation. Because only firms with ready access to capital could benefit from the investment credit, the plan was also attacked as inequitable. Smaller and financially weaker companies, which would have more difficulty securing funds, feared that the incentive credit would help the bigger enterprises grow still larger.[7] The sliding-scale formula proposed by the administration involved the same revenue loss as would a 7 percent across-the-board credit. Industrialists who did believe in the value of a tax credit preferred a simple flat-percentage allowance, but most insisted that an even more liberal credit was necessary to provide the desired growth.[8]

Trade and industry associations representing retailers, wholesalers, and service organizations supported the president's proposal as a positive step toward the acceptance of the "plowback" principle. Small entrepreneurs had for many years urged a tax credit for profits reinvested in a company. Small business also wanted the investment credit applied to the purchase of used as well as new equipment.[9]

Liberal and labor groups opposed the investment tax credit. Spokesmen for the Americans for Democratic Action and the AFL-CIO argued that tax relief for middle- and low-income citizens would increase purchasing power and do more to stimulate growth and reduce unemployment than a handout of billions of dollars to business.[10]

The lack of enthusiasm by business for the incentive plan astonished the administration. Assistant Secretary of the Treasury Stanley S. Surrey, chairman of Kennedy's preinauguration task force on tax reform and chief author of the president's 1961 tax recommendations, defended the investment credit against both liberal and industrial critics. Describing the plan as an aid both to recovery and to future growth, he predicted that in the long run the taxes from larger business profits would offset the immediate loss of tax revenues by a wide margin. Surrey, an eminent tax lawyer, discounted the claims of business leaders that faster depreciation write-offs were superior to the tax-credit formula, noting that for investors accelerated depreciation would be merely a loan to be repaid in later years, while the credit would be an outright deduction.[11]

Spurred by critical conditions in the textile industry, the nation's second largest employer, the Treasury Department complied with the president's request to review depreciation allowances. On October 11, 1961, the White House announced that the estimated average life for most textile machinery equipment had been substantially reduced. By July of the following year, new depreciation schedules were ready for all industries, the first administrative modernization of tax levies in twenty years. Calling the action "permanent change in the light of technological advance," President Kennedy estimated savings of $1.5 billion in the first year for businessmen and farmers.[12]

The *Wall Street Journal* "roundup" of executives in major industrial corporations reflected a curious apathy toward the new depreciation guidelines, although most spokesmen called the decision a forward step and granted that it would be helpful. Some business leaders complained that the revision did not go far enough and worried that surplus capacity would slow investment despite accelerated depreciation.[13]

When Congress reconsidered the president's tax proposals in 1962, most business witnesses who appeared before the Senate Finance Committee in April continued to oppose the investment tax credit as excessively complex and a form of government subsidy.[14] However, as it became obvious that the administration would keep its promise to revise depreciation allowances, the investment credit gained favor among businessmen.[15]

Business nevertheless exhibited little initial enthusiasm about final congressional approval of the investment incentive plan which substituted a flat 7 percent credit for the sliding-scale formula originally proposed by Kennedy.[16] But a sharp increase in orders for machine tools in October 1962, the month the president signed the tax bill, seemed to prove the skeptics wrong. Industrial surveys in the spring of 1963 indicated that capital investment was 7 percent ahead of the 1962 rate and suggested that the long-term plans of business were expansive in mood. Companies questioned cited the liberal depreciation allowances and the tax incentive program as important reasons for their increased investment.[17] With business prospects brighter than for many years, *Business Week* editorialized that the gathering speed of capital spending underlined the contribution that government tax policies can have on economic growth.[18] The brisk investment in early 1963 was no temporary stroke of luck; by 1964 capital spending reached $44.90 billion, compared with a disappointing $34.37 billion in 1961.[19]

TAX REFORMS

Business groups essentially expressed their own special interests in supporting or opposing the president's investment credit, but they formed almost a solid phalanx against the tax reform measures requested at the same time. In general, management officials representing both small and large firms believed that the plan to close tax loopholes created a false impression that upper-income taxpayers and businessmen escaped their fair share of the tax burden. In turn this image fostered the use of taxes to manipulate the social and economic structure in America. Business waged a successful fight against the administration's reform package as Congress first delayed, then substantially emasculated, key reform proposals.

As stated in the previous chapter, seventy business witnesses testified against the proposal to eliminate tax-deferral privileges for American companies with subsidiaries in developed foreign countries, while only one business group spoke for the measure. A similar solidarity existed concerning most of the other reform suggestions.

Although the restaurant industry led the assault on the proposal to tighten expense-account allowances, other business groups were also vigorous in their objections. While not denying that illegal expense deductions should be controlled, business representatives maintained that this could be accomplished best by strict, but flexible, administrative action rather than by legislative fiat. They particularly believed that only business could judge what was "ordinary and necessary" expense. Businessmen regarded the attempt to define justifiable expenses by legislation as illogical and dangerous.[20] One business editorial declared that the administration seemed "preoccupied with the Hollywood image of business, complete with champagne, yachts, safaris, and luxury suites."[21]

The law eventually passed by Congress limited company gifts and required that strict records be kept of specific expenses, especially for eating, drinking, lodging, and entertaining. Management officials admitted that they could "live with" the new rules, but viewed them as expensive, annoying, and a penalty on the honest businessman, while allowing the tax swindler to continue cheating.[22] Director Mortimer Caplin of the Internal Revenue Service proved to be both fair and reasonable. He successfully moderated the antagonism of businessmen by his willingness to heed their advice in formulating the details of administering the new legislation.[23] Surveys reported that cheating and lavish spending on expense accounts had declined sharply because of both government and company crackdowns, and restauranteurs and hotelmen across the country quickly complained about falling revenue.[24] If the term "it's deductible" did not pass completely from the American vernacular, the reform measure at least made it more uncomfortable for those who sought to abuse expense accounts.

In principle, business readily agreed that taxes should be paid on interest and dividends. But when Kennedy attempted to obtain withholding of taxes due at the source of such payments, the business community mounted an energetic campaign to defeat the proposal. Objections to the plan were numerous. Allegedly, the measure would frustrate the thrift motive, nullify the growth of savings accounts through compound interest, deprive savers of the use of money during the year, be expensive and complex for the institutions required to withhold the taxes, involve complicated claim procedures to recover funds withheld from persons having no tax liability and be an unfair hardship on low-income citizens relying on dividends and interest for living expenses. Business spokesmen also protested the administration's recommendation to repeal the dividend credit and exclusion allowance. Business argued that the credit and exclusion provided necessary relief against double taxation of dividend income and that elimination of these benefits would weaken enthusiasm for investing.[25]

Savings and loan associations, using misleading advertising and scare tactics, led the assault on the withholding provision with an extensive —and expensive—grass-roots campaign.[26] Their actions angered the president, who caustically noted that only those evading taxes on dividends and interest would be affected by withholding. Kennedy heatedly criticized the savings and loan associations for deceiving the people by innuendos that withholding was a new tax or a tax increase which would harm the elderly, widows, orphans, and those with low incomes.[27]

Administration officials estimated that at least $600 million per year in lost revenue could be collected if the provision was adopted. Stanley Surrey speculated that about 9 percent of dividend income and approximately 35 percent of interest income went unreported annually. The Treasury spokesman countered business claims that withholding would be a burdensome expense by observing that it would be a deductible cost of operation. And, he argued, the task was part of a company's obligation in a democratic society.[28]

Despite the efforts of the chief executive, Surrey, and others to correct false impressions about the proposal, Congress yielded to the swell of public opposition and eliminated the withholding provision from the Revenue Act of 1962. In addition, the dividend credit and exclusion loophole, which the administration wished to close, was left open.[29] As a consolation to the president, the legislators decreed that institutions paying an individual more than $10 per year in interest and dividends must report the payment to the Internal Revenue Service.[30]

The business community's attitude toward his tax proposals, especially its lack of energetic support for the investment credit bonanza, displeased Kennedy. But except for the harsh comments he made about the savings and loan associations, he was restrained in his criticism.[31] He disappointed his liberal supporters by calmly accepting what Congress offered rather than using his personal popularity in an appeal for public support to save important reform measures.[32] When he signed the tax bill, the president pointedly endorsed the new law as making "a good start on bringing our tax structure up to date."[33] To secure the tax reductions that would stimulate economic growth, Kennedy was plainly willing to sacrifice tax reforms.

6

An Oblique Approach to Antitrust

The history of the antitrust movement in America clearly repudiates the myth of a monolithic business community. While nearly all defenders of the free enterprise system give nominal support to antitrust laws, their opinions as to scope and method of enforcement vary greatly. Small business has consistently attacked the growing tendency toward concentration, warning of the evils inherent in monopoly.[1] Big business, although finding antitrust regulation annoying and expensive, has so far never launched a full-scale campaign against antitrust laws per se.[2]

During the Kennedy years, spokesmen for large companies repeatedly urged a reexamination of laws infringing on their right to merge and to operate efficiently in the international market.[3] Small operators, hoping for additional legislative protection against competitive pressure from giant firms, joined in the call for public hearings, amendment, and constant review of antitrust statutes.[4] Both sides agreed, as *Fortune* magazine colorfully phrased the problem, that "Antitrust—the Sacred Cow Needs a Vet," but they sharply disagreed about the type of treatment needed.[5]

At the beginning of the twentieth century, the formation of massive business combinations caused deep concern in America. The trend toward bigness continued through the century with few interruptions, accelerating its pace in the years following the Second World War.[6] Numerous studies have stressed the substantial control over the nation's industrial wealth by a relatively small number of individuals, both by direct ownership and by interlocking directorates.[7] But the public, perhaps because the perils of monopoly pale in comparison with explosive issues like civil rights and world peace, has shown little enthusiasm for a tough new antitrust crusade.[8] In the goods-oriented modern world, bigness seems to have become endowed with the ultimate economic values: efficiency, productivity, stability, expansion, technical progress, and social responsibility.[9] As a result, competition has lost much of its attractiveness and monopoly has lost much of its terror.[10] Some economists, contrary to traditional theory, even argue that the concentration of business may increase, not diminish, competition.[11]

Because President Kennedy regarded growth as an important cure for America's economic ills, he had to weigh the virtues of bigness against its faults. He appeared to agree with the growing belief in government ranks that big business is desirable because it is efficient. In addition, requirements for national security prompted decisions by the Kennedy administration which strengthened the market position of major corporations. The complexities of modern weapons systems tend to benefit the large companies which possess the facilities, personnel, and resources necessary to handle huge and complicated projects. This condition has accelerated the trend toward concentration, despite antitrust laws. Federal research and development funds have also been disbursed to a few large companies. By limiting research work, the government has allowed the favored firms to gain a dominant technological position if they later choose to bid on production contracts.[12]

Strongly influenced by his desire for economic growth and by defense needs, Kennedy, particularly in his last year in office, promoted closer relations between government and big business. In so doing he helped set the stage for what has been labeled a "new partnership" between these two forces under President Johnson.[13]

PRICE FIXING

The Kennedy administration had barely assumed office when the conviction of executives from twenty-nine electrical supply companies for price conspiracy made national headlines. The action against the electrical supply firms had actually been initiated by the Eisenhower Department of Justice. But since many of the rigged sales were to gov-

ernment agencies, it was up to the incoming Democratic administration
to recover the overcharges on the federal contracts.[14]

As noted previously, business made no attempt to justify this price-
fixing behavior, and a few influential executives used the opportunity
to urge companies to improve their ethical standards. While the Senate
Subcommittee on Antitrust and Monopoly, chaired by Estes Kefauver
(Democrat, Tennessee), a veteran opponent of business, conducted
extensive hearings on the electrical industry affair, the administration
took steps to prevent any repetition of price conspiracy on government
contracts.[15] On April 24, 1961, President Kennedy issued an executive
order requiring government agencies to advise the attorney general of
any identical bids received on contracts for over $10,000.[16]

Administration officials did not attempt to conceal their anger that
the price fixing could have existed so long without detection. The
Justice Department let business know that it intended to report identical bids to the news media to arouse public feeling, and would award
contracts to the smallest company bidding, instead of by lot, whenever
uniform bids were received. The *Wall Street Journal* agreed that conspiracy to fix prices was wrong but warned that uniform prices could
also occur because of tough competition and should not be taken
automatically as a sign of illegal price rigging.[17]

ADMINISTRATIVE ANTITRUST POLICY

The appointments of Lee Loevinger as chief of the Antitrust Division
and Paul Rand Dixon as chairman of the Federal Trade Commission
drew little applause from the business community. Dixon had been
staff director for the Kefauver Subcommittee on Antitrust and
Monopoly, which had long harried key industries with its investigations.[18] But Loevinger, a former Minnesota judge with pronounced
antibigness convictions, became the administration member who worried big business the most.[19]

The new antitrust director challenged the policies of some of the
largest corporations in the country, instituting suits against General
Motors, General Electric, Minnesota Mining and Manufacturing, and
United States Steel. Rather than concentrating on efforts to prevent
future mergers, he gave special attention to conspiracy violation, involving identical bidding, and reciprocity cases, concerned with companies who pressured suppliers to buy from them.[20] Loevinger, settling
swiftly into his new job, filed forty-two suits in his first nine months in
office.[21] Bluntly informing business that he intended to enforce the

antitrust statutes vigorously, he disagreed sharply with the argument that the laws against monopoly were inconsistent. He took particular exception to executives who complained that each business situation was different, but who wanted a clearer delineation of what government expected and demanded from business. The antitrust chief declared that it was "futile and logically absurd" to expect more flexibility and more certitude from the same law at the same time.[22]

A speech by Attorney General Robert F. Kennedy in November 1961 added to the anxieties of big business. The president's younger brother harshly rebuked businessmen who engaged in price conspiracies, equating such action with crooked gambling. He emphasized that although the administration was not antibusiness, it would vigorously prosecute violators of the antitrust laws.[23]

The president's angry response to the price increase by the steel industry in April 1962 provided an excellent opportunity for a dramatic speedup in antitrust efforts, had he been so inclined. But despite the fear of many executives, no antitrust onslaught on business materialized. *Business Week,* noting that Kennedy had made little effort to change the traditional antitrust approach of government, saw signs that the antibusiness charges against the administration following the steel crisis had produced a cautious new attitude in the Antitrust Division.[24] While antitrust problems are not strictly quantitative, the examination of case statistics is a common measure of antitrust activity. In 1962, records were established for the number of cases filed, terminated, and pending. But the quantities in each category were only marginally higher than during the last year of the Eisenhower administration.[25]

In May 1963, Loevinger was moved to the Federal Communications Commission, a promotion ostensibly designed to give the FCC the advantage of his experience as it became more involved in regulating the new Communications Satellite Corporation. The change came at a time when Kennedy was trying to convince business that it had nothing to fear from his administration. Businessmen regarded Loevinger as a "crusader" and sensed that his transfer signaled a transition in antitrust policy.[26]

William H. Orrick, Jr., who replaced Loevinger in the Antitrust Division, established a unique planning section to identify industries in which mergers would apparently be harmful to competition. Orrick's action indicated that attention would not be directed toward older industries that had already passed through the merger cycle. Big business welcomed Orrick's more flexible approach to the issue of bigness. While freedom of competition was considered essential to free enterprise, businessmen generally supported the right to merge and to acquire assets as a vital ingredient for a dynamic economy.[27] Even small businessmen wanted the right to grow larger.

Kennedy was aware that the increasing trend toward economic concentration frightened small entrepreneurs, and shortly after taking office he appointed a special White House committee to study the problems of the small operator.[28] The New Frontier stepped up activities of the Small Business Administration, especially its lending authority, and increased the number of "set-asides"—federal contracts specifically reserved for small companies.[29] These efforts provoked sharp criticism from some business sources as unwarranted special benefits, unwise government interference, and a detriment to genuine competition.[30] The president was proud of his administration's efforts on behalf of small business, but large firms continued to receive the overwhelming preponderance of federal awards.[31]

Administered Prices and the Kefauver Subcommittee

During the last years of the Eisenhower administration and during the Kennedy years, about two-thirds of all antitrust cases filed concerned price fixing.[32] The conspiracy scandal involving the electrical supply companies was a highly publicized part of a series of probes into administered prices in selected industries which was conducted by the Kefauver Subcommittee between 1957 and 1962. The concept of administered prices, first suggested by economist Gardner Means in the 1930s, was rescued from near oblivion by the Kefauver investigations and blamed for contributing to inflation.[33] The inquiries by the Kefauver Subcommittee focused on three points: (1) whether the prices charged by all sellers in an industry were approximately simultaneous and identical; (2) whether price behavior indicated the absence of independent competitive behavior by various firms; (3) whether price increases were necessary to compensate for higher costs.[34]

On two occasions, the Kefauver investigations resulted in embarrassing episodes for President Kennedy. One involved the steel industry in the summer following the government-steel confrontation in April 1962. Searching for possible price collusion, the Kefauver Subcommittee subpoenaed cost records from major steel manufacturers. However, four of the companies refused to release the information on grounds that the demand constituted unreasonable search and could seriously damage the competitive position of both the individual firms and the steel industry of the United States. The Subcommittee voted to recommend that the offending companies be cited for contempt of Congress, but the full Judiciary Committee refused to accept the recommendation.[35] This incident occurred while the president was attempting to improve his strained relations with the business community and made his task more difficult.

The passage of the Drug Regulation Act of 1962 followed two years of investigation by the Subcommittee on Antitrust and Monopoly and caused the second embarrassing incident involving the president, Kefauver, and business. Hearings on drug regulation in 1960 and 1961 drew sharp criticism from Republicans, the medical profession, and the drug industry. Efforts to pass a regulatory measure were fruitless until the frightening thalidomide incident in early 1962 mobilized public opinion for stronger controls over drugs.[36]

Kefauver, firmly believing that profits of drug manufacturers were generally excessive, prescribed keener competition as the remedy required to lower the high administered prices of drugs. He argued that this could be accomplished by shortening the life of patents from seventeen to three years and by simplifying the confusing array of product brand and generic names.[37]

Pharmaceutical company officials focused their opposition on proposals to reduce the life of patents and to require government licensing of drug manufacturers. Patent protection was stoutly defended as vital to provide incentive and to offset the high costs and risks of research. Other business groups, sensing the threat that similar restrictions might be applied to additional industries, joined in expressing hostility to these key provisions.[38]

President Kennedy supported the strong Kefauver bill originally, but at no time did he endorse the key patent-life reduction provision.[39] To Kefauver's intense chagrin, this item was deleted from the bill by agreement between representatives of the Health, Education, and Welfare Department and the Judiciary Committee at a meeting at which he was unrepresented. Kefauver angrily attacked this maneuver in a speech to the Senate. Warning that there was nothing left in the bill to bring the price of drugs down, he demanded to know why personnel from an administrative department were at the secret meeting, and just what was the administration's position on the bill.[40]

With Kennedy's blessing, Congress subsequently passed an act which substantially tightened laws governing the labeling, advertising, and testing of drugs. But the measure considerably softened the original Kefauver bill, and it totally excluded the proposal to reduce the period of exclusive patent ownership. While the measure further extended government authority over the pharmaceutical industry, it did not require federal licensing of drug makers.[41]

The president expressed pleasure with the final version of the bill, calling it "a major step forward toward giving necessary protection to the American consumer."[42] As passed, the act also won praise from the drug industry. The president of a major pharmaceutical manufacturing company labeled it good legislation in the public interest.[43] Kennedy's approach to drug regulation was to worry more about the health than the pocketbook of the American consumer.

CONGRESS AND COURT

Kennedy, like his predecessors in the White House, rendered lip service to strong antitrust enforcement but actually paid oblique, rather than direct, attention to the problem. He neither launched an administrative assault on big business nor forwarded recommendations to Congress for new tools to police and control the trend toward concentration. During the New Frontier years, legislative proposals to combat monopoly were initiated on Capitol Hill, not in the White House. The president did strongly endorse an unsuccessful attempt to authorize the Federal Trade Commission to issue temporary cease-and-desist orders against the continuance of unfair business practices while the cases concerned were pending.[44]

He also urged congressional approval of a useful antitrust enforcement measure to require companies planning merger action to notify government authorities in advance, a measure strongly supported by Loevinger, Dixon, and Attorney General Kennedy.[45] On this bill the business community divided predictably. Big business defended the right to merge, while small business warned that uncontrolled mergers weakened the free enterprise system.[46] Premerger notification did not become law, but Congress did approve a bill authorizing the Justice Department to compel businesses to surrender their records for civil antitrust investigations. The consensus of business regarding this act centered on concern that the removal of traditional judicial safeguards might lead to abuses. Since both the Eisenhower and the Kennedy administrations backed such a bill, its ultimate passage, in 1962, can scarcely be classed as an antibusiness move by Kennedy.[47]

Late in his first year in the White House, Kennedy was asked how much more he would have to do to assure American business that he was not antibusiness. The president quipped that if it was necessary to cease enforcing the antitrust law, then he supposed the cause was lost.[48] But as the New Frontier story unfolded, it became apparent that neither the chief executive, Attorney General Robert Kennedy, nor Congress seemed interested in a really aggressive campaign against bigness. The most serious threat to concentration in business during the Kennedy administration resulted from neither administrative nor legislative activity but from a decision by the Supreme Court. In 1962, the high tribunal affirmed a trial court's verdict in *Brown Shoe Company* v. *U.S.*, a case originally instituted by the Eisenhower Antitrust Division seven years earlier. The decision prohibited the merger of a manufacturer and a retailer, not on the basis of the share of the market that the merged firms would control, but because the vertical and horizontal aspects of the merger were deemed to further oligopoly.[49]

7

Business and the Kennedy Labor Policy

The Public Interest

As management appraised the candidacy of Kennedy in 1960, a Democratic president supported by organized labor presaged trouble for the business community. The pervasiveness of this belief, carefully cultivated among businessmen since the New Deal, caused Kennedy to deny explicitly and repeatedly that his administration would be oriented toward either business or labor.[1] Instead, he envisioned a new dimension to the labor-government-business triangle; the New Frontier would emphasize public, not private, interest.

In his early messages to Congress, Kennedy presented no specific recommendations for labor-management relations, but as he sketched his program "to move America forward," his basic labor policy began to take shape. He intended for labor, management, and the public to work together to combat high unemployment, to promote free and responsible collective bargaining, to keep the industrial peace, and to develop sound wage and price policies that would insure America's competitive position in the world markets.[2]

To emphasize the importance of the public interest in industrial relations, Kennedy appointed representatives of the public, along with union and business leaders, to the prestigious

Advisory Committee on Labor-Management Policy.[3] During the New Frontier years, the committee, under the alternating chairmanship of the secretaries of labor and commerce, issued reports on automation, collective bargaining, private pension plans, and foreign trade, and sponsored educational conferences and seminars. Unfortunately, because union officials feared any suggestion that labor would be subject to antitrust laws, the committee decided not to study private monopoly power. Even more important, the advisory group failed to complete a report on wage-price policies. Significantly, the committee provided business and union leaders with an informal opportunity to become better acquainted.[4]

The designation of cabinet secretaries to head the Labor-Management Committee reflected Kennedy's determination that the government should play an active role in industrial relations. It soon became apparent that the administration's involvement would be more extensive than mere efforts by the secretary of labor and the federal mediation service to settle strikes.

UNEMPLOYMENT AND INFLATION

Both business and labor agreed with the president that high unemployment needed to be reduced and inflation held in check, but they differed on how these goals were to be achieved. Business leaders argued that if labor costs were kept low, production increases through technology would reduce prices. Lower prices would in turn increase sales and profits, creating more jobs to meet the growing demand for goods. Following this line of reasoning, business groups united in opposing the Kennedy administration's minimum wage bill in 1961, emphasizing that a higher minimum wage was immaterial to a man without a job.[5]

To rebut this argument, proponents of the measure, including organized labor, stressed the need for increased purchasing power to stimulate demand.[6] Referring to the proposed $1.25 minimum rate, President Kennedy later asserted ". . . who's going to buy our automobiles and refrigerators if people are getting less than $50 a week?"[7]

Although the president sided with labor against business on the minimum wage issue, he consistently opposed the recurring suggestions by union officials for a shorter workweek to cope with automation and unemployment. Kennedy insisted that the forty-hour week was essential to economic growth, although he observed that a shorter week might be feasible in the future. In particular, he deplored the twenty-five-hour-week contract negotiated by the electrician's union in New

York City in early 1962, terming it clearly outside of the realm of productivity increases, and hence inflationary.[8] The Labor-Management Advisory Committee backed the president in his stand against a shorter workweek; however, labor members on the committee qualified their agreement by warning that if unemployment was not substantially reduced in the near future, shorter hours might be necessary.[9]

Despite the impressive economic recovery in 1961, a high level of unemployment continued to frustrate administration officials. To supplement fiscal programs designed to stimulate economic growth, Kennedy proposed measures to attack structural unemployment that occurred as industries became obsolescent or as automation eliminated jobs. Congress enacted an area redevelopment bill in 1961 and manpower retraining and public works measures in 1962 but refused for three years to pass a recommended bill to provide employment training for young people. The legislators also failed to extend the area redevelopment program in 1963.[10]

In theory both business and labor agreed that the hardships caused by structural unemployment should be ameliorated by vocational retraining, improved educational opportunities, and aid in relocation.[11] But national business groups opposed government financing and direction of programs to create employment. Fearing that government involvement would accelerate the trend toward a controlled economy, business urged federal authorities to lower taxes and curb abuses of union power but leave job training and area redevelopment in the hands of local governments and private industry.[12] Not all businessmen were hostile to the administration's proposed measures. For example, a number of local chambers of commerce which had benefited from area redevelopment strongly supported its extension in 1963.[13]

The programs suggested by Kennedy to curb structural unemployment were essentially designed to help over a period of several years. As a result, even the measures that did gain congressional approval were of small help in cutting the numbers of jobless during the Kennedy administration.[14] The manpower training program was able to place 70 percent of its graduates, but in fiscal 1964 only enough funds were provided to train 80,000 persons.[15] The administration's attempts to reduce the number of unemployed were so futile that labor leaders, despite their ties with the Democratic party and their fondness for Kennedy, repeatedly charged that the president's efforts were excessively timid.[16]

Kennedy had greater success than his predecessor in stifling inflation.[17] Some economists believe that stable prices in a time of rising demand are possible only when there is slack in the economy. According to this argument, the wage-price-profit spiral originates when firms with a strong market position bargain with strong unions. As the economy nears capacity, advancing wages provide oligopolistic firms with an inducement to increase prices.[18]

But the economy's operating at less than maximum capacity reduces the chance of reaching a position of full employment. Kennedy's vigorous efforts to stimulate economic growth emphasized his unwillingness to accept slack in the economy as a check on inflation. He was not obsessed with the problem of inflation above all others. As a presidential confidant, Theodore C. Sorensen noted, Kennedy "paid no heed to those who said inflation was a greater danger to our economy than unemployment."[19]

THE WAGE-PRICE GUIDEPOSTS

Although he put jobs first in importance, Kennedy nevertheless realized the danger of uncontrolled inflation. In its *January, 1962, Annual Report,* the Council of Economic Advisers presented guideposts designed to insure wage and price stability.[20] Chairman Heller of the CEA later explained that the guidelines, though having the chief executive's blessing from the start, only gradually became a full presidential objective.[21]

Although they advocated free collective bargaining as the proper vehicle for settling industrial disputes, the council insisted that wage and price decisions must be tied to productivity advances in order to be noninflationary. The guidelines could thus provide a useful standard for both the public and the government in determining if wage and price increases were justified.[22]

The initial reaction from the private sector was negative, but not frantically so.[23] The economy was just emerging from the 1960–61 recession; profits were down, unemployment was high, and inflation seemed a remote threat.

Both labor and business rejected the premise that the guidelines were complementary to strong and free collective bargaining.[24] The CEA's proposal looked like an excuse for greater federal interference, and even with a Democrat in the White House, unions preferred that the government keep out of its negotiations with management. Labor, as Joseph A. Beirne, president of the Communications Workers of America, told a Senate hearing, has traditionally fared better when bargaining with private employers than with the government.[25] Perhaps union officials also pondered the possibility that their leadership might seem unnecessary to rank-and-file members if wage increases were limited to producitvity increases.

Business believed that it was already at a disadvantage in negotiations with unions and feared that the wage-price guidelines would add to its difficulties. Management complained, as it had for years, about labor's exemption from antitrust laws. For big and small companies alike, the leverage that organized labor exerted in industrywide bargaining testified to the monopoly status of unions.[26] Not all firms within a specific industry could necessarily afford the wage increases that general productivity advances might indicate. Also, if all production gains were passed along to the workers, what financial benefits could be given to the consumers and stockholders?[27]

After government pressure helped force the steel industry to rescind its announced price increase in April 1962, the business community watched skeptically to see if the Kennedy administration would be as firm with labor demands for wage increases that exceeded the guidelines.[28] It soon became obvious that an obstinate union, oblivious to public opinion and government persuasion, could obtain a bigger wage package than the guidelines justified. The International Longshoremen's Association, stubbornly arguing that the prospects for reduced sizes of work crews "qualified" the 3 percent increase recommended by the administration, won an approximate 5 percent pay raise after a lengthy strike in 1962–63.[29] The guideposts were just that; they were not laws. Regardless of his inclination, the president simply had no legal power to enforce wage restraint.

Kennedy had more success in restraining inflation than in solving the unemployment riddle. Ironically, his successor had exactly the opposite results. The guideposts were still relatively new when Kennedy was assassinated. Although they proved useful in preserving wage and price stability during the abbreviated New Frontier, the guidelines received a much sterner—and critics would say fairer—test under President Johnson.

The Kennedy Council of Economic Advisers prescribed no arithmetic number, though the 3 percent average increase in producitvity between 1947 and 1960 was generally accepted as the standard. In 1966 the CEA specifically recommended a benchmark of 3.2 percent. But the sharp escalation of the Vietnam War unleashed strong inflationary tendencies and badly undermined the effectiveness and prestige of the guidelines. The following year, the council abandoned any precise percentage but stoutly reaffirmed its faith in the guidepost principle.[30]

Labor has been especially hostile to the wage-price recommendations. The AFL-CIO has charged that the guidelines aimed directly at the working man by unfairly limiting wage increases, while rising prices and corporate profits more than absorbed the fruits of greater productivity.[31] Conversely, management has complained that the government has allowed wage settlements in excess of productivity advances while using the guideposts to restrict price raises in conspicuous industries like steel manufacture. Business spokesmen have also called the guidelines ill-advised substitutes for unpopular political policies like tax increases, expenditure reductions, and tight money.[32] But suggested alternatives to the guidelines—accepting inflation arising from full employment, keeping unemployment high, using mandatory controls instead of voluntary guidelines, and toughening the antitrust laws to break up giant corporations—have attracted little enthusiasm.[33]

Many observers contend that better measurement tools will be needed if the guidelines are to improve their performance in the future. It is also possible that other factors, such as cost-of-living changes, may have to be merged with productivity variations to arrive at more valid standards.[34]

In his detailed examination of the guidepost controversy, John Sheahan concluded that, although not satisfactory as they stand, "The guideposts represent an intelligent gamble in an important direction."[35] He and other economists, in answering what is perhaps the fairest question about the value of the guidelines, have maintained that had they not been used, wage and price increases since 1962 would probably have been even greater.[36]

From their inception during the Kennedy administration, the guideposts were prematurely buried many times by their opponents.[37] But despite sharp criticism from both labor and management, the Johnson administration continued to use the wage-price standard. President Nixon, however, shortly after his inauguration in 1969, announced that his administration would no longer depend upon the laudable but ineffective voluntary guideline approach as a weapon to combat inflation.

KENNEDY AND COLLECTIVE BARGAINING

President Kennedy took office as a supporter of the "new arsenal of weapons" concept for dealing with labor-management disputes, particularly national emergency strikes.[38] He did not request new labor legislation, however, because his past congressional experience convinced him that the existing mood in Congress might produce an even worse law.[39] Lacking an ultimate weapon, such as the power to impose arbitration or to seize strike-bound firms, the president sought to make collective bargaining procedures more effective. The far-ranging efforts at personal diplomacy by Secretary of Labor Arthur J. Goldberg, and later by his successor, W. Willard Wirtz, proved useful in resolving labor disputes. However, negotiators increasingly tended to mark time pending the arrival of the secretary.[40]

Kennedy's action in the strike threat against several aerospace companies in 1962 won him no friends in the business community. The president supported labor's demands for a union shop and hinted at the loss of government contracts to prod the recalcitrant manufactures into agreement. While the unions were not wholly satisfied with the settlement, government pressure appeared to fall much more heavily on management than labor. The administration's intervention did minimize time lost by the strike.[41]

Controversies over "featherbedding" (make-work practices) in the airline and railroad industries presented the Kennedy administration with its most difficult challenge in industrial relations. The impact of automation on employment was reflected in the growing tendency among unions to concentrate on job security instead of wage issues. Kennedy's formula for dealing with "featherbedding" concentrated on protecting the men, but not the jobs. Workers were not to be laid off without regard for their needs and rights. The president's solution involved the employer's carrying employees through a period of adjustment, where necessary, and giving them first claim to remaining jobs.[42]

In the summer of 1963, Kennedy asked Congress for legislation to prevent a crippling railroad strike. Congress endorsed the president's request after labor and management yielded to pressure at the last minute and voluntarily submitted the two central issues to arbitration. The chief executive requested a two-year ban on strikes over work rules and asked that all unresolved points in the dispute be referred to the Interstate Commerce Commission for binding interim decisions. The joint resolution passed by the legislators, however, reduced the ban to six months and limited the scope of arbitration to the two key issues, then proposed a return to traditional collective bargaining with the right to strike.[43]

The president drew considerable criticism from business because of actions by the National Labor Relations Board. Kennedy's appointments to the board in 1961 resulted in the reversal of several key decisions made during the Eisenhower years. Businessmen complained that in reversing decisions, the NLRB was playing politics. A further objection was that the Kennedy board tended to "make policy," instead of merely rendering decisions. Particularly annoying to business was the ruling circumscribing the rights of an employer to speak freely against attempts by a union to organize his employees.[44]

The Kennedy NLRB used a case-by-case approach, which made it more difficult for either management or labor to be certain of its rights or obligations.[45] But the board also made substantial improvements in the efficiency of its regulations and appeal procedures.[46] Defenders of the Kennedy board have pointed out that it is difficult not to reverse a decision when the board disapproves, while policy determinations are inevitable in the administration of the National Labor Relations Act.[47] As for the charge that the board played politics, this was nothing new; both liberals and conservatives have traditionally solicited its favor.[48]

Labor's relationship with the Kennedy administration was on the whole congenial. Both of the men who served as secretary of labor during the New Frontier were noticeably influential in developing government policies. Union leaders were given appointments of importance and invited in increasing numbers to White House functions. In sum, Kennedy, who added a new dignity to so many facets of the presidency, also elevated the stature of labor.

The chief executive felt more comfortable in his relations with labor than with business, but he did not steer a prolabor course.[49] Despite apprehension in the ranks of entrepreneurs regarding a Kennedy-labor alliance, unions received no spectacular concessions from government. The New Frontier often appeared to be "neutral" on the side of labor in industrial disputes. But businessmen could at least be gratified that the president made no effort to secure changes to the Taft-Hartley Act long desired by unions, though he was reported to favor such amendments.[50] In his handling of strike threats which endangered the public interest, Kennedy's protection of the free collective bargaining process rated with his maintenance of stable prices among his most illustrious accomplishments.

EQUAL EMPLOYMENT OPPORTUNITY

When Kennedy became president, the rate of unemployment among nonwhite workers was, characteristically, double the average for whites.[51] The chief executive recognized that perhaps the most valuable assistance that could be given to minority groups was to help provide more and better jobs. On March 6, 1961, the president signed an executive order pledging the federal government to take the lead in ending racial discrimination in employment.[52]

The executive order combined the old committees on Government Contracts and Employment into the President's Committee on Equal Employment Opportunity (CEEO) and required contractors on government projects, with certain exceptions, to end discrimination in their employment practices. While nondiscriminatory clauses had been included in government contracts for years, the Kennedy directive made greater demands of contractors. It also provided for more effective enforcement, including publishing the names of violators, terminating contracts, and requiring government agencies to refrain from recontracting with those breaking the agreement until deficiencies were corrected.[53]

Programs to win the voluntary cooperation of American business and labor supplemented the government's mandatory requirements. On May 25, 1961, after initial negotiations with fifty of the largest government contractors, the CEEO and Lockheed Aircraft Corporation signed the first Plan for Progress. Aimed especially at firms holding no federal contracts, agreements were concluded with 115 companies employing more than 5.5 million workers by the end of the Kennedy administration.[54] Late in 1962, leaders of the AFL-CIO and 115 affiliated unions, representing about 11 million members, reached a similar agreement, the Union Program for Fair Practices.[55]

The first concrete test of effectiveness for the Plan of Progress occurred at Lockheed's Marietta, Georgia, plant shortly after the first agreement was signed. Responding to charges of discrimination by the National Association for the Advancement of Colored People, the aircraft manufacturer desegregated its facilities and pledged to open its training program to all qualified persons.[56] In the next six months, Lockheed reported a 26 percent increase in total Negro employees.[57]

Neither labor nor business rushed to embrace the president's equal employment program. Despite the attempts of A. Phillip Randolph, of the Brotherhood of Sleeping Car Porters, to hasten the adoption of a code endorsing the ending of segregation by AFL-CIO unions, the big labor federation moved slowly.[58] A similar apathy pervaded the business community. A survey of nearly four hundred Southern defense contractors in early 1962 revealed that at least one-fourth hired no Negroes.[59] Over a year later, a Pentagon probe into the policies of the Atlanta branches of national companies with defense contracts found only four of twenty-four firms not disregarding the employment regulations.[60] During its first year of operation, the Kennedy Committee on Equal Employment Opportunity handled more grievances than the former Committee on Employment had in six years.[61] But the CEEO functioned largely as a clearinghouse for complaints and an agency for persuasion, only occasionally disciplining violators.[62]

Companies participating in the voluntary Plan for Progress provided encouragement for the future. Reports filed in July 1963 by members of the program showed that larger numbers of Negroes were being hired than in the past, especially for salaried positions.[63] Surveys of businesses made in 1964 and 1965 indicated a gradually changing attitude in racial policies. While many elements contributed to the change, the government's policy of barring discrimination on Federal projects was commonly cited as a major reason.[64] In general, business followed, rather than led, the Kennedy administration in promoting equal employment opportunity for minority groups.

8

Steel, Stocks, and Confidence

The widely publicized confrontation between the government and the steel industry, in mid-April 1962, followed fifteen months of growing disenchantment with Kennedy in the business community.[1] Within months after he became president, the economy had reversed its direction and had begun a steady movement upward. But despite the end of the recession, the chief executive's policies drew more criticism than praise from businessmen, and the recovery's loss of momentum in the winter of 1961–62 added to the mounting discontent.

During the late months of 1961, the president sensed a growing loss of rapport with private enterprise. He emphatically denied that his administration was antibusiness and stressed that America could not prosper unless business prospered. As the first occupant of the White House since McKinley to speak at an annual convention of the conservative National Association of Manufacturers, Kennedy made repeated overt efforts to solicit the support of entrepreneurs.[2]

The chief executive's declared goal of faster economic growth within a noninflationary framework appealed to business. Higher sales meant little if rising costs prevented a company from holding or improving its margin of profit, and the "profit squeeze" was a particular worry for business in the

early 1960s.[3] Some business spokesmen pointed with horror to the contemporary trend toward welfare statism, but all businessmen worried
about making an adequate profit.

In few industries was the alarm over shrinking profits more pronounced than among steel manufacturers.[4] Steel had not raised its prices
since 1958, absorbing, at the urging of Vice President Richard M.
Nixon, the forty-cent hourly package pay increase granted steelworkers
in January 1960. The contract then signed scheduled wage boosts at
staggered intervals during the thirty-month duration of the agreement.

Observers in both business and government anticipated a price
increase by the steel manufacturers to compensate for the final wage
step-increase due October 1, 1961.[5] In a late-summer press conference,
Kennedy expressed hope that the companies would voluntarily maintain existing price levels, adding that his economic advisers believed
that the steel industry could withstand the higher wage costs and still
make a good profit.[6]

Early in September, the president clearly stated his views in identical
letters to top officers of twelve major steel companies. Terming steel
a "bellwether" of industrial costs, he reminded the executives that by
forgoing a price increase, they would be able to boast of three and a
half years of price stability when they negotiated a new contract with
labor for the following spring. "It would clearly then be the turn of
labor representatives," Kennedy counseled, "to limit wage demands
to a level consistent with continued price stability."[7]

The president's letter was released to the news media and was
attacked in business journals as unwarranted government interference
in management responsibility.[8] David J. McDonald, president of the
United Steelworkers of America, applauded the position of the chief
executive, and pledged the union to consider the public interest in
wage negotiations.[9] Replies by the steel company executives ranged
from a simple, curt acknowledgment of receiving the president's communication to Roger M. Blough's meticulously detailed defense of
United States Steel's urgent need for greater profits to "make up for
serious inadequacies in depreciation allowances, repay borrowings,
pay dividends, and buy new equipment."[10]

As the chief executive officer of the nation's largest steel manufacturer, Blough frequently served as spokesman for his industry.[11] He
agreed that inflation was a matter of serious concern, but he charged
that the causes of inflation were clearly associated with government
fiscal policies. In particular the steel executive chided Kennedy's eco-

nomic advisers for selecting "return on net worth" as the basis for evaluating steel's profit position. Noting the 50 percent depreciation of a dollar invested twenty years ago, he recommended using "profit as a percentage of sales" as the most meaningful measurement in an inflationary period. On this basis, the steel industry equaled the 8 percent level of 1940 profits in only one year through 1960, averaging only 6.5 percent between 1955 and 1960.[12]

Although the steel industry argued that it needed more profits, it did not raise prices in 1961. In January 1962, the formal presentation of the New Frontier's wage-price guideposts by the Council of Economic Advisers symbolically coincided with the beginning of bargaining between the steel companies and the union for a new contract. The administration was particularly anxious for a new steel-labor pact to be concluded early, so that users of steel could plan without resorting to stockpiling. But as the president explained to newsmen, all the government could do was to indicate the public interest; the companies and the union were free to negotiate as they pleased, unless there was a strike which threatened the national health and safety.[13]

The White House stayed in close touch with the contract talks, and when the negotiators agreed on a new, noninflationary pact in late March 1962, Kennedy enthusiastically telephoned his congratulations to labor and management leaders.[14] The settlement, which included significant benefits to protect worker job security, was generally estimated to cost 2.5 percent, considered by the Council of Economic Advisers to be safely within the recently introduced wage-price guideposts. Significantly, the agreement seemed to relieve the threat of a price increase by steel. Coming without a strike, three months before the old contract expired, the settlement was an impressive victory for free collective bargaining.[15]

THE STEEL CRISIS

The president's pleasure with the demonstration of economic responsibility by labor and management was short lived. On April 10, 1962, Roger M. Blough personally advised the chief executive at the White House that United States Steel was increasing prices six dollars per ton across the board. The drama that unfolded in the subsequent seventy-two hours ranked among the top headlines of the Kennedy years.[16]

Seven large steel manufacturers, following the lead of United States Steel, promptly raised their prices. Initial editorial response to the action among business journals was mixed. Some defended the decision by steel as necessary and just, while others labeled the move a serious blunder in public relations.[17]

Kennedy indignantly denounced the price increase as "a wholly unjustifiable and irresponsible defiance of the public interest."[18] The frenetic activities of government officials reflected the president's strong feeling against the action by the firms. Privately, members of the administration, by telephone and in person, explained the chief executive's opposition to acquaintances holding executive positions and directorships with steel companies.

Secretary of Defense Robert McNamara announced that his department was directing defense contractors to switch their steel purchases to manufacturers who did not raise prices. The Justice Department immediately subpoenaed documents relating to the price increase and ordered a grand jury investigation of the incident. Agents of the Federal Bureau of Investigation called reporters early in the morning to verify stories that a top official of Bethlehem Steel Company had denied the need to raise prices only hours before his firm announced an increase. On Capitol Hill, Democratic congressmen denounced the steel producers' action, promised investigations, and threatened legislation to protect the public interest.

In a genuinely competitive industry, the almost instantaneous action of the major steel manufacturers in raising their prices would have appeared blatantly conspiratorial. But for many years, steel has been an oligopolistic industry, with United States Steel clearly functioning as the price leader. The surprising thing in April 1962 was that several of the big steel producers did not rush to join the leader in the price boost. Inland Steel, a small but highly efficient manufacturer, followed quickly by Kaiser Steel, announced that it would maintain prices. Armco, another key member of the industry, also decided to hold firm. These decisions started a chain reaction of companies rescinding their price increases. The crisis ended on April 12, when United States Steel determined that its prices, too, would revert to their previous levels.

Although many business spokesmen questioned the wisdom of the steelmen's strategy, most agreed that responsible company officials must be free to make the decisions deemed necessary to assure adequate profits. The administration's swift coercion of the steel firms frightened the business community and severely strained relations between private enterprise and the president. A *Business Week* survey of executives reported the general mood to be that "the damage is irreparable." Some were unwilling to talk, even anonymously, for fear of reprisals on government contracts.[19]

MARKET PRESSURE OR GOVERNMENT PRESSURE?

Conditions in the steel industry were not economically healthy in 1962. Profits were off badly, exports were substantially lower, and production was sharply below the high marks of the mid-1950s.[20] Most steel executives explicitly denied that they had succumbed to government coercion to rescind the price increase, stressing the competitive pressure of the market as the determining factor. At the same time, industry spokesmen sharply condemned the president's attempt to interfere in management's right to set prices as an attack on the free enterprise system.[21]

In telling his side of the steel price story, both in early May and later, Roger M. Blough agreed that the decisions by some leading steel producers to hold prices "actually settled the whole issue." The steel official avoided a tone of harshness, at least publicly, in describing the affair, repeatedly pointing to his continuing cordial relations with Kennedy. Defending the higher steel prices as important to the economic health of the steel companies and actually in the public interest, Blough emphasized that at no time in the preceding months had he tried to give the president the impression that United States Steel would not raise prices. He also emphatically denied that the price increase had political overtones intended to embarrass or pressure the administration or the chief executive.[22]

Despite Blough's insistence that economic factors alone dictated the price rise, Kennedy regarded the action, coming as it did within days after the steel industry had accepted the union's wage restraint, as a double cross and a personal affront to the presidency. It underminded his prestige with labor and his whole program for controlling inflation. Since he had concentrated his greatest effort for price-wage stability on the steel negotiations, his failure seriously weakened his position with all other industries and unions.[23]

In his study of the steel crisis, Grant McConnell argued that the administration came "perilously close to an exposure of impotence" and was actually saved by the real power, the power of the market.[24] This seemed to imply that the president had used substantially all of his executive authority, and that further action of significance would have had to come from Congress. But if market pressure, not government pressure, forced the rescinding of the price increases, then the "scare" charges made by business that Kennedy was threatening the decision-making privileges so sacred to free enterprise were considerably exaggerated.

The chief executive had at least two obvious and potent administrative weapons remaining. He could have threatened to withhold policies favorable to business, such as the pending investment tax credit and faster depreciation write-offs. And he could have continued harassment of the steel companies by federal departments and agencies. Public condemnation by a popular president, combined with aggressive administrative action in antitrust, tax matters, and other areas, would have been embarrassing, annoying, and damaging to profits.

Unknown, as yet, is what specific leverage the administration applied against Inland, Kaiser, and Armco. It is possible, for example, that fear of spoiling the probable passage of the investment tax credit weighed heavily in the decisions of these companies to hold the price line. When such inside information is revealed, historians will be able to make a more valid judgment on Kennedy's role in the steel affair. A reasonable guess is that both federal pressure and market pressure played key parts in thwarting the price increase.

EASING STRAINED BUSINESS-GOVERNMENT RELATIONS

At least on the surface, the outcome of the steel crisis marked an important victory for the New Frontier and the public interest. Had he so chosen, Kennedy could have used his triumph to launch a hostile attack on business in general, and on big business in particular.

If the president contemplated a significant swing to the left—and there is no indication that he did—he quickly determined against such a course. At a news conference on April 18, 1962, he emphatically declared that his administration harbored "no ill will against any individual, any industry, corporation, or segment of the American economy." Although specifically denying that recriminations would serve any purpose, the chief executive did hint that had the steel companies held firm in their price increases, the prospects for passage of the investment tax credit and for rewriting the depreciation allowance schedules would have been dim.[25]

Businessmen had scarcely had time to appraise and digest the president's consoling words when a story began to circulate that Kennedy had used highly derogatory language in referring to businessmen on the night the price increase was announced. The chief executive's alleged remark that his father had always told him that all business-men were sons-of-bitches, but that he had never believed it until then, was first printed in the *New York Times* on April 23, 1962.[26] At a news conference two weeks later, the president agreed to answer a question about his remark. Noting that his father was a businessman himself, Kennedy declared that he, like his father, had confined the statement not to include "all" businessmen. That he found the term appropriate to apply to steelmen on the occasion of the price raise, the president did not try to deny.[27]

It is not unnatural for men in public life, even American presidents, to invoke, privately, comparable or even harsher epithets when angry.[28] But Kennedy's remark, since it became known publicly, provided a battle cry for those wanting to accentuate the anti-Kennedy sentiment in the business community. No other single incident connected with the steel crisis aroused so much hostility, although the middle-of-the-night calls to reporters by FBI agents ran a close second.[29] Within a short time, buttons emblazoned with the letters "S.O.B."—Sons of Business or Save Our Business—began to appear. Business cards, bumper stickers, and sly jokes combined wit and sarcasm to attack the president, the administration, his advisers, and his family.[30]

More sophisticated business spokesmen bluntly warned that Kennedy had lost the confidence of entrepreneurs. The business community generally agreed with the commentator who described the "brutal exercise" of presidential power in the steel price episode as "a pretty hairy, scary performance in a nation which presumably operated a relatively free enterprise system."[31] More caustically, a retired tire manufacturing company executive charged, "Lip service to free enterprise is belied by the steady march to socialism."[32] More temperate business criticism focused on what Henry Ford II described as the dangerous implications of government intervention in wage-price decisions.[33]

At a conveniently scheduled appearance, April 30, 1962, before the annual meeting of the United States Chamber of Commerce, Kennedy again sought to allay the apprehensions of the business community. The president made no effort to evade the fact that relations between business and government were strained. But he reminded his listeners that government relied heavily upon business earnings for its revenue and could not afford to create an atmosphere that penalized profits. Denying that his administration wanted the additional burden of setting prices for individual products, Kennedy declared that business was essential to the nation and urged the executives to work with government to create a climate of understanding and cooperation.[34]

Influential business leaders meanwhile attempted to check excessive animosity toward the president. Ladd Plumley, president of the National Chamber of Commerce, proclaiming his desire to "rebuild the bridge between business and government," conferred during May with Kennedy and other top administration officials.[35] A random sampling of executives at the May meeting of the Business Council revealed wariness, but not real hostility, toward the president. Roger M. Blough significantly led a toast to the president at the Council's banquet meeting.[36]

Other executives publicly warned that friction between government and business might seriously damage economic growth and seconded Kennedy's call for understanding and cooperation between the two antagonists.[37] The president repeatedly emphasized this theme in remarks before business audiences and in news conferences during the weeks that followed the steel crisis.[38]

THE STOCK MARKET CRASH

A bearish stock market aggravated Kennedy's already difficult task of closing the rift between the business community and the government. After reaching a record high in late December 1961, the stock market began a gradual trend downward during the following month. When the president reacted negatively to the steel price increase, many financial analysts quickly blamed his actions for further weakening investor confidence.[39] In May the market decline quickened. On Monday, May 28, 1962, a wave of selling resulted in the sharpest drop in stock values in one day since October 29, 1929.

At first the chief executive refused to comment on the falling market averages, except to emphasize his belief that the nation's economy was basically strong.[40] But as the decline continued, he asserted that the drop reflected recognition by investors that inflation was ending.[41] Many respected stock analysts had warned for several months that stocks, relative to earnings, were overvalued.[42] Some of Kennedy's sternest critics admitted that the ingredients for a "crash" had been present for a long time; only the prospects of inflation could justify artifically high stock prices.[43]

As the president later noted, he received several thousand letters complaining about the "Kennedy Market" when stock prices went down, but not one communication crediting him with its recovery.[44]

Kennedy's actions in the steel crisis undoubtedly caused investors, both large and small, real concern over the course of the economy. Emotion plays a vital role in determining the prices of stocks. Prices, relative to earnings, were overvalued at the start of 1962; but investor psychology often overrides the hard realities of prices and earnings, and, for a brief cycle, forces the market up on the strength of confidence in the future.

Kennedy may reasonably be blamed for quickening the decline in the market. The withdrawal of the price increase by the steel companies underlined the fact that inflation, at least momentarily, was checked. Since, over the the long cycle, the market tends to discount temporary emotional influences and adjust itself to realistic investment values, it is incorrect to make the president the villain for the market's six-month decline. The real culprit was the recession of 1960–61, which sharply depressed corporate earnings. A special Securities and Exchange Commission committee, authorized by Congress in 1961 to conduct a detailed examination of the nation's securities markets, stressed that the high prices of stocks to earnings contributed critically to the May 1962 market break. The investigators, under the direction of Milton H. Cohen, a Chicago lawyer, uncovered no evidence of market manipulation by brokers or exchange officials during the 1962 stock crisis. The lengthy report issued by the SEC committee in 1963, although making numerous recommendations to correct weaknesses in stock market operations, was generally favorable to the securities industry. As profits increased dramatically during late 1962 and in 1963, market averages responded by climbing to a new record shortly before the president's assassination.[45]

RESTORING BUSINESS CONFIDENCE

The stock market crash on the heels of the steel crisis intensified the ugly business mood regarding Kennedy and his administration. Some free enterprisers tended to blame the president's advisers for his alleged antibusiness actions, and others held the chief executive personally at fault.[46] But despite their political bitterness, entrepreneurs were generally optimistic and confident about the future of the economy.[47] A poll of 30,000 members of the business community revealed that over 88 percent believed the administration was strongly or moderately antibusiness. Yet a significant majority of those surveyed favored the president's foreign trade bill and his investment tax credit proposal.[48] Questioned about this apparent inconsistency, Kennedy suggested that although most businessmen were Republicans, they recognized what was in the best interests of business and the country.[49]

In his celebrated Yale University speech of June 14, 1962, in which he sharply attacked economic myths, the president spoke candidly about business confidence. He rejected the idea that "any and all turns of the speculative wheel" were the result of a lack of confidence in the national administration. The economic downturns of 1929, 1954, 1958, and 1960, Kennedy noted, occurred when business had full confidence in the administration in power. Referring to the recent differences between business and government, he urged a serious dialogue between the two forces that would produce useful collaboration in promoting economic progress. It was time, he warned, to stop the trend toward meeting present problems with old clichés—"before it lands us all in a bog of sterile acrimony."[50]

Many responsible business leaders were receptive to the call for open channels of communication and active cooperation between the administration and the business community. Executives of large corporations who were active in such groups as the President's Labor Management Advisory Committee, the Committee for Economic Development, and the Business Council—organizations designed to facilitate the flow of ideas between government and business—played a significant role in relaxing taut relations. As a result, the really savage attacks on the administration were largely confined to back rooms, clubs, and board meetings.

Long before the steel crisis, Kennedy, both by public statements and by legislative proposals such as the investment tax credit, had attempted to encourage business support for his administration. Once the steel companies withdrew their price increase, the president and ranking government officials resumed energetic efforts to convince entrepreneurs that the New Frontier was neither dangerous nor unfriendly.[51]

Within months, business received the benefits of new, liberal depreciation allowances, the long-delayed tax credit bill, lower margin requirements for buying stocks on credit, and a new trade bill. In addition, the president supported a drug bill satisfactory to drug manufacturers and backed communications satellite legislation favorable to the private communications industry.

The following year, Kennedy laid the groundwork for tax revision that substantially lowered corporate and personal income taxes. Business was also pleased that he did not recommend changes in the existing labor laws or pursue aggressive antitrust action against the steel industry or against business in general. Among important reforms desired by liberals, only civil rights was vigorously pushed by the president during the remainder of his administration. In April 1963, one year to the month after the steel crisis, the president, although still warning against the inflationary danger of an across-the-board increase in steel prices, gave his tacit approval to selective price boosts by steel companies.[52] With the stock market and business profits edging toward new highs in late 1962 and in 1963, the backlash of bitterness over the steel and stock market affairs subsided into history for most businessmen.

9

Planning, Controls, and Regulation

Business Suspicion of Kennedy

Businessmen viewed the phenomenal growth of the federal government in the twentieth century with suspicion and, sometimes, with outright hatred. While most members of the business community accepted the existence of a "mixed" economy, they continued to guard jealously their prerogatives as managers. With the election of a Democratic president in 1960, most businessmen unhappily anticipated the impact of more vigorous federal efforts in the private sector.[1]

Not all increased government activity was viewed as necessarily detrimental to the interests of business. Expected higher federal spending for defense requirements would be beneficial, as would additional support for research and development projects.[2] But business leaders worried about the prospects of the government's using its massive powers to protect the underdog, socially and economically.[3]

What business wanted from government was a political climate in which economic growth could take place without direct or indirect controls, except when necessary to prevent an imminent threat to national security. When controls were essential, most businessmen preferred that they be derived from Congress, not the executive branch. In general, the business community agreed that the continuing trend toward a welfare state made it imperative to resell the virtues of a competitive economic system to Americans.[4]

Much of the friction that developed between Kennedy and business resulted from confusion over the differences between government planning and direct government controls. James Tobin, a member of the Kennedy Council of Economic Advisers, was one of many administration officials who tried to clarify the misunderstanding. Stressing the distinction between plans and controls, Tobin noted, "clearly there is a great difference between planning one's own actions and coercing the actions of others, between using forethought and using force."[5] Kennedy recognized the advantages of planning, and both during the campaign and during the period between election and inauguration, he depended heavily upon study groups and task forces for ideas and advice.[6] As president, he continued to rely upon conscious and coherent planning.

To some businessmen, planning conjured up unpleasant visions of Washington bureaucrats directing the affairs of private companies and private individuals within tightly circumscribed limits.[7] But other members of the business community accepted the wisdom of some degree of central planning if America was to maintain its position as the champion of the free world. In particular, enlightened executives of blue-chip corporations admitted the inevitability and the necessity of planning by the federal establishment in a complex economy. But they urged that government reconcile its social and economic objectives with the traditional American free enterprise system.[8]

BUSINESS AND THE KENNEDY REGULATORY AGENCIES

Like Presidents Truman and Eisenhower, Kennedy hoped to remodel the executive branch to make it function more efficiently. Early in his administration, he submitted seven reorganization plans to Congress, including five concerned with regulatory agencies. The president's measures closely followed the preinauguration report on the subject prepared by James M. Landis. Drawing upon his years of service with regulatory bodies, Landis urged the creation, within the executive department, of an Office of the Oversight of Regulatory Agencies. Kennedy, perhaps sensing congressional opposition to the overtone of centralization inherent in the suggestion, deleted it from his own proposals.

The president did use two of the report's most important recommendations. He urged that the authority of each agency chairman be greatly expanded and clearly defined and that the chairman be responsible to, and serve at the pleasure of, the chief executive. To reduce the long delays required to secure decisions by regulatory agencies, Kennedy proposed that they be allowed to delegate authority to subordinate panels.[9] Reorganization plans were submitted for the Securities Exchange Commission (SEC), the Federal Communications Commission (FCC), the Civil Aeronautics Board (CAB), the Federal Trade Commission (FTC), and the National Labor Relations Board (NLRB). The proposals were substantially identical, and similar objections were advanced for each.

Business representatives spoke firmly against any shift of control over the regulatory agencies from the legislative to the executive branch and urged Congress to conduct extensive studies and write its own legislation to meet the requirements of changing industries. Spokesmen for business also warned of the danger of the sweeping delegation of rulemaking and adjudicatory functions to persons who bore no public responsibility.[10] Despite the parallel nature of the measures, only two —the reorganizations of the CAB and the FTC—won approval in both the Senate and the House; enough Democrats joined opposition Republicans to kill the other three bills.

Private enterprise remained ever alert for signals indicating a shift in policy by regulatory agencies.[11] The colorful speech by Chairman Newton Minow of the Federal Communications Commission in May 1961, in which he described American television as a "vast wasteland," seemed to the *Wall Street Journal* to be an implied "plug" for government censorship.[12] Minow's remarks earned him the antagonism of much of the broadcasting industry and fueled its opposition to the president's reorganization plan for the Federal Communications Commission.[13] No censorship resulted, and discriminating viewers of television continued to see considerably more waste than quality on their screens.

The powerful utility industry was vociferous in warning of the threat of New Frontier incursions upon private business.[14] Kennedy's attempt to appoint a former counsel of the Tennessee Valley Authority, Joseph C. Swidler, as chairman of the Federal Power Commission provoked a controversy early in the new administration. The holdover chairman from the Eisenhower years refused to resign his position, and Republican congressmen threatened a court suit if the president tried to force the resignation. Although the recalcitrant official subsequently reconsidered and vacated the post, the incident underscored the anticipated change in public power philosophy when a Democrat replaced a Republican in the White House.[15] Not only did the business community challenge Swidler's objectivity in questions involving public versus private power, but it also regarded the Interior Department, under Secretary Stewart Udall, as a bastion of pro-public-power sentiment.[16]

Kennedy's pronouncements did not suggest a revolutionary expansion of public power. He insisted that he would support a public power project only if it were proved that a power site could not be developed competently by private interests or that private service would not be satisfactory and competitive.[17] The president placed the greatest stress on making sure that the nation planned adequately for its rapidly growing power needs. To this end, the FPC made completion of a comprehensive national power survey—public, private, and cooperative—its primary objective during the New Frontier.[18]

The administration's moderate policy on power issues gradually eased anxiety in private industry, while irritating champions of public power. By late 1962, a utility executive was willing to concede that not as many public power projects had come into being as expected.[19] But FPC Commissioner Howard Morgan, in advising the president that he did not wish to be considered for reappointment, tartly implied that the Power Commission was dominated by utility interests.[20]

PROTECTING THE CONSUMER

In March 1962, the president sent a broad program to Congress emphasizing the protection of consumer interest, including a recommendation for larger staffs for all major regulatory agencies and approval of legislation to strengthen controls concerned with food and drugs and unfair business practices. He also announced that a Council of Consumer Advisers would be appointed to assist and advise the government, thus fulfilling a promise he made during the 1960 presidential election campaign.[21]

In the same message, the chief executive endorsed two measures— "truth in lending" and "truth in packaging"—that had long been favored by liberals and strenuously opposed by large and vocal numbers of the business community.[22] The lending bill, in particular, aroused the wrath of businessmen to a degree that appeared out of proportion to the severity of the measure. Sponsored for many years by Senator Paul Douglas (Democrat, Illinois), the bill required full disclosure of all interest charges on installment contracts and demanded that interest be stated in terms of the simple annual rate. Management objections stressed the complexity of computing simple annual interest and the argument that the measure would spawn a whole series of related federal policing bureaus and regulations. Business strongly urged that the problem of enforcing honest and ethical lending practices be left to the states.[23]

Opponents of the packaging bill pointed out the problem of standardization of size relative to quality. Further, they stressed that the small number of abuses in packaging found by Federal Food and Drug Administration investigation made expensive detailed regimentation by government unnecessary.[24] The president made no additional public appeal for support of the two bills, and interest groups were again able to prevent passage of the measures.

PLANNING AND PERSUASION IN ACTION

Modern presidents have often been accused of using powers neither prescribed by the Constitution nor sanctioned by Congress. But in 1946, the chief executive was given an explicit legislative mandate to provide economic planning. The Employment Act of that year, passed with strong bipartisan support, specifically directed the president to send to Congress each January an economic statement reporting the existing levels and foreseeable trends of employment, production, and purchasing power, along with a program to promote positive progress in all three. To advise the president and prepare the report for Congress, the act established a three-man Council of Economic Advisers to be chosen by the chief executive and accepted by the Senate.[25]

Ably chairmaned by Walter W. Heller, a respected economics professor from the University of Minnesota, the Kennedy Council and staff were heavily Keyesian in orientation.[26] As described in an earlier chapter, the CEA was firmly committed to the new economics—the positive management of demand by government through fiscal and monetary policies. Planning was important to the Council's policies. But contrary to the fears of some in the business community, planning did not mean federal regimentation of the American economy.[27]

Once the nation began to emerge from recession in 1961 the Council drew up a model of a high utilization employment economy for 1963, projecting the performance levels required by all sectors of the economy to achieve a 4 percent minimum unemployment. Asked to criticize the forecasts, business economists cautiously agreed to provide data on anticipated output in their own industries.[28] The CEA presented its wage-price guideposts in its portion of the president's 1962 *Annual Economic Report* in an effort to inform management, labor, and the public of ways the wage and price decisions could voluntarily be adapted to productivity increases which would avoid a price-wage spiral. To stimulate faster economic growth, the Council took the lead in urging a tax revision for both corporations and individuals.[29]

In none of these proposals did the Council suggest new, direct controls. Instead, the CEA relied upon the prestige of an active president to shape traditional budget, tax, and monetary controls into tools that would secure the objectives of the administration.

To adapt monetary controls—concerned with interest rates and the quantity of money and credit—to his purposes, the president depended upon the cooperation of the independent Federal Reserve Board and its respected chairman, William McChesney Martin. Traditionally the Democratic party has favored low interest rates. During the presidential campaign in 1960, Kennedy repeatedly attacked the policy of using high interest charges as the sole means of controlling inflation. Warning that high costs of borrowing seriously retarded economic growth, he promised a more flexible approach. But he pledged there would be no changes in the constitution of the Federal Reserve Board.[30]

Businessmen frankly expected to see the president and the conservative-minded Federal Reserve clash over policies if the administration attempted to assume a direct role in setting interest rates.[31] Kennedy confounded the skeptics; he not only reappointed Martin but included him in the so-called Quadriad—the secretary of the treasury, the director of the budget, and the chairmen of the CEA and FRB—which advised the president on high-level economic policy.[32] The White House made no attempt to undermine the independence of the Federal Reserve, and Martin cooperated in providing a more expansionist monetary policy.[33]

Easily the preeminent cause for the private sector's persisting anxiety about planning and controls was Kennedy's repeated call for restraint on prices and wages. Long before the Council of Economic Advisers unveiled its guideposts, business spokesmen were warning that the administration intended to intervene in the essential right of management to set prices.[34] The emphasis of the Antitrust Division on price conspiracies added to this concern.

The president's swift and vigorous action when the steel manufacturers raised prices brought the fear of additional federal controls to a new peak. Scare headlines, such as "Planned Economy—How It

Will Work," both reflected and provoked alarm.[35] The *American Banker* described in detail what lay ahead:

First, stand-by controls over prices, wages, and profits, under the third man's rule (i.e. the public interest): this is a pattern of how socialism enters the government of a democratic state.[36]

Although not all free enterprisers painted such a terrifying picture, there was no question that business was seriously worried.[37]

KENNEDY'S SUPPORT OF PRIVATE ENTERPRISE

The president personally led efforts to convince entrepreneurs that his administration had no desire to substitute government direction for management's discretion. To a business audience he emphasized:

I regard the preservation and strengthening of the free market as a cardinal objective of this or any other administration's policies.

. . . .

The free market is a decentralized regulator of our economic system. The free market is not only a more efficient decision maker than even the wisest central planning body, but even more important, the free market keeps economic power widely dispersed. It thus is a vital underpinning of our democratic system.[38]

Responding to statements that the chief executive had no right to interfere in private economic issues, Kennedy liked to remind business-men that no one had ever defined what the president's business was. But, he reasoned, since he would be blamed for the nation's economic difficulties, he and the government had a right to present proposals which might prevent or lessen such difficulties.[39]

Businessmen almost unanimously agree that the government should not be in competition with private companies.[40] Kennedy, aware of business sentiment on this subject, took pleasure in announcing the discontinuance of federal operations that competed with private enter-prise.[41] After reviewing the practice of using federal contracts with private companies to provide services to the government, his adminis-tration continued the policy, set forth in a Bureau of the Budget bulletin issued in 1959, of not having the government engage in commercial or industrial efforts unless necessary or advisable to do so in the public interest.[42]

The business community was less harmonious in its views on gov-ernment aid to private industry. A president of the United States Chamber of Commerce sharply condemned "the seduction by subsidy" of business by government, but this did not prevent certain industries from welcoming specific federal assistance.[43] Likewise, few company officials demanded the end of research and development grants, which benefited businesses both directly and indirectly. Many business spokesmen criticized the proposed increase in federal funds in 1961 for loans to small businesses through the Small Business Administration, but small entrepreneurs warmly supported the measure.[44]

President Kennedy's most unequivocal endorsement of private rather than government ownership of an enterprise concerned the development of the communications satellite system. In 1962, the chief executive recommended that Congress enact a bill chartering a privately owned corporation with a government-sanctioned monopoly to own and operate the American portion of the planned international space satellite communications network. According to the president's plan, both the general public and the nation's communications industry would be allowed to buy stock in the company. To protect the public interest, Kennedy proposed close federal regulation.[45]

Despite the administration's stand for private ownership, many of the commercial communications companies qualified their endorsement of the plan, objecting both to sharing ownership with public stockholders and to "excessive" government control.[46] However, business spokesmen in general applauded the president's position as a victory for private enterprise.[47]

A small but determined band of liberal senators waged a stout fight against surrendering government ownership of the satellite system. But backed by the firm support of Kennedy, legislative leaders were able to invoke cloture against the filibustering opponents of the bill and obtain its passage.[48] Subsidized by the taxpayers, but privately owned, the unique Comsat Corporation has been described as a broker of public services operating for a private profit.[49]

Kennedy also cast a vote of confidence for private enterprise in 1963 when he protected the private ownership of patent rights developed by companies working on federal projects. Some congressmen and some members of the administration argued that the government should hold title to valuable patents and reap the benefits.[50] The president compromised the differences. He issued a policy memorandum giving private contractors a maximum of three years to make practical application of new discoveries. If a contractor complied with this requirement, the protection of the patent would last for the customary seventeen years.[51] Small business, hoping to weaken the power of the giant companies who almost monopolized federal contracts, favored government ownership of the patents, but most companies welcomed the decision.[52]

The president showed a willingness to rely upon private market forces to cope with problems in the transportation industry. In both 1962 and 1963, he asked Congress to remove inequities in interstate commerce minimum rate regulations which placed railroads at a disadvantage compared with water and motor carriers. Stressing the need for equal competitive opportunity, he explained that other laws were sufficient to protect the public interest against predatory trade practices by the carriers.[53]

The *Wall Street Journal* hailed the action as a commendable step toward breaking the shackles of regulation.[54] The transportation industry responded to the proposal along predictable lines—railroads for, trucks and water carriers against.[55] Spokesmen for the Chamber of Commerce and retail groups endorsed the principle of equal competition and lower freight rates while hedging support for the specific administration measure.[56] Unable to secure agreement within the industry, Congress failed to act on the president's request to remove government regulation of the private sector. Ironically, in this case the avowed champions of capitalism, not the president accused of wanting to extend federal controls over business, struck a blow against competitive free enterprise.

10

Trade
or
Fade

In contemporary America, tariff policy fails to excite attention or enthusiasm among the general public as it did during the nineteenth and early twentieth centuries.[1] For powerful interest groups with their persuasive Washington lobbies, however, the question of high or low protection continues to be of vital importance. But, as a recent study of foreign trade attitudes among executives observed, it is overly simplistic to say, "Tell me what a businessman makes, and I will tell you what foreign trade policy he stands for." Other factors—ideological and social—fuse with self-interest to influence attitude, further splintering the image of a monolithic business community.[2]

Considering the diversity of opinion among business interests, the enactment of the Trade Expansion Act of 1962 was an especially impressive legislative triumph for President Kennedy. Never before had Congress given a chief executive such extensive discretionary authority to reduce tariff barriers. Passed by great majorities in both the House and the Senate, the measure provided a resounding bipartisan endorsement of free world trade.[3]

THE NEED TO INCREASE EXPORTS

Throughout his first year in the White House, Kennedy pointed out that an increase in the balance of trade would be the best and most painless means of eliminating the nation's persistent payments deficit, which threatened to undermine world confidence in the value of the dollar (see chapter 4).[4] Since the end of World War II, the United States had enjoyed a large excess of exports over imports.[5] The president recognized that stiffening competition for world markets made it increasingly difficult to improve, or even to maintain, this healthy margin. The organization, in the late 1950s, of the European Economic Community (EEC or Common Market) and the European Free Trade Association by two groups of six and seven Western European nations seeking greater economic collaboration heralded even tougher competition for American traders in the future.[6]

At the president's urging, the Senate approved a treaty in March 1961, aligning the United States with Canada and eighteen Western European states in the Organization for Economic Corporation and Development (OECD). With economic relations between European countries literally at "sixes and sevens," the overlapping OECD hoped to bridge these divisions, stimulate world trade, and program foreign aid contributions made by its members to underdeveloped nations.[7]

Kennedy, denying charges that participation in the organization was a maneuver to secure American membership in the Common Market, emphasized explicitly that his concern was to prevent American sellers from being locked out of lucrative markets in Western Europe.[8] Nor did the president neglect valuable trade ties with Japan; he dispatched Secretary of State Dean Rusk to head the American delegation to the Tokyo meeting of the United States-Japanese committee on trade and economic affairs.[9]

To encourage business to concentrate on raising exports, the administration sponsored trade missions, market surveys, and export promotions.[10] To provide recognition to companies who contributed significantly toward producing and selling in international markets, the president initiated the practice of awarding "E" flags—the same emblem that flew over factories making notable records in production during wartime.[11]

A more tangible asset to businessmen was the inauguration of an effective system of export credit insurance. Major insurance companies voluntarily joined with the government's Export-Import Bank to supply protection for sales to foreign credit risks, and the bank alone agreed to offer safeguards against political risks on sales to foreign buyers. In addition, the "Eximbank" instituted a system of guarantees to commercial banks and financial institutions willing to finance exports. By the end of 1962, nearly 1,200 protection policies, worth $500 million, had been issued.[12]

Officials in business and government were keenly aware that a major problem confronting domestic exporters in the intense struggle for sales was the high cost of American products, caused chiefly by the higher wages paid American workers. For many years, the technical superiority of American industry made possible successful competition with foreign goods made by cheap labor. But technology in other developed countries was beginning to overtake, and in some cases surpass, that of American companies. The obsolete condition of sizeable segments of industrial capacity in the United States further compounded the dilemma.

Kennedy launched a two-pronged campaign to make home products more comeptitive. To stimulate needed modernization and expansion of plants and facilities, he proposed an investment tax credit and promised a favorable rewriting of depreciation allowances. Since it was obviously not feasible, politically or economically, to lower the wages of American workers, his economic advisers urged labor and management to contain price and wage increases within the boundaries of productivity gains.

THE OTHER SIDE OF THE COIN: IMPORTS

While exporters favored measures to increase their volume, industries plagued by the growing inroads being made in domestic markets by foreign producers wanted added government protection. The problems of textile manufacturers, in particular, gained national publicity. Having been in an economic slump for many years, the industry blamed much of its trouble on cheap foreign imports. Both management and labor spokesmen were almost unanimous in pleading for import quotas and restrictions.[13]

Although many textile concerns suffered from sadly antiquated equipment, they were important sources of jobs and income. Congressmen from states where the industry was important were under constant pressure to provide relief for the struggling companies. In May 1961, Kennedy announced a broad program of government assistance for textile makers, including aid to stimulate research, help in securing financing for modernization, a tariff inquiry, early review of depreciation schedules, and an attempt to arrange a conference of the world's principal textile exporting and importing countries.[14] Later in the year, the president raised the import duty on cotton textiles, in spite of strong protests by Japan.[15]

Although the size of the textile industry made it a particularly powerful political force, it was not alone in facing economic difficulties stemming in part from foreign competition. Small manufacturers in many industries were at a serious disadvantage in an era of increasing emphasis on research and rapid technological development. They strongly favored flexible tariff protections based on differentials in wage costs paid by domestic and foreign producers.[16] Among larger manufacturers, the indications were that in 1961 a majority tended to oppose protection, although a solid minority believed that high tariffs were necessary to give American companies a fair competitive chance.[17]

THE TRADE EXPANSION ACT OF 1962

Kennedy disappointed some of his advisers by choosing to make trade legislation, not a controversial political issue such as Medicare or federal aid to education, his major legislative target in 1962.[18] The Reciprocal Trade Agreements Act, initiated by Franklin D. Roosevelt in 1934 and extended eleven times, was due to expire in midyear. Howard Peterson, the president's special aide on foreign trade, counseled another extension of the act while waiting to see if the Common Market accepted the United Kingdom's bid for membership. Kennedy, however, believed that it was time for the United States to take the lead in promoting expanded world trade.[19]

The entry of Britain, America's leading trade partner, into the European Economic Community threatened to intensify trade problems for the United States. But London's international commitments promised to incline the Common Market to cooperate more with the rest of the world, rather than to become a high tariff, inward-looking economic unit. In the chief executive's judgment, political reasons clearly outweighed the potential trade disadvantages. It was imperative that the defensive shield of the Atlantic Community not be shattered by the existence of two angry European trade blocs.[20]

From the start of the New Frontier, protection-minded industries feared an effort to lower tariff barriers. The early statements by Kennedy urging increased exports looked to many business leaders, both those for and those against free trade, like trial balloons for a change in trade policies.[21]

For many weeks in the late fall of 1961, the president talked about trade tactics with his advisers and with political leaders. Early in December, speaking on consecutive days to the National Association of Manufacturers and the AFL-CIO, he declared his intention not to seek renewal of the Reciprocal Trade Act and urged support for a fresh and vigorous trade law.[22] Business journals favorable to free trade greeted Kennedy's disclosure with qualified approval, withholding critical judgment until they learned more specifics of his plan.[23]

On January 25, 1962, the chief executive unveiled his program in detail. His bill asked for two basic kinds of presidential authority to invigorate foreign trade: a general power to cut existing tariffs by up to 50 percent in reciprocal negotiations, and a specific authority for use with Common Market countries to reduce or eliminate totally tariffs on groups of products where the United States and the EEC together accounted for 80 percent or more of world trade, as measured by a representative period. To safeguard American industries from excessive hardship resulting from lowered tariffs, the measure proposed to continue a modernized version of "escape clause" and "peril point" procedures. In addition, the president introduced a new dimension into tariff policy by asking for a varied program of federal readjustment assistance for both workers and businesses damaged by foreign competition.[24]

Kennedy emphasized that the rapid development of the European Economic Community made clearly inadequate a trade policy designed to negotiate item-by-item tariff reductions with a large number of small countries. If the United Kingdom entered the EEC, the Common Market would be able to speak with one voice for a market almost as large as the United States. The president also reminded Congress that the nation must attempt to offset outlays for overseas defense and assistance with dollar sales in order to strengthen the international position of the dollar and to prevent a steady drain on American gold reserves.[25]

As special interest groups girded themselves to fight for or against the administration plan, it was obvious that the business community was widely split in opinion.[26] The influential business journals generally endorsed the concept of expanded free trade, although several condemned federal largesse for readjustment.[27] Many of the individual companies and industry associations which strongly supported the bill before congressional hearing committees also spoke against the assistance proposal.[28]

Organizations that transcended industry boundaries were in the particularly difficult position of trying to represent a wide diversity of interests. For instance, the National Association of Manufacturers declined to comment on the tariff issue, confining its remarks to opposition to the readjustment assistance feature of the trade bill and stressing the need to curb union power and excessive federal spending.[29] The United States Chamber of Commerce, however, expressed its approval of the principles of the bill, including the retention of escape clauses and assistance for workers, companies, and industries injured by tariff concessions to foreign competitors. But the Chamber remained consistent in its traditional beliefs and urged that aid to displaced employees be administered by state governments.[30]

Protesting the new trade measure were representatives from a wide variety of industries ranging from the American Knit Handwear Industry to the Rolled Zinc Manufacturers Association. Spokesmen for the opposition argued that reduced tariffs would make the balance of payments worse by reducing the favorable American balance of trade, increase inflation at the present exchange rates, ruin domestic companies and drive the unemployment rate upward, and weaken national security by making it impossible for essential industries to continue to operate. A special concern to opponents of the bill was the surrender of congressional controls over tariffs.[31]

Although he had frequently been criticized for failing to fight for his legislative recommendations, Kennedy waged a vigorous campaign for the Trade Expansion Act. Repeatedly—in news conferences, brief remarks, statements, and formal speeches—he sounded the urgency of expanded world trade. On opening a new dockside terminal in New Orleans, Louisiana, he warned, "In May of 1962, we stand at a great dividing point. We must either trade or fade. We must either go backward or go forward."[32] He also showed his willingness to use more than rhetoric. Tariff decisions traditionally have provided a fertile breeding ground for charges of "political deals," and the manueuvering in 1962 was no exception. The president's decision to raise tariffs on certain glass and carpet imports looked like a divide-and-conquer tactic to split the ranks of protectionists and woo support for his trade bill.[33]

The chief executive's decision to push hard for a major trade revision in 1962 paid unforseen dividends during the months following the steel crisis and stock market slump. By midsummer, enthusiasm for the proposed trade measure was growing perceptibly among businessmen.[34] With relations between the White House and the business world still strained, the mutual interest in expanded trade provided a useful rallying point for attempts to restore rapport.

The final version of the Trade Expansion Act gave the president great satisfaction. Even the readjustment allowance provision, included in the bill as an appeal for labor support and for possible bargaining purposes, received congressional approval.[35] Only a stipulation that the chief executive should act as soon as practicable to suspend most-favored-nation trade benefits granted to any country dominated by communism conflicted with Kennedy's wishes.[36]

THE HARD ROAD TO FREE TRADE

The president termed the new trade law "the most important international piece of legislation . . . affecting economics since the passage of the Marshall plan."[37] In a shrewd move to insure continued bipartisan support during the long and hard negotiations with the Common Market, he named Christian Herter, former secretary of state under Eisenhower, as special representative for trade negotiations. Kennedy also took care to warn that significant bargaining accomplishments would come slowly.[38]

The trade bill had been framed on the assumption that Britain would be part of the European Economic Community.[39] The decision made by Charles de Gaulle of France early in 1963 to block the entrance of the United Kingdom into the Common Market added a new dimension for American trade negotiators. Judged purely by short-run economic considerations, the exclusion of the British from the EEC promised to benefit American traders by making it possible to consolidate traditional British-American trade ties. But it significantly weakened the president's hopes for transforming Western Europe, including Britain, into a unified political and economic entity that would join with the United States to bulwark the free world's defensive posture.[40]

Perhaps because of his desire to secure passage of new trade legislation, Kennedy raised the expectations of American business too high. By mid-1963, much of the early excitement among businessmen over the trade program had waned. De Gaulle's blackballing of the United Kingdom made it clear that favorable trade concessions would be difficult to obtain from the EEC. Although optimistic about the ability of American companies to compete for world markets as a whole, executives were much less confident about future trade with Europe.[41]

In crucial talks between the United States and the EEC in May 1963, the Common Market spokesmen put an end to any remaining American illusions that the path to free trade would be easy. Although the bargainers successfully compromised differences over procedures to be followed in multilateral trade negotiations scheduled in 1964 under the General Agreement on Tariffs and Trade, the Europeans plainly displayed a stubborn attitude.[42] Another early warning note was sounded when the EEC countries refused to lower their high levies on frozen poultry imports. The "chicken war" which followed when champions of American agriculture demanded retaliatory action created grave concern for future negotiations.[43]

The effectiveness of the Trade Expansion Act of 1962 as a diplomatic instrument to strengthen the free world was weakened almost as soon as it became a reality. Economically, total American exports and imports continued to rise in the years after Kennedy's death, as did the rate of trade between the United States and the Common Market countries;[44] but the inclination of the EEC to concentrate on establishing supranational control over its own economy, rather than lowering trade barriers, proved frustrating. The so-called Kennedy Round of trade bargaining, which began in 1964 and lasted until 1967, reduced tariffs on 6,300 items by an average of 35 percent over a period of five years. Although the results of these negotiations were encouraging, they did not live up to American hopes and expectations.[45]

Neither President Kennedy nor his advisers expected expanded trade alone to reverse the nation's unfavorable balance of payments position. But by emphasizing the critical role that world trade played in the payments dilemma, they hoped at the very least to prevent the loss of foreign markets that would make the gold drain even worse. And since the trade bill of 1962 focused on the need to make American goods more competitive internationally, it also played a key role in Kennedy's program for noninflationary economic growth.[46]

11

Business and the Cold War

THE DEBATE OVER IDEOLOGY

Substantial bipartisan support has marked the conduct of American foreign policy since the early days of the Second World War. Despite sharp —at times bitter—dissent about tactics, the basic strategy of protecting the "free world" against the threat of communism has won overwhelming approval. Kennedy continued this policy, stressing the necessity of powerful military forces to deter aggression. But at the same time, like Eisenhower, he attempted to thaw the cold war.

Even without the threat of a shooting confrontation, businessmen oppose communism as a philosophy implacably hostile to the free enterprise profit system. Business greeted Kennedy's efforts to relax tension between the Western democracies and the Communists with skepticism and feared that the president was unwise in failing to drive hard bargains in negotiations with the Soviet bloc. A small but vocal minority of the business community endorsed the charges of the Radical Right that an internal communist conspiracy was undermining the nation's security. But, significantly, many more entrepreneurs considered "creeping socialism" and moral and spiritual decay to be the real danger to the American way of life.[1]

The conservative National

Association of Manufacturers devoted the bulk of its 1961 convention to a forum on the perils of communism. The program linked the spending proclivities of the federal government, the drift toward centralized control of the national economy, and the dependence of citizens on Washington for social needs with warnings that the contest between capitalism and communism would end only when one side was vanquished. The implication was unmistakable: big government—as represented at the time by the Kennedy administration—increased the danger of a communist victory. Business was urged to become more active in prodding the United States to take the offensive in the cold war.[2]

For businessmen already concerned about some of Kennedy's liberal advisers and his bent for higher federal spending, his action against the steel manufacturers in April 1962 heightened alarm about socialist-style regulation by government. Steel company executive Allison Maxwell warned that socialistic governments "do not spring up over night" but "come gradually by stealth."[3] Another corporate official called upon the historical examples of the decline of Israel, Athens, and Rome to show where the flow toward centralization was leading the United States. Declaring that businessmen needed political courage to stop the trend, he stressed, "If we work together, we can turn the course of this nation. If we don't, we may ourselves live to see the American dream perish."[4]

A few companies used advertising in an attempt to educate the public about the evils of collectivist systems; others tried to explain the advantages of free enterprise in employee publications.[5] The financial analyst for the *New York Herald-Tribune* delivered a scathing attack on the practice of companies' sponsoring liberal news commentators and buying ads in "welfare-state loving" magazines and newspapers. He warned businessmen,, "Don't finance your own corporate demise."[6] The great majority of firms, however, believed that advertising was an ineffective way of putting across the business view on basic issues and an unjustified waste of the stockholders' money.[7]

Business has long been anxious for free enterprise to play a vigorous part in foreign affairs, as witnessed by the familiar "Open Door" and "Dollar Diplomacy" policies.[8] When Senator Alexander Wiley (Republican, Wisconsin) suggested in 1961 that American firms operating internationally be mobilized to spread ideas and information about the United States and its economic system, he received enthusiastic response from a host of blue-chip companies.[9]

Kennedy agreed that private enterprise could and should play an important role in the development of other countries.[10] But as he told a group of visiting foreign students, although the United States preferred profit enterprise, other nations should be free to decide their own means of providing progress. This included socialism, so long as the people were not denied their basic civil liberties and the right to choose the kind of government they wanted.[11]

The president's willingness to cooperate with socialist regimes abroad and his faith in big government at home made it difficult for many businessmen to accept in good faith his repeated strong assertions of support for the free enterprise system.[12] Few members of the business community seriously doubted his sincerity about defending the United States against military aggression. But the feeling persisted that he was soft on socialism and not tough enough in his dealings with the Communists.[13]

TRADE WITH THE COMMUNIST BLOC

During the presidential campaign in 1960, Kennedy called for more flexible economic tools to deal with communist countries. He especially hoped to encourage peaceful change in nations behind the Iron Curtain.[14] Shortly after his inauguration, his administration became embroiled in an embarrassing controversy involving the sale to the Soviet Union of machinery for making precision ball bearings. Eisenhower's secretary of commerce had initially approved the transaction, but delivery had been delayed because of Defense Department objections. Kennedy's new secretary of commerce, Luther H. Hodges, overruled the Defense Department in February 1961 on the grounds that since comparable machinery could be purchased elsewhere, the sale did not undermine American security. The resulting publicity, and the introduction in the Senate of a resolution to stop the shipment, prompted Hodges to suspend the license again pending further study.[15]

Questioned at a press conference about the incident, Kennedy agreed that improved procedures were needed to prevent the recurrence of such confusion.[16] But the administration made it clear that it favored an increase in controlled trade with Soviet bloc nations. Secretary of State Dean Rusk, outlining the government's position on such trade, assured the House Committee on Export Control that no licenses for goods with potential military value would be approved. Rusk defended commerce with communist countries as valuable to the United States. He explained that it earned needed foreign exchange, helped American businessmen to sell goods that would otherwise be purchased else-where, dramatized the administration's stand for maximum freedom of trade, provided a lever for use against the Soviet Union in crisis situations like Berlin, and emphasized the desire of the United States for world peace.[17]

The business community solidly opposed selling strategic or semi-strategic materials to the Soviets or their allies, but most executives reasoned that companies should be allowed to engage in commerce involving nonstrategic goods.[18] As the National Machine Tool Builders Association argued, if European competitors could supply an item, clearly there was no security advantage to be gained by prohibiting American manufacturers from reaping the profits of sales to com-munist countries.[19]

Kennedy's 1963 proposal to license private grain dealers to sell sev-eral million tons of surplus American wheat to Russia propelled United States-Soviet trade relations into the national spotlight. The president stressed the sale's advantages to the taxpayer, since the wheat had already been purchased by the government at higher than market price. In addition, he noted the benefits to the balance of payments deficit, to farmers, and to the transportation industries that would handle the shipment of the grain.[20] Most business journals, even those usually hostile to the administration, approved of the sale.[21] *Business Week* reported that its survey of businessmen revealed that "in general the ayes have it" relative to the sale of wheat, surplus foods, drugs, and soft goods to the Soviets.[22]

Arch conservatives, complaining that Kennedy blindly refused to acknowledge the Soviet Union's use of trade as a key tactical weapon, heatedly opposed attempts to increase American-Russian trade.[23] Iron-ically, before the wheat sale, the largest annual volume of American exports to the USSR and Eastern Europe during the cold war occurred in 1960, under Eisenhower, not under a Democratic president.[24]

Right-wing extremist groups relied on more than rhetoric in their campaign to stifle trade with the Communists, actively organizing boy-cotts against stores selling imports from Iron Curtain countries. Ken-nedy attacked this practice as an ineffective way to fight the spread of communism and suggested that advocates of such tactics would accom-plish far more by assisting the Alliance for Progress or joining the Peace Corps.[25] Although many merchants yielded to the pressure and removed communist-made goods from their shelves, others refused to do so.[26]

RANSOMING THE CUBAN PRISONERS

Relations with Cuba brought Kennedy both his greatest embarrass-
ment—the Bay of Pigs debacle—and his finest triumph—the missile
crisis—in foreign affairs. The first incident led to a quiet, but far-
reaching, example of business-government cooperation, with overtones
of administration pressure on private industry.

In May and June 1961, the private Tractors for Freedom Committee
attempted to trade agricultural tractors for men captured by Cuba in
the Bay of Pigs invasion. The effort failed when Cuban Premier Fidel
Castro raised his demands. President Kennedy, although carefully noting that the government could not be a party to the negotiations, pro-
claimed his full support for the humanitarian motives of the proposed
exchange, but many Republicans in Congress condemned the maneuver as disgraceful blackmail and damaging to American prestige.[27]

Attempts to liberate the prisoners were revived in the summer of
1962. James B. Donovan, a lawyer, assisted by an advisory committee
headed by retired General Lucius Clay, succeeded in reaching a pre-
liminary agreement with Castro to trade food and drugs for the incar-
cerated men.[28]

In late November, Donovan appealed to Attorney General Robert
Kennedy for help in consummating the transfer. In a whirlwind campaign of little over three weeks, the attorney general, "without using
government funds or supplies," mobilized the Justice Department and
other administrative agencies to assist in raising food and drug donations worth $53 million from private industry.

The younger Kennedy was able to supply the invaluable assurance
that the president regarded the exchange as in the national interest.
The Internal Revenue Service ruled favorably on the gifts as tax deductions, and the Justice Department provided trade associations, who
took the lead in prorating company donations, with letters exempting
them from the antitrust consequences of cooperation. Administration
officials stressed that their role was strictly humanitarian and cautioned
firms which donated to expect no future favors.

At the last minute, a demand by Castro for an additional $2.9 mil-
lion in cash threatened to hold up the prisoner exchange. However,
within twenty-four hours, Clay, Robert Kennedy, and others raised the
money, with the attorney general reportedly securing a one-million-
dollar donation from one source. The almost 1,200 prisoners were all
in the United States by Christmas.

To minimize the political repercussions, the whole 1962 exchange procedure was handled with little publicity until it was accomplished. Business cooperated extensively in the affair. Reportedly, 20 railroads, 10 airlines, and 15 steamship lines provided free transportation for merchandise and men, and 139 food and drug companies contributed the ransom goods. Companies took the government's promise to allow tax deductions equal to the goods and services donated to mean either market price or an arbitrated price. In either case, the firms expected to realize a larger allowance than was usual for charitable contributions.[29] *Fortune* cynically pointed out that since the government got 52 percent of corporation profits, the taxpayer really paid the ransom.[30]

Despite strong denials of any pressure by the administration on private business to give to the prisoner exchange, the existence of federal tax, antitrust, and regulatory powers over the affairs of companies doubtless caused many executives to question the wisdom of refusing to help.[31] Although justifiable for strictly humanitarian reasons, the government's unofficial, but very active, role in the ransom affair seems both irregular and improper.

THE GOVERNMENT AND THE DEFENSE INDUSTRY

Congress has frequently refused to enact presidential proposals for pump-priming expenditures designed to invigorate a slumping economy, but since World War II it has seldom seriously challenged requests for additional funds to bolster national security. Thus in 1961 Kennedy used the Berlin crisis to justify a sizeable increase in military spending.[32] His action had a double purpose: to strengthen America's position in its cold war confrontation with the Soviet Union, and, he hoped, to stimulate business and relieve unemployment. Business, while quick to criticize the trend toward ever-larger federal budgets, has, like Congress, consistently supported massive appropriations for defense needs. Throughout the New Frontier years, outlays for national security accounted for well over half of the federal budget.[33]

The demands of the cold war have significantly blurred traditional relationships between the private and public sectors of the economy. Major segments of the business community have benefited hugely from defense spending. In some instances entire industries, as well as individual companies, operate in a market with only one customer—the federal establishment. The question may properly be asked whether a firm doing nearly 100 percent of its business with the government is actually engaged in free enterprise.

The frantic pace of improving technology, which commonly makes weapons obsolescent before they can be mass-produced, places great emphasis upon extensive research and development. Since traditional competitive bidding is seldom feasible on items not yet invented, the government relies heavily upon negotiated contracts with selected suppliers on a cost-plus-fixed-fee basis. Because of the uncertainty for the contractor and the high stakes for national security involved in research projects, the federal government has assumed the normal role of business as innovator and risk-taker.[34]

Exempted from risks, private industry has found government research and development work highly attractive. Direct dollar profit alone has been sufficient to interest business, despite the large amount of red tape involved. Often even more beneficial, federal research contracts have provided access to information otherwise denied, revealed new developments sometimes valuable in commercial business, and frequently led to lucrative production contracts.[35]

In 1961 President Kennedy, recognizing the hazy line of government control over negotiated contracts, directed Budget Director David E. Bell to head a high-level administration committee to study federal contracting and procurement, with special attention to research and development.[36] The report of the committee judged the nation's interest to be well served by research and development contracts with private institutions but urged that management and control of federally financed programs rest in the hands of full-time government officials. The extensive use of cost-plus-fixed-fee agreements, which obviously provided little or no incentive to reduce costs, was sharply criticized. The committee also suggested that high salaries paid to employees on federally subsidized projects should be specifically approved by the head of the government agency making the contract.[37]

By fiscal year 1963, the Kennedy administration had achieved a small but significant increase in the number of defense contracts let by competitive bidding, although nearly two of every three contracts were still being negotiated. Secretary of Defense Robert NcNamara estimated that savings averaging 25 percent resulted when bidding procedures could be used. In testimony before a congressional committee, McNamara stressed that to realize substantial savings on negotiated contracts it was necessary to cut costs, not profits, since private contractors averaged only a low 3.5 precent return from such work. To stimulate interest in reducing costs on projects where competitive bidding was not feasible, the administration utilized more contracts with incentive bonus features. By this arrangement, the contractor could earn additional profits by keeping his expenses below the negotiated amount.[38]

During the Kennedy administration, the federal government provided almost two-thirds of the funds invested in research and development in the United States. Military and space needs dominated the spending.[39] Although individual companies benefited handsomely from such contracts, executives recognized the accompanying loss of operational freedom and flexibility.[40] Many observers, both in and out of private industry, worried that not enough research was being performed in nonmilitary areas. Since costly weapons systems do not increase a nation's basic productivity, the emphasis on defense threatened to weaken the fundamental structure of the economy for long-range growth.[41]

Most government money, both for research and for production, went to a relatively few large corporations. Kennedy attempted to spread the flow of federal funds, especially to small enterprises.[42] His administration increased the number of contracts "set aside" for small business and required prime defense contractors to report regularly on their efforts to solicit bids from subcontractors classified as "small." During the New Frontier, small firms received a record dollar amount of prime federal contracts. But in terms of percentage of total contract awards, small business did not fare as well as it had in the mid-1950s.[43]

With the business lives of many companies depending upon defense spending, firms which lost valuable contracts often complained loudly and charged political bias.[44] The selection of General Dynamics Corporation for the billion-dollar TFX aircraft award led to forty-six days of congressional hearings over a nine-month period. Despite heated charges that political considerations had dictated the award, the president stood firmly behind the decision of Secretary of Defense McNamara.[45]

Another congressional investigation of defense-related contracts—for the stockpiling of strategic raw materials—produced few more concrete results.[46] Kennedy instigated the probe when he charged that stockpiling procedures during the Eisenhower administration had resulted in a $3.4 billion surplus over requirements and "unconscionable profits" for some private firms.[47] The Senate hearings featured a bristling exchange between the investigators and George Humphrey, Eisenhower's secretary of the treasury, who was also the former head of the Hanna Nickel Company, which had profited heavily from stockpiling.[48] No flagrant, partisan conflict of interest was established by the Senate inquiry, and the report of the investigating subcommittee, criticizing the stockpiling policies of the previous administration, failed to win the approval of the full committee.[49] Many businessmen, mindful of the dollar-and-cents value of government contracts, remained quiet about the probe. But others strongly believed that political considerations had motivated the action.[50] The congressional investigation did call attention to the pressing need for a vigorous and continuous review of federal stockpiling requirements.[51]

The New Frontier's efforts to streamline the federal establishment's erratic and often wasteful procurement and supply procedures were consistent with traditional business philosophy. McNamara, the efficiency-minded secretary of defense, created a single Defense Supply Agency to eliminate costly duplicate purchasing by the separate armed services. He also closed or reduced military installations not essential to national security and attempted to reorganize the National Guard and the Reserves, despite the objections of state and national politicians and the carping of communities adversely affected economically.[52]

THE ECONOMIC IMPACT OF DISARMAMENT

The possibility of an ultimate slowing or ending of the cold war arms race created a dilemma for the United States. Few responsible citizens advocated war. But the conjunction of an immense military establishment and a large arms industry, which President Eisenhower warned about in his 1961 farewell address, dramatically influenced almost every part of American life.

Two government reports, released in 1962, stressed the awesome impact of defense activities upon the economy. Spending for national security absorbed nearly 10 percent of the gross national product and accounted for over 85 percent of all federal purchases. Including armed services personnel, over 9 percent of the total labor force was engaged in defense-related operations. Applying the familiar multiplier concept, economists estimated that a five billion dollar cutback in military outlays might generate a total decline of between ten and twelve billion dollars in aggregate demand, if compensating policies were not brought into play. The economies of a large number of states, including virtually the entire Pacific region, rested heavily upon defense production.[53] The significance of the reports was not lost on businessmen, politicians, or labor leaders. However welcome an arms détente might be for world peace, it would clearly raise the fear of depression.

Kennedy's announcement, in July 1963, of an agreement with Great Britain and the Soviet Union to suspend above-ground testing of nuclear weapons stimulated renewed prospects for substantial disarmament.[54] That same month, the president asked Walter Heller of the Council of Economic Advisers to organize an informal committee to review and coordinate the work of federal agencies concerned with the economic impact of defense and disarmament. Shortly after Kennedy's death, President Johnson gave the committee permanent status.[55]

Enlightened business leaders, even those with major military contracts, shunned any bald attack on the principle of arms reduction. A survey of corporation executives indicated overwhelming support for the test-ban provided a foolproof inspection system, including on-the-spot checks, could be guaranteed. A large majority expressed their confidence in America's armed forces as the greatest protection against the outbreak of world war. But they split almost evenly in their opinions about the probability that the United States and the Soviets would eventually reach a limited agreement on the control of conventional weapons.[56]

The test-ban treaty included no restrictions on nuclear research and, in itself, was a small threat to military suppliers. *Business Week* reasoned that the demand for monitoring devices caused by the suspension of tests should actually stimulate government buying.[57] Publicly, large defense contractors generally declined to seriously consider the possibility of any sizeable cutback in armaments. Few companies reported having underway any long-range planning to smooth the conversion to civilian production, and many corporate spokesmen, either by hints or by direct statements, noted that government direction would be welcomed.[58] Lockheed Aircraft Corporation, the nation's largest defense supplier at the time, suggested that proper government and private planning could make advantageous new uses of the defense industry's great technical and systems competence. Lockheed looked optimistically to prospective federally financed programs, like supersonic air transport, for future work if arms spending was reduced.[59]

The *Morgan Guaranty Survey* reminded businessmen that defense expenditures, as a percentage of gross national product, reached 42 percent during World War II and almost 14 percent during the Korean War, but industry managed a healthy adjustment after both conflicts. Government help, including financial aid, would probably be essential if the cold war subsided substantially, but, the *Survey* declared, it "ought to be one of lubricating the friction points, rather than stoking the engine." The banking publication sagely warned the business community that it would be a shame if "faint-faithed capitalists" used the old communist line—that armaments kept the capitalist economies going—to resist defense cuts.[60]

12

The Crisis in Foreign Aid

THE CHANGING PATTERN OF OVERSEAS ASSISTANCE

By the time John F. Kennedy entered the White House, the United States government had provided almost $80 billion in post–World War II foreign aid.[1] Defended by various sources as essential to the free world's defense and as a great humanitarian contribution, foreign assistance was supported in principle by both Republicans and Democrats. The Marshall Plan to bolster war-ravaged Europe was cited by theologian Reinhold Niebuhr as a prototype of national enlightenment, in which "prudent self-interest was united with concern for others in a fashion which represents the most attainable virtue of nations."[2] But the task of getting aid appropriations through Congress grew harder each succeeding year, as the incessant charges of "giving away the taxpayers' money" chipped away at the foundations of public support for the program.

The direction of foreign aid changed dramatically during the 1950s. By the end of the decade the areas needing substantial assistance were no longer the industrialized countries of Western Europe but were the emerging underdeveloped nations. Many Americans had felt a deep cultural rapport with the people of Europe. This factor, combined with Europe's face-to-face confrontation with Soviet communism, made the wisdom of United States aid relatively easy to accept. But Americans were markedly less enthusiastic about the efforts of African and Asian states to raise their standards of living.[3]

A majority of businessmen supported foreign aid during the Eisenhower administration, although with reservations. Influential members of the business community frequently charged waste and inefficiency in the operation of aid programs; indicated their preference for loans, not grants, to foreign nations; and urged that private, instead of public, investment be utilized to a greater extent.[4]

Private investment by American firms did play an important part in the recovery of Europe. But as the focus of foreign needs shifted to backward areas, free enterprise proved ill-equipped to handle critical requirements such as roads, schools, and medical care. Improvements in these and related areas were essential to raise the economic and social environment in new states to a point where private investment, except for extractive and plantation industries, could be profitable. The situation was further complicated because some of the developing nations did not favor capitalism as the most advantageous economic arrangement for coping with their particular problems.[5] In these circumstances, American business had little choice but to admit the necessity of public, or joint public-private, aid efforts in the nonindustrialized countries.[6]

THE NEW FRONTIER APPROACH TO FOREIGN AID

Kennedy believed that foreign assistance activities under Eisenhower had concentrated too heavily upon military and short-term political programs. As a result, long-term development and constructive economic and social advancement had been slighted. The new president was determined to change the impact of American aid by more vigorously supporting the needs of the emerging less-developed nations.[7] In his first foreign aid message to Congress, Kennedy did not shun the politically expedient appeal to American self-interest, warning that communism stood poised to benefit in areas plagued by chronic poverty and chaos. But he signaled a fresh policy, incorporating a new idealism, by stressing that the fundamental task of foreign assistance should be to make the 1960s a "decade of development," not solely to fight communism in a negative sense.[8] During the New Frontier years, the funds devoted to economic development exceeded dollars spent for military aid by a sizeable margin, thus reversing the trend of the preceding eight years.[9]

To administer his program for development more efficiently, the president proposed to gather the scattered foreign assistance operations into an efficient Agency for International Development (AID) within the State Department. Kennedy also envisioned ambassadors in the field taking a leading role in formulating the priorities of individual nations.[10] The chief executive originally planned to include the exciting new Peace Corps project and the Food for Peace operation in the Agency for International Development, but he subsequently decided not run the risk of the programs' losing their zeal by being submerged within the bureaucracy of the sprawling AID organization. As autonomous agencies, the Peace Corps and Food for Peace proved highly successful as concrete examples of American goodwill to people in backward lands. The former, in particular, captured the fancy of world opinion.[11]

Equally exciting, and potentially much more significant as a symbol of the New Frontier approach to foreign aid, was the Alliance for Progress. For years the United States had channeled little aid to her neighbors to the south. Aware of the threat posed to hemispheric stability by Castro and communism, Kennedy hoped to substantially improve economic and social conditions in Latin America. In his inaugural address, he pledged "to assist free men and free governments in casting off the chains of poverty." But he also warned that the United States would oppose subversion and aggression.[12]

By March 1961, the president was ready to formalize the ideas developed by an early task force and by his advisers, notably Richard Goodwin.[13] Speaking to Latin American members of the diplomatic corps, the chief executive outlined a massive cooperative ten-year program for the Americas. Homes, work and land, health and schools, as well as democratic reforms, were cited as the goals for the new plan.[14] Five months later, twenty nations at the Punta del Este, Uruguay, Inter-American Conference agreed to establish the *Alianza para Progreso*.[15]

Congress funded a multitude of measures designed to implement this ambitious program, but despite early optimism, the Alliance failed to live up to expectations. Although he continued throughout his administration to encourage Latin American reforms, Kennedy was frankly disappointed in the results.[16]

Businessmen did not question the desirability of improving life in underdeveloped lands. But they worried that democratic reforms might undermine capitalism in these countries. If governments dedicated to

anticommunism were deposed by revolutionary change, private investments by United States companies might be gravely imperiled.[17] This
concern by business strongly influenced future assistance requests for
all nonindustrialized nations.

The president proposed to make long-range planning a key part of
his foreign aid strategy. He requested congressional approval of five-
year borrowing authority to make dollar-repayable loans to underdeveloped countries at low or no interest and for terms up to fifty years.[18]
Neither Congress nor the business community looked favorably upon
granting the administration a "backdoor" borrowing privilege, regarding it as a clever technique to avoid legislative control over spending.
The United States Chamber of Commerce testified that it welcomed
the concept of long-range planning but felt that multiyear authoriza-
tions and appropriations would adequately serve the purpose. This
would clearly leave the burden of proof upon AID to justify its requests for funds for specific projects.[19]

Congress eventually agreed to give AID authority to make long-
term commitments for development, with the reasonable assurance—
but not the guarantee—that the commitments would be honored by
the annual appropriation of funds. The president approved the action
and expressed satisfaction that the senators and representatives recognized "the magnitude of need" in the developing countries.[20]

In 1962, Congress attempted to ease the anxiety of American businessmen who feared that revolutionary change in underdeveloped nations might threaten their investments. The legislators accepted an
amendment sponsored by Senator Burton B. Hickenlooper (Republican, Iowa) to prohibit American aid to any country that expropriated
property owned by United States nationals without immediate and
effective compensation.[21] The administration opposed this restriction
on the grounds that it would unduly circumscribe the government's
freedom of action. Secretary of State Rusk argued that such problems
could be handled most effectively by normal diplomatic procedures.
The law, he warned, would provide the Communists with a powerful
propaganda weapon, by making it possible for them to brand United
States assistance programs as mere tools to facilitate exploitation by
American capitalists.[22] The administration also failed to beat back
congressional action substantially tightening controls on the extension
of foreign aid to communist-bloc nations.[23]

Kennedy grew increasingly vexed by the annual struggle with Congress over the size of appropriations for foreign aid. In both 1961 and

1962, economy-minded legislators succeeded in substantially lowering his requests for aid.[24] In September 1962, the president lashed out sharply about the drastic cut recommended by the House Appropriations Committee: "It makes no sense at all to make speeches against the spread of communism . . . and then vote . . . to undermine the efforts of those who are seeking to stave off chaos and communism in the most vital areas of the world." Warning that a mutilated aid program would seriously damage the nation's security, he urged bipartisan support in Congress to correct the "irresponsible action" of the House committee.[25]

The fight over the assistance program in 1962 convinced the chief executive that some means must be found to rebuild congressional and grass-roots enthusiasm for foreign aid. Against the advice of some of his close advisers, he resorted to a device used successfully by President Eisenhower in similar circumstances. He appointed a committee, heavily weighted with conservative, private-enterprise-minded citizens, headed by the respected General Lucius Clay, to examine the scope, operation, and purpose of American overseas aid.[26]

The Clay committee declared its support for "properly conceived and administered" assistance programs but concluded that the United States was trying to do too much for too many countries. With undiplomatic bluntness the report urged that foreign aid not be extended to nations whose attitudes were inconsistent with American beliefs and policies and flatly asserted that aid should be pursued on the basis of enlightened national self-interest.[27] Kennedy, aware that the negative tone of the Clay report would serve to sharpen the knives of congressmen who annually fought to cut aid appropriations, reduced his original foreign assistance budget recommendation of $4.9 billion by $400 million.[28] However, Clay told the House Committee on Foreign Affairs that the administration's request could safely be lowered still further.[29]

When Congress showed distinct signs of making even larger reductions than he recommended, Clay rallied vigorously to the defense of the aid program, warning that cuts below $4.3 billion would seriously endanger American foreign policy.[30] Despite Kennedy's strenuous efforts to arouse public support for his revised figure, Congress appropriated only $3 billion for foreign aid for fiscal 1964.[31] This represented the sharpest slash of a presidential request for overseas assistance funds since the program began with the Marshall Plan.

The chief executive's gamble with the Clay committee obviously backfired, doubtless inspiring opponents of foreign aid to greater en-

ergy. Quipped the liberal journal, *New Republic,* "when an administration breeds with Big Business, you get a Clay Report."[32] But other
factors were also significant in fomenting congressional opposition to
mutual assistance in 1963. Rising partisanship, the balance of payments crisis, a rebellion against government spending in general, and
the antagonism of southern legislators toward Kennedy because of his
pending civil rights bill contributed to the legislators' stubborness. In
addition, there were embarrassing failures of foreign policy, such as
those in Cuba, Vietnam, and Pakistan, to remind Americans of the
past shortcomings of aid programs.

BUSINESS AND FOREIGN AID

The attitude of business toward foreign aid during the New Frontier
years provided few surprises. The Clay report was in effect a mani-
festo of free enterprise sentiment regarding overseas assistance. Only
one national business group, the National Federation of Independent
Business, representing small entrepreneurs, flatly rejected foreign assistance.[33] The Chamber of Commerce of the United States, the largest
organization speaking for businessmen, and the conservative National
Association of Manufacturers half-heartedly endorsed the aid program
in their annual policy statements.[34] The Chamber acknowledged the
value of America's international support activities to the defense of
the "free world." But, perhaps in keeping with the business image of
tightly controlling expenses, Chamber spokesmen appeared before congressional hearings on foreign aid each year with recommendations on
how to save money by cutting the "fat" from administration requests
for funds.[35]

Big business substantially supported foreign aid spending, both military and economic, just as it had during the Eisenhower and Truman
administrations. Executives of major corporations continued to be active in developing assistance policies and in promoting public backing
for the program.[36] In the summer of 1963, a survey of more than 1,400
business leaders from a variety of industries revealed that 75 percent
fully or generally opposed eliminating foreign aid.[37] For some, this
position was a matter of enlightened self-interest. Managers of companies with millions of dollars invested in profitable foreign assets had
no desire to see American influence in other nations diminished by an
end to foreign aid. Countries receiving support from the United States
were obviously less likely to discriminate against American property
owners.

By 1963, United States private investments in other nations totaled more than $66 billion, compared with $60 billion in 1962 and only $19 billion in 1950.[38] Foreign facilities of American companies were usually more modern than their home counterparts, and sales by the overseas subsidiaries of most firms exceeded export sales by the parent company by a considerable margin.[39] During the late 1950s and early 1960s, when the profit return on domestic assets slumped painfully for the majority of companies, foreign investments continued to earn a high yield.[40]

Businessmen thus strongly approved of the investment guarantee program of the Agency for International Development, which protected American firms operating abroad against loss from expropriation, war, revolution, civil strife, and restrictions on converting foreign currency earnings into dollars. The business community also viewed the Hickenlooper amendment as a useful tool for stimulating confidence in private investment overseas.

Both the Clay committee and the Commerce Department's Committee for the Alliance for Progress, also composed principally of executives from large corporations, commended private intiative, both by American companies and by foreign enterprises, as capable of making the greatest overall contribution to a nation's rapid economic growth and general development.[41] But informed business leaders also recognized that nonprofit investment for improvements in education, roads, and sanitation systems must receive heavy emphasis in backward countries.[42]

Kennedy's recommendations in 1963, to enlarge and extend private investment guarantees and to provide special tax credits for companies operating in developing nations, seemed to acknowledge the merit of business thinking on foreign aid.[43] But the proposed use of aid funds by India to build a publicly owned steel mill appeared to contradict the American emphasis on private enterprise. The president defended the plan—subsequently specifically disapproved by the House—by pointing to the distinction between a government's constructing a mill and its taking over a facility already operated by private owners.[44] The chief executive's argument convinced few businessmen. It was against basic free enterprise to encourage other nations to turn to socialism, and foreign aid should clearly not be used to promote public activities that could be profitably developed by private initiative.[45]

Business spokesmen frequently lamented the hazy goals of American foreign policy. They generally took a realistic, practical position, urging that tax dollars spent for overseas assistance should reinforce the foreign policy of the United States. This could be done by drawing uncommitted nations away from the Soviet bloc, strengthening America's friends and allies, and gaining economic advantages for the United States.[46]

Multilateral action by noncommunist nations, to spread the heavy load of providing assistance for economic advancement in nonindustrialized regions, increasingly appealed to businessmen.[47] Besides offering the possibility of reducing the amount of American funds necessary to accomplish desired development, an aid program operated by multiple governments also promised to be more efficient. As one banking leader explained, whereas the Soviet bloc was unified in its foreign economic policy, the Western democracies wastefully "scattered their shots."[48] A multilateral assistance organization, the Clay Report observed, would have the advantage of having no political or commercial interests of its own to serve and would thus be able to concentrate objectively on securing the maximum return in terms of economic and social benefit for underdeveloped regions.[49]

OVERSEAS COMMITMENTS AND THE PAYMENTS DEFICIT

The American balance of payments deficit, which became critical in 1958, added a new dimension to foreign aid spending by the United States. Neither Kennedy nor any other ardent defender of the assistance program attempted to deny that aid did not adversely affect the nation's payments position. But the president argued that the United States could not strengthen its balance of payments at the expense of the developing countries without incurring even greater danger to national security.[50] Answering questions before a business audience in 1963, he responded sharply to an implication that foreign aid "giveaways" were undermining the value of the dollar and causing a serious loss of American gold reserves. The chief executive agreed that assistance spending contributed to the problem, but he reminded his listeners that huge private investments abroad by American citizens and companies also added significantly to the deficit.[51] A number of influential executives joined with Kennedy to argue that the benefits of foreign aid outweighed the detrimental effect upon payments.[52]

The president also struggled to convince Congress and the public that foreign assistance was not the chief culprit in the gold drain problem. Secretary of State Rusk and Secretary of the Treasury Dillon carefully explained to congressional committees that at least 80 percent of all aid funds were actually spent for goods and services in the United States, not abroad.[53] The president was not loath to remind critics of the benefits that accrued to the American economy as a whole from assistance spending.

To be sure, foreign aid is in our economic self-interest. It provides more than a half a million jobs for workers in every State. It finances a rising share of our exports and builds new and growing export markets. It generates the purchase of military and civilian equipment by other governments in this country. It makes possible the stationing of 3½ million troops along the Communist periphery at a price one-tenth the cost of maintaining a comparable number of American troops.

But the president also insisted that aid to other countries had a deeper purpose than American economic interest.

The Family of Man . . . cannot survive, in the form in which we know it, a nuclear war—and neither can it long endure the growing gulf between the rich and the poor. . . . The gulf between rich and poor . . . is an invitation to agitators, subversives, and aggressors. It encourages the ambitions of those who desire to dominate the world, which threatens the peace and freedom of us all.[54]

13

Compromise— 1963: Tax Revision

Early in the summer of 1962, Kennedy rejected the concept of a balanced budget as the keynote of economic prosperity. Instead, he adopted the frankly Keynesian policy of seeking a massive, deficit-producing tax cut. He was hopeful that such an action would provide the thrust necessary for long-term economic growth.[1] His decision to move for a tax reduction represented a signal change in thinking by the chief executive. Only a year before, he had come close to requesting a tax increase to finance the additional defense spending required by the Berlin crisis.

On June 7, 1962, when the president publicly acknowledged his intention to ask Congress for new tax legislation, the nation's momentum of economic recovery appeared to have stalled.[2] His announcement came only days after the drastic drop in the stock market had further undermined optimism about the future of the economy. Kennedy obviously hoped that his commitment to a net tax reduction, along with tax reform, would bolster economic confidence, even before the actual implementation of a tax cut. Although he pointed to 1963 as the target date for revision of the tax rates, the president did not wholly rule out the possibility of asking for a tax cut in 1962, if circumstances dictated the necessity for such action.[3]

Having complained chronically that excessively high tax rates were destroying individual initiative, businessmen might have been expected to rally vigorously in support of the president's proposal.[4] But, ironically, opinion in the business community regarding an immediate tax cut was split.[5] Malcolm Forbes editorialized in *Forbes,* a financial journal, that he could not understand the opposition of many political and business leaders to the projected tax cut. "The thinking of the administration," he wrote, "is just what the Republican party spokesmen have been proposing for years."[6]

Business Week reported that "150 high ranking executives," surveyed in sixteen cities, lined up six to four against any "quickie" tax reduction in 1962, because of the lack of assurance that the government would make commensurate cuts in federal spending. For the long run, however, the businessmen interviewed were almost unanimous in hoping for a general tax reform. Many favored something like the Herlong-Baker bill, which would gradually reduce personal income taxes to a 15–38 percent range and work the corporate income tax maximum down to 45 percent.[7] According to a Gallup poll, an even larger percentage of the general public—72 percent—opposed a tax reduction if it meant going further into debt.[8]

Among the president's advisers there were differences of opinion as to where the focus of the tax cut should be. Secretary of the Treasury C. Douglas Dillon favored tax reduction as an adjunct to tax reform. He opposed hasty action to cut taxes in 1962 for fear that such action might endanger the chance for a careful and comprehensive reform of the entire revenue structure. Although lower taxes would unbalance the budget, Dillon agreed that a cut could play an important role in reaching full employment, spurring production, and preventing an economic slump.[9] Chairman Heller of the Council of Economic Advisers—the president's chief teacher of Keynesian economics—concurred that tax reduction would help to prevent a recession. But he insisted that the real case for a basic tax cut "rested on the longstanding gap between capacity and spending, and the absence of any reason to believe that the gap would close itself."[10]

Wilbur Mills (Democrat, Arkansas), who as chairman of the House Ways and Means Committee was the key figure in any prospective tax cut, showed little enthusiasm for a "quickie" tax bill. He agreed that tax rates were too high, blunting incentive and stifling initiative, but, like Dillon, he favored a careful examination of the whole tax structure. The congressman observed that although he could not comment specifically until he actually saw the president's plan, a major tax bill *might* pass the next year.[11]

Kennedy, seeing the signs of lukewarm support in Congress for an immediate tax reduction, vetoed the recommendation of his Council of Economic Advisers for tax action in 1962.[12] On August 13, 1962, in a radio and television address to the American people on the state of the national economy, the president declared that "in the absence of a clear and present danger to the American economy today," he would recommend no emergency tax cut at the time. But he promised to submit to Congress the following year a full-scale reform bill, including an across-the-board, top-to-bottom cut in both corporate and personal income taxes.[13] Somewhat surprisingly, the chief executive did not emphasize tax reduction while campaigning for the Democratic party in the fall congressional elections, mentioning the issue infrequently, and then only briefly.[14]

DOUBT AND DECISION

During the final months of 1962, while administration officials hammered out the details of the tax bill, doubt continued to plague the president about the advisability of cutting taxes.[15] But in mid-December, in a significant speech to the Economic Club of New York, he reaffirmed his intention to seek tax reform and reduction. At the same time, he laid the foundation for the administration's defense of its tax plan.

Kennedy acknowledged that economic indicators reflected a healthy American economy, but he insisted, "we can and must do better, much better than we have been doing for the last 5½ years." Referring to the responsibility of the government to aid economic growth, he rejected the idea of increasing federal expenditures more rapidly than necessary as demoralizing both to government and to the economy: to spend more than could be justified by national need or be used with maximum efficiency would undermine the people's confidence in government. "The final and best means of strengthening demand among consumers and business," he continued, "is to reduce the burden on private income and the deterrents to private initiative which are imposed by our present tax system."[16]

What was necessary, he assured his listeners, was not a "quickie" or temporary tax cut to forestall an immediate recession. Drawing upon the rhetoric and ideas of his Keynesian advisers, principally Heller, the chief executive explained:

I am talking about the accumulated evidence of the last 5 years that our present tax system, developed as it was, in good part, during World War II to restrain growth, exerts too heavy a drag on growth in peace time; that it siphons out of the private economy too large a share of personal and business purchasing power; that it reduces the financial incentives for personal effort, investment and risk-taking.

In short, to increase demand and lift the economy, the Federal Government's most useful role is not to rush into a program of excessive increases in public expenditures, but to expand the incentives and opportunities for private expenditures.[17]

Answering questions after his speech, Kennedy defended the logic of a tax cut at a time when the budget was already operating at a deficit. Noting that 1958 and 1960 proved that the biggest deficits come because of a recession, he warned that an economic downturn "would really knock our budget out of shape."

The businessmen also queried the president about the advisability of coupling reform with tax reduction, since congressional debate over reform promised to significantly slow action on rate revision. Admitting that reform would be a longer task, he hinted that he was anxious enough to get a tax reduction that he would accept whatever reform Congress chose to give.[18] Kennedy's early indication that he would be willing to sacrifice reform for reduction proved to be a serious tactical error. By revealing his hand early in the game, he left the administration few high cards to play in the final bargaining over the bill.

In the dark about precisely what the president's tax proposal would involve, business adopted a hopeful "wait-and-see" attitude. Roger M. Blough of United States Steel found the talk of tax reduction encouraging as a sign that Washington was increasingly aware that profits meant jobs and more rapid growth.[19] But *Business Week,* surveying hundreds of businessmen regarding their spending plans for 1963, found not a single one who contemplated any change because of the promise of a tax cut.[20] The *Wall Street Journal* reminded its readers that the surest way to a fiscally responsible balanced budget was not really, as the president maintained, to cut taxes, but rather to cut government spending.[21] Most of the other influential business journals favored a tax cut in 1963, but as *Fortune* cautioned, its endorsement did not mean that deficits should be accepted as a way of life.[22]

JUSTIFYING TAX REDUCTION

On January 24, 1963, Kennedy, unveiling the details of his tax package in a special message to Congress, reiterated the sentiments of his December speech.

The largest single barrier to full employment of our manpower and resources and to a higher rate of economic growth is the unrealistically
heavy drag of Federal income taxes on private purchasing power, initiative, and incentive.

His plan, scheduled to begin in 1963 and become fully effective by
1965, provided for tax cuts of $13.6 billion—$11 billion for individuals and $2.6 billion for corporations—plus reforms expected to
produce a revenue gain of $3.4 billion, leaving a net reduction of $10.2
billion.[23]

Loopholes in the existing tax code provided lucrative—and sometimes ludicrous—advantages for certain interests, and generous personal itemized deductions lowered the government's revenue potential
by $40 billion in 1962.[24] Tax expert Joseph A. Pechman described the
reform recommendations as, "the first serious attempt by a president
to reverse the erosion of the individual income tax base."[25] Five of the
reforms—those concerned with capital gains, dividend exclusion and
credits, itemized deductions, taxation of the aged, and minimum
standard deductions—were particularly significant and attracted the
greatest attention.[26]

House hearings on the tax measure began almost immediately, and
the business community quickly showed that it had its own ideas about
how tax revision and reform should be accomplished. Specific reform
proposals were supported, opposed, or ignored according to their effect on the special interest position of business groups. But a general
mood of business did emerge: basic approval of tax reduction, but only
if coupled with meaningful cuts in government spending; displeasure
with the amount of relief recommended for middle and high income
taxpayers; and a desire to secure tax reduction immediately but to
leave tax reform for later.[27] The president told a press conference in
late February, "at least there is a consensus there should be a tax cut,"
despite the argument over "who should get the cut and how it should
be divided."[28]

Flavoring the national debate over the tax proposal was Heller's
comment regarding the need for public education in the field of economic policy. The CEA chairman spoke of the "basic Puritan ethic" of
the American people as causing them to want to deny themselves tax
reductions because of their fears of deficits and the increase in the
national debt. Heller emphasized that, in fact, the tax cut offered the
best opportunity for the growth and full employment that would secure
a balanced budget.[29]

Heller's remark antagonized conservatives, and prompted the president to warn of the danger of recession to defend his fiscal intentions. Kennedy denied that he was attempting to abandon the "Puritan" ethic of thrift, declaring that he too, like the American people, was concerned about the size of the national debt. But he stressed that he was more worried about the prospect of another recession, like the one in 1958 which produced a really massive deficit.[30] Ironically, this was the argument that Heller precisely hoped to avoid. The CEA strongly believed that the main purpose of the tax cut should be the removal of fiscal barriers to long-term economic expansion, not short-run anticyclical adjustments.[31]

The differences in opinion over reform proposals made it clear that tax legislation, if passed at all, would not come swiftly. Kennedy indicated concern that extended debate over reform might delay the tax bill until the prime opportunity to stimulate the economy by tax reduction was lost. Although he did not specifically say that he would accept reduction without reform, several of his statements implied as much.[32] By midspring economic indicators reflected a strong upward movement and caused speculation that Congress might decide to postpone action on the tax program. The president hastened to credit the prospect of a tax cut as an important reason for the vitality of the economy; the important thing, he emphasized, was the long-range promise offered by the reduction.[33]

In his efforts to combat congressional and public apathy toward tax reform and reduction, the president welcomed the help offered by two private committees—the Business Committee for Tax Reduction in 1963 and the Citizens Committee for Tax Reduction and Revision in 1963.[34] The businessmen's group—labeled by a prominent Republican congressman as a lobby organization inspired by the executive branch —refrained from taking a stand on reform in order to concentrate on the need for an immediate lowering of tax rates.[35] By the fall of 1963, the organization boasted almost three thousand members, from every state in the Union and every segment of private enterprise. Headed by the auto magnate Henry Ford II and the railroad executive Stuart T. Saunders, the Business Committee included many of the top officials of America's blue-chip corporations.[36]

By early summer, business spokesmen in favor of the tax reduction bill had grown increasingly critical of the administration's handling of the measure. Some charged that the president's opportunistic defense of the tax cut as a way to head off a recession appeared shallow in view of the strength of the economy. Much sounder, editorialized *Business Week,* was the statement in his original message to Congress pointing to the economy's "unrealized potential" as the vital reason for a tax cut.[37] Equally harmful, from a business vantage point, was the administration's tendency to condone needless federal spending.[38]

Kennedy attempted to rebut charges of loose government spending policies. In a letter to Wilbur Mills, the influential chairman of the House Ways and Means Committee, the president insisted that a tight rein on federal expenditures would accompany tax reduction. Despite the loss of revenue that would result from enactment of the tax bill, he assured Mills that improved business conditions and prudent control of government spending would enable the administration to submit a budget for fiscal 1965 with an estimated smaller deficit than was forecast for fiscal 1964.[39]

Theodore Sorensen noted that Mills's slow and deliberate pace exasperated the president. Finally, in mid-September, the Ways and Means Committee reported out a bill basically in harmony with the administration's reduction plan but substantially shorn of the proposed reforms.[40] As the House deliberated, Kennedy appealed by radio and television for public support of the tax measure. He described the individual benefits to typical families in easily understood detail. But he put the most emphasis on the ability of the tax cut to provide jobs, stimulate business, deter recession, and make possible a balanced budget.[41] The president thus stressed both long-range growth and short-term recession prevention.

FAREWELL TO REFORM

As if in answer to the president's plea, public opinion polls in September reflected solid majority support for a tax cut.[42] Late in the month, the House approved the bill and sent it to the upper chamber. But final action on the measure was still months away. The Senate Finance Committee began hearings in October, and the committee's fiscally conservative chairman, Harry Flood Byrd (Democrat, Virginia), made it clear that the hearings would be both comprehensive and lengthy. No friend of any action that might encourage deficit finance, Byrd did not intend to be rushed.[43]

Representatives of some two hundred business firms or associations testified before the Senate committee or sent communications expressing their views on various aspects of the tax plan. In general, business found the reform provisions of the bill much more palatable after their modification by the House of Representatives. Almost without exception, the business spokesmen endorsed the tax cut as vital to the nation's economic health. But they also continued to urge Congress to exert firm determination to limit federal spending.[44]

Stuart T. Saunders, co-chairman of the Business Committee for Tax Reduction in 1963, emphasized that most businessmen regarded the vote on the tax bill as a test of government confidence in the private enterprise system. "If tax reduction is not passed," he warned, "they will take it as a sign that our national policy is to achieve faster growth through massive federal spending." Seconding the general business plea, Saunders explicitly affirmed the committee's belief that to reap the benefits of tax reduction, government spending should be rigidly controlled.[45] Buoyed by the endorsement of some of the most influential executives in America, the Business Committee deserved signal credit for its work in rallying free enterprise support for the tax bill.[46]

From the long debate over tax reduction and reform in 1963 emerged a classic example of the American compromise tradition. Kennedy, the practical politician, sacrificed reform in order to obtain what he considered to be more important—a tax cut to stimulate economic growth and provide jobs. Business proved to be an equally pragmatic antagonist. Having won on tax reform, private enterprise paid loud lip-service to restraints on budget-unbalancing federal spending but strongly endorsed the desired tax cut, despite the administration's frank forecast of budget deficits for several years.[47]

President Kennedy did not live to see his tax bill become law. Senator Byrd kept his promise to hold extensive hearings on the measure, and Lyndon Johnson had occupied the White House for almost three weeks before the last witness appeared before the Finance Committee. As a result, final congressional passage of the act did not come until early in 1964.

Kennedy had recommended reducing personal income tax rates from a 20–91 percent scale to 14–65 percent and the corporate rate from 52 percent to 47 percent.[48] As enacted, the individual scale ranged from 14 to 70 percent and the corporate levy was set at 48 percent.[49] The administration's reform proposals were drastically whittled down by the legislators. For example, on personal income taxes the president had suggested reforms to net $2.3 billion. The final net estimated income was only $290 million.[50]

The failure to obtain badly needed reform of the internal revenue structure disappointed many Americans. But the nation's economy received a dramatic impetus from the Revenue Act of 1964, just as Kennedy and his advisers had predicted. The impressive results which followed the revolutionary tactic of a tax cut in face of a budget deficit provided a persuasive argument for the value of the new economics. The annual rate of growth in 1964 surged to 5 percent; subsequent years saw an even more powerful acceleration. By March 1966, the unemployment rate at last dropped to Kennedy's 4 percent goal, with almost five and a half million more persons employed than in 1961. Corporate earnings soared in a spectacular fashion. Between 1961 and 1965, profits before taxes increased by 50 percent and profits after taxes improved by almost 70 percent.[51]

14

The Legacy of Practical Politics

When John F. Kennedy was murdered, on November 22, 1963, Congress was still in session, and most of the president's 1963 legislative requests were awaiting final action. The legislators were not saying no to his proposals, but they were stubbornly delaying final action.[1]

The large number of controversial and crucial measures, such as the nuclear test ban, tax reduction, and, especially, civil rights, plus an unusually refractory congressional attitude toward foreign aid, contributed heavily to the delay. In some instances, Kennedy had made serious tactical errors in his dealings with Capitol Hill. The Clay committee, named by the chief executive to investigate foreign aid, undermined the assistance program by urging a smaller appropriation than that originally recommended by the administration and by focusing national attention on past failures of overseas aid. And the president's premature acknowledgment that he would not fight to save loophole-closing reforms weakened his bargaining position in the latter stages of debate on the tax revision bill.

Kennedy's legislative program had fared much better in both sessions of the previous Congress, with 62 percent of his requests becoming law in 1961 and 70 percent in 1962.[2] But many of these statutes, notably those concerned with tax revision, reorganization of the regulatory agencies, and federal supervision of the drug industry, were emasculated by the deletion of key reform provisions. In many instances, although the acts remained the president's in name, their substance bore the stamp of Congress.

Particularly during the first two years of the New Frontier, liberal critics attacked the chief executive for not "spending" his personal popularity in an attempt to win grass-roots support for his program.[3] In 1963, Kennedy did make more direct pleas for public backing—for foreign aid, the nuclear test ban treaty, civil rights, and a tax cut—but his efforts appeared to have little effect on Congress.[4] And, as he increased the tempo of his appeals to the voters, his popularity declined to its lowest point.[5] Since more than half of the congressmen held relatively "safe" seats, effectively protected from any pressure generated by the White House, the value of such a strategy was probably overrated.[6]

Shocked by Kennedy's assassination and prodded by the parliamentary wizardry of Lyndon Johnson, Congress eventually approved a sizeable number of the bills requested by the administration. It is impossible to say with certainty that they would have been enacted had Kennedy lived.[7] His defenders have pointed to assertions by Democratic and Republican leaders that the measures would have passed.[8] But in a nation mourning the loss of a martyred president, any less favorable statements by the legislators would have seemed tasteless.

KENNEDY'S POPULARITY WITH BUSINESS

As was said previously, business accepted Kennedy's election as president calmly, although with misgivings about his attitude toward big government and his reliance upon liberal advisers. The post-election "honeymoon" between the White House and the business world proved only a brief interlude. Despite the end of the recession in the spring of 1961 and the steady upward movement of the economy, increasing charges that the administration was antibusiness signaled the steady deterioration of government-business relations.[9]

The faltering pace of economic recovery early in 1962 made the situation worse. The chief executive's incisive action against the steel industry's price increase in April 1962, followed by the sharp drop in the already slumping stock market, sank the administration's popularity with businessmen to its lowest ebb. Bitter anti-Kennedy sentiment continued throughout the summer of 1962, while powerful leaders of major corporations, alert to the need for communications between business and government, labored to repair frayed relations between the antagonists.

An assortment of legislative enactments and administrative actions favorable to business followed, including private ownership of the Communications Satellite Corporation, the issue of more liberal depreciation allowances, the trade expansion bill, the investment tax credit, and a drug bill palatable to private industry. In addition, the president promised to reduce both corporate and personal income taxes in 1963. With economic activity and business profits moving steadily upward by early 1963, the New Frontier's stock in business circles began a slow but perceptible rise (see chart 1).

Criticism of Kennedy by business spokesmen continued in 1963, but it was neither as pervasive nor as harsh as it had been during the preceding eighteen months. There was a more general recognition that, as one financial columnist wrote, "The Kennedy Administration is cooperating and trusting U.S. business to a degree unprecedented in modern times. . . . To accuse Mr. Kennedy of being anti-business is almost akin to accusing Senator Goldwater of being pro-Communist."[10]

Nation's Business reported that many businessmen polled in early 1963 believed that the Kennedy administration was growing more responsive to business.[11] A random survey taken at the annual convention of the Chamber of Commerce indicated that at least two of every three delegates interviewed felt that relations between management and the New Frontier were better than during the previous year.[12] And the corporate executives at the spring meeting of the Business Council were reported to seem less nervous about Kennedy.[13] *Fortune* noted with satisfaction that government and business had avoided a full-scale war after the 1962 steel crisis, and that, as a result, business prospects for the future looked favorable.[14]

Speaking to the Florida Chamber of Commerce only three days before his death, Kennedy said that he wondered why, despite his efforts to the contrary, the antibusiness image of his administration persisted.[15] The *Wall Street Journal,* an indefatigable critic of most of his policies, editorialized that it was not sure that such a negative attitude existed in the business world. At least, explained the *Journal,* management understood and appreciated the government's attempts to improve the business climate.[16]

Ironically, relations between private enterprise and the Kennedy administration were gradually improving during the same period when

CHART 1

Comparison of Trends: President Kennedy's Popularity with Business and the Public; Corporation Profits before Taxes

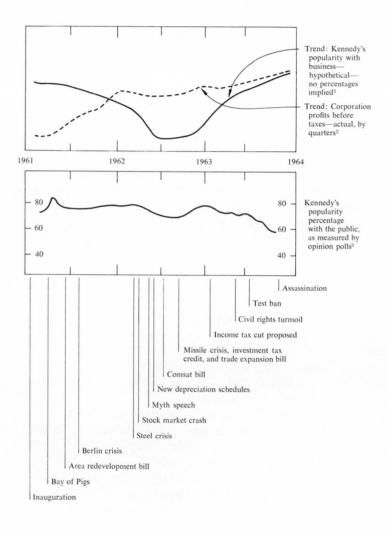

SOURCES: [1] Author's Impressions.
          [2] *Business Statistics, 1965,* p. 6.
          [3] American Institute of Public Opinion, *Public Opinion News Service.*

the president's popularity with the general public was sinking, his legislative program was seriously bogged down in Congress, and news
analysts were depicting the New Frontier as in serious trouble.[17] During
the final months of 1963, business spokesmen were among the most
active defenders of proposals for tax reduction, foreign aid, and the
sale of wheat to Russia.

THE LOCUS OF POWER

To gauge precisely a president's popularity with *the* business community is impossible; there are actually many business communities.
The great majority of American enterprises are small in size and of
various formats.[18] Small businessmen not only have different problems
and, hence, different views from the managers of large firms, but they
also have immensely less bargaining power to exert on national
polices.[19] In 1963, United States Steel Company alone employed more
workers than the total membership of the largest national organization
representing small businessmen—the National Federation of Independent Business.[20]

Largely untouched by international and nationwide pressures upon
his daily business decisions, the small entrepreneur is able to enjoy the
luxury of ideological rigidity far more than his counterpart in big business. Large companies, recognizing that their policies directly affect the
lives of thousands, perhaps millions, of persons—employees, stockholders, customers, and the public at large—have been forced for many
years to grapple with the problems of social responsibility.[21]

With their global commitments and their preeminence in the massive
space and defense market, the majority of big-business executives have
become increasingly aware that government and business depend upon
and need one another in order to achieve their respective objectives.[22]
Before, during, and after the Kennedy years, leaders of major corporations dominated the official and unofficial business committees providing advice to the federal government on a wide variety of issues.
Opinions expressed by a Henry Ford II or a Roger M. Blough attract
national attention. Key executives with proved administrative talent
shuttle easily between large private firms and the federal government.[23]

A rough assessment would be that Kennedy was accepted more
readily by the eastern establishment wing of private enterprise than by
the businessman in the hinterlands.[24] Although New York City no
longer dominates commerce and industry as it once did, the nation's
largest city still remains the chief nerve center for American business:

the headquarters of the largest corporations and the leader in banking, advertising, and publishing.

On the surface it might appear that the personal style of a Massachusetts-born, Harvard-educated president with respected intellectual qualities and cultured tastes would be accepted quite naturally by the eastern establishment corporation official. But David Bazelon and others have suggested that business responded more warmly to Lyndon Johnson than to Kennedy because it liked the Texan's style better.[25]

Perhaps Bazelon's observation is true if the nation's businessmen are judged collectively. But for the eastern establishment executive, it is likely that results were more important than style, and business prospered even more under Johnson than it did under Kennedy.

Theodore White had described the establishment businessmen: "Republicans almost to a man, the Wall Street bankers and corporate executives must learn to live in a world of constant adjustments."[26] One of the adjustments they began to make during the New Frontier was to accept the new economic policies advocated by the president and his advisers. A tax cut—like the one suggested in 1963—which increased an existing budget deficit was contradictory to all traditional economic theories and precedents. But the tactic provided huge dividends for business during the longest economic expansion in American history. Kennedy's policies stimulated the boom, and enlightened executives learned to appreciate his efforts. Johnson basically continued the economic programs of the New Frontier. And the officials of the blue-chip corporations grew even more responsive to the new economics—and to the chief executive who used it.

A Shade of Difference

The fate of all extremes is such: men may be read, as well as books, too much.

—Alexander Pope

It would be an error to read too much into the ideological rhetoric that has described Kennedy's 1,037 days in the White House and to overlook his basic political pragmatism. In his celebrated "myth" speech at Yale University in 1962, the president was credited by some with declaring his independence of the old economic restraints and signaling his conversion to the new, Keynesian brand of economics.[27] But in the same address, he paid high respects to the practical attainment of essential national needs.

What is at stake in our economic decisions today is not some grand warfare of rival ideologies which will sweep the country with passion but the practical management of a modern economy. What we need is not labels and cliches but more basic discussion of the sophisticated and technical questions involved in keeping a great economic machinery moving ahead.[28]

Kennedy was liberal in his willingness to experiment and in his receptiveness to change. He had a particular talent for combining pragmatism with idealism—as he did with the Peace Corps—and making it not only popular but productive. As the premier representative of a new generation of leaders, he was impatient to achieve success and to remedy obvious ills—to reduce unemployment, to provide equal opportunity, to eradicate poverty, and to protect the public against exploitation. One of his favorite parables, woven again and again into his speeches, concerned Marshal Lyautey, the former French commander in North Africa. When Marshal Lyautey suggested that his gardener plant a tree, the servant answered, "Well, why plant it? It won't flower for one hundred years." Lyautey replied, "In that case, plant it this afternoon."[29]

Like the Marshal, Kennedy was anxious to "begin"—to move America forward. But as a sensitive politician, the president was also conservative. He recognized plainly that education and reorientation must precede the uprooting of firmly held traditions. And, above all, he revealed his respect for the place of compromise in America's history and thought.

He moved comfortably in the mainstream of America while pursuing his economic goals with vigor and a keen sense of the politics of the possible. Although left of center of the business community as a whole, at no point did he venture far from easy hailing distance of the business leaders whose help he needed most—the influential titans of the major corporations.

Notes

The following code abbreviations are used in the notes:

BW	*Business Week*
CED	Committee for Economic Development
CFC	*Commercial and Financial Chronicle*
CR	*Congressional Record*
HBR	*Harvard Business Review*
J of C	*Journal of Commerce*
MWS	*Magazine of Wall Street*
NAM	National Association of Manufacturers
NFIB	National Federation of Independent Business
NICB	National Industrial Conference Board
NPA	National Planning Association
NYT	*New York Times*
PONS	American Institute of Public Opinion, *Public Opinion News Service*
Pub. P.	*Public Papers of the Presidents* (code followed by the year)
USCC	United States Chamber of Commerce
USNWR	*United States News and World Report*
VS	*Vital Speeches*
WSJ	*Wall Street Journal*

Chapter 1

1. John Kenneth Galbraith suggested this in his discussion of countervailing power and government in *American Capitalism* (Boston, 1952).

2. During his whistle-stop tour of California in early September, Kennedy began to use the "moving America forward" theme frequently. *Senate Reports*, 87 Cong., 1 sess., no. 994, part 1, *The Speeches, Remarks, Press Conferences, and Statements of Senator John F. Kennedy, August 1 through November 7, 1960*, pp. 163–93.

3. One measure of Republican predominance among businessmen was the survey by Stephen A. Greyser, "Business and Politics, 1964," *HBR* 42 (Sept.–Oct., 1964): 22–32. Greyser sampled 5,000 subscribers to the *HBR* and received a 31 percent response, with 78 percent listing their affiliation as Republican. A sampling of business and professional citizens by *PONS,* July 21, 1960, indicated that 55 percent believed that the Re-

publican party was the party with their best interests at heart. When the same question was asked two years later, the percentage had increased to 58 percent. Ibid., Sept. 8, 1962.

4. Theodore C. Sorensen, *Kennedy* (New York, 1965), p. 178. For the content of the Democratic platform, see K. H. Porter and D. B. Johnson, *National Party Platforms, 1840–1960* (Urbana, 1961).

5. *Senate Reports,* 87 Cong., 1 sess., no. 994, part 1, pp. 1053–54. Kennedy asked individual businessmen and trade and industry association officials for their opinions on problems directly affecting the welfare of the business community.

6. *Senate Reports,* 87 Cong., 1 sess., no. 994, part 3, *The Joint Appearances of Senator John F. Kennedy and Vice-President Richard M. Nixon, Presidential Campaign of 1960,* pp. 73–92. Kennedy emphasized that domestic problems were directly involved in the struggle with communism.

7. *Economic Indicators,* Mar. 1961, p. 9; *Business Statistics, 1965,* p. 6.

8. *Senate Reports,* 87 Cong., 1 sess., no. 994, part 1, pp. 557–58.

9. Ibid., pp. 559–62. In an advertisement which appeared in the *New York Times* on October 18, 1960, Kennedy declared that he did not believe it was time for a tax increase. He stressed that he favored measures to aid small business and had no desire to change the American free enterprise system. Ibid., pp. 659–63.

10. Ibid., p. 1225.

11. Ibid., p. 826.

12. *Pub. P., 1962,* p. 348. The speech was delivered April 30, 1962, at Washington, D.C. A *Dun's Review* president's panel of nearly two hundred leading corporation executives was asked which American political leader most closely reflected the attitudes and philosophies of America's businessmen. Forty percent of the executives listed Barry Goldwater; 33 percent, Nixon; 17 percent, former President Eisenhower; 6 percent, Kennedy; and 4 percent, Nelson Rockefeller. *Duns Review,* Mar. 1961, p. 30.

13. *BW,* Nov. 19, 1960, pp. 42–43.

14. Robert W. Galvin, president of Motorola, Inc., quoted in *Iron Age,* Nov. 17, 1960, p. 107.

15. Neil C. Harley, president of Thor Power Tool Company, Ibid., p. 108.

16. Ibid.

17. *WSJ,* Nov. 10, 1960, pp. 1, 16. The "lack of a mandate" was a popular theme with many business publications. See *J of C,* Nov. 10, 1960, p. 4; *NAM News,* Nov. 18, 1960, p. 2; *MWS,* Nov. 19, 1960, p. 215; *BW,* Nov. 12, 1960, p. 194; *CFC,* Nov. 17, 1960, p. 1.

18. The best prepresidential biography of Kennedy is James Mac-Gregor Burns, *John Kennedy: A Political Profile* (New York, 1960).

19. *PONS,* Jan. 28, 1961.

20. *WSJ,* Nov. 10, 1960, p. 16.

21. Sorensen, *Kennedy,* p. 296.

22. Narrated without source in Hobart Rowen, *The Free Enterprisers: Kennedy, Johnson and the Business Establishment* (New York, 1964), p.

20. Leon Keyserling, an economist with strongly Keynesian views, was chairman of the Council of Economic Advisers under President Harry Truman. Rowen's book drew heavily upon off-the-record comments, frequently anecdotal, by business and government contacts. Although hesitant about documentation, Rowen presented a sparkling account of the business-government relationship.

23. *Senate Hearings,* 87 Cong., 1 sess., Committee on Labor and the Public Welfare, *The Nomination of Arthur Goldberg to be Secretary of Labor.*

24. David T. Stanley, *Changing Administrations* (Washington, 1965), pp. 3–4.

25. *American Banker,* Jan. 18, 1961, p. 4; Jan. 25, 1961, p. 4. Also see *CFC,* Jan. 19, 1961, p. 1. *Printers' Ink,* May 19, 1961, p. 11, reported that its survey of 451 client and advertising executives indicated that 30 percent rated the Kennedy appointees as excellent; 52 percent, good; 14 percent, fair; and only 4 percent, poor. Seventy-nine percent of the executives had voted for Nixon.

26. *CR,* 87 Cong., 1 sess., pp. 1657–58. For statements by Representative Thomas M. Pelly (Republican, Washington), see ibid., p. 1799. Schlesinger had presented similar views many years previously in an article, "The Future of Socialism: The Perspective Now," *The Partisan Review,* 14 (May–June, 1947): 229–42.

27. John E. Swearingen, president of Standard Oil of Indiana, "Government and American Business," *VS,* Nov. 1, 1961, pp. 39–42.

28. *Management Review,* Nov., 1962, p. 14. Richard Hofstadter has written that while the hostility toward intellectuals by businessmen may be interpreted in the narrow sense as mainly a political phenomenon, it may more broadly be interpreted as part of the American devotion to practicality and direct experience. *Anti-Intellectualism in America* (New York, 1962), p. 236.

29. George J. Stigler, "The Intellectual and the Market Place," *National Review,* Dec. 3, 1963, p. 476.

30. *PONS,* various releases. Kennedy's public popularity index was 69 percent in January 1961; reached a high mark of 83 percent in April 1961; and hit a low of 57 percent in October 1963.

31. Adolf A. Berle, Jr., "Businessmen in Government: The New Administration," *Reporter,* Feb. 3, 1953, p. 8.

32. Seymour E. Harris, *The Economics of the Political Parties* (New York, 1962), p. 25. Harris calculated that of 199 early high-level Kennedy appointments, only 6 percent came from business, finance, and insurance, compared with 36 percent of 180 comparable Eisenhower appointees. Conversely, 47 percent of the New Frontiersmen were from government and 18 percent from academic and nonprofit institutions, compared with 28 percent and 6 percent, respectively, under Eisenhower.

33. Calculated by the author.

34. *USNWR,* Feb. 4, 1955, p. 37, reported the guest lists at thirty-eight Eisenhower stag dinners. Over half of the 555 guests were businessmen. For comments on Kennedy's White House entertaining, see Sorensen,

Kennedy, pp. 430–32; Arthur M. Schlesinger, Jr., *A Thousand Days* (Boston, 1965), pp. 730–38.

35. Charles A. Nelson, *Developing Responsible Public Leaders* (Dobbs Ferry, New York, 1963), pp. 52–54, 59–72. Among the businessmen interviewed were LeRoy Collins, Marion B. Folsom, Gabriel Hauge, Eric A. Johnston, Stanley Marcus, and Charles Percy.

36. Colonel W. F. Rockwell, chairman of the Rockwell Manufacturing Company. Quoted in *Iron Age,* Nov. 17, 1960, p. 107.

CHAPTER 2

1. Henry Steele Commager, ed., *Documents of American History* (New York, 1963), 1: 625.

2. *Statistical Abstract of the United States, 1966,* p. 229.

3. The two most important contemporary American business ideologies are the classical, essentially the nineteenth-century economic view of private, competitive capitalism without government interference; and the managerial, which accepts many new economic ideas and emphasizes the role of professional managers directing economic forces for the common good. See R. Joseph Monsen, Jr., *Modern American Capitalism* (Boston, 1963), especially pp. 16–47. There are numerous valuable studies of business ideology. Among the most useful are Francis X. Sutton, et al., *The American Business Creed* (Cambridge, 1956); Edward S. Mason, ed., *The Corporation in Modern Society* (Cambridge, 1959); Earl F. Cheit, ed., *The Business Establishment* (New York, 1964); John H. Bunzel, *The American Small Businessman* (New York, 1962).

4. V. O. Key, Jr., *Politics, Parties, and Pressure Groups* (New York, 1964), p. 84.

5. Six national organizations which attempt to speak for business are the United States Chamber of Commerce, the National Association of Manufacturers, the National Federation of Independent Business, the Committee for Economic Development, the National Industrial Conference Board, and the National Planning Association. All are frequent contributors to congressional hearings. The NFIB attempts to speak for small businessmen. The CED, NICB, and NPA are small but influential organizations which concentrate on technical analysis of national problems. The CED and NICB are composed largely of executives of major corporations. The NPA membership includes corporate executives, labor union leaders, farm leaders, and public representatives.

6. Raymond A. Bauer, Ithiel de Sola Pool, and Lewis A. Dexter, *American Business and Public Policy: The Politics of Foreign Trade* (New York, 1963), pp. 156–62. Circulation figures for business publications are provided in *Ayer's Directory of Newspapers and Periodicals,* published annually. In 1963, the *Wall Street Journal,* with a circulation of 798,169, was the most-read business publication. Others included: *Business Week,* 401,776; *Fortune,* 378,904; *Harvard Business Review,* 62,857; *Duns Review,* 120,576; *Barron's,* 141,185; *American Banker,* 9,600; *Nation's Business,* 768,263; *New York Journal of Commerce,* 27,883.

7. Sorensen, *Kennedy,* pp. 353–59. During the Cuban missile crisis, Assistant Secretary of Defense for Public Affairs Arthur Sylvester referred to news management as "part of the weaponry" available to the government. Sorensen observed that Kennedy felt that Sylvester's terms were both unclear and unwise.

8. *Magazine of Wall Street* is an example of a business publication which repeatedly alluded to the evils of the New Deal and modern economic ideas. Editor-publisher C. G. Wyckoff, Feb. 10, 1962, p. 542, speculated that Keynesian economics was a Russian plot to bankrupt the United States. Keynes married a Russian, and Wyckoff believed that she was capable of having a cloak and dagger influence on her husband.

9. *Senate Reports,* 87 Cong., 1 sess., no. 994, part 1, pp. 1053–54.

10. C. Wright Mills, *The Power Elite* (New York, 1956), p. 276.

11. Ibid., p. 267.

12. Arnold M. Rose, *The Power Structure* (New York, 1967), p. 492.

13. *Pub. P., 1960–1961,* pp. 1038–39.

14. For a pro-Goldwater tract castigating the eastern establishment, see Phyllis Schlafly, *A Choice Not an Echo* (Alton, Illinois, 1964), especially pp. 82–116. The role of the eastern Establishment was also examined by Theodore H. White, *The Making of the President, 1964* (New York, 1965), pp. 82–89. For a sprightly account of the Establishment, see Richard H. Rovere, "Notes on the Establishment in America," *The American Scholar,* 30 (August, 1961) : 489–95. Some readers suspected that Rovere's article was half-spoof.

15. See Paul Jacobs and Saul Landau, *The New Radicals: A Report with Documents* (New York, 1966); Mitchell Cohen and Dennis Hale, eds., *The New Student Left* (Boston, 1967).

16. David J. Galligan, *Politics and the Businessman* (New York, 1964), pp. 11–12, 67–72. Also see J. J. Wuerthner, Jr., *The Businessman's Guide to Practical Politics* (Chicago, 1961). Wuerthner was the spark plug of the Syracuse Plan.

17. Galligan, *Politics,* pp. 5–6.

18. Ibid., pp. 73–77; USCC, *Action Course in Practical Politics* (Washington, 1959).

19. James C. Worthy, *Big Business and Free Men* (New York, 1959), pp. 165–66.

20. Charles R. Barr of Standard Oil of Indiana, "A Post-Election Look at Businessmen in Politics," *VS,* Apr. 1, 1961, pp. 378–81. Also see Robert K. Gray of Hill & Knowlton Agency, "We Are Growing Up in Public Affairs," *Printers' Ink,* Apr. 28, 1961, p. 66

21. Speech by Donald J. Hardenbrook, new president of the National Association of Manufacturers, *NAM News,* Dec. 15, 1961, pp. 1 ff.

22. Alan F. Westin, "The John Birch Society (1962)," in *The Radical Right,* ed. Daniel Bell (New York, 1963), p. 249, n. 1. Although sixteen of the twenty-five directors of the society were corporation executives or former executives, they were from family firms or companies headed by a single entrepreneur.

23. Alan F. Westin, "Anti-Communism and the Corporations," *Commentary*, Dec. 1963, pp. 481–82, 484.

24. *Steel*, June 25, 1962, pp. 76–79.

25. Peter C. Reid, "Employees in Politics: A Survey of Company Policy," *Management Review*, Nov. 1962, pp. 5–13.

26. William A. Mann, a General Electric executive, "Creating and Maintaining a Good Business Climate," *Advanced Management-Office Executive*, May 1963, pp. 8–10.

27. *NYT*, Aug. 5, 1963, p. 1.

28. Kenton R. Cravens, "A New Force in Politics," *Bankers Monthly*, Apr. 15, 1964, pp. 17–22.

29. Greyser, "Business and Politics," p. 23.

30. Luther H. Hodges, *The Business Conscience* (Englewood Cliffs, 1963), p. 14.

31. Ibid., pp. 14–15.

32. Carl Reiser, "Luther Hodges Wants to be Friends," *Fortune*, Aug. 1961, p. 108.

33. *BW*, Apr. 8, 1961, p. 27.

34. Department of Commerce press release, May 16, 1961 (mimeographed).

35. *NYT*, July 6, 1961, p. 16; July 7, 1961, p. 1; *WSJ*, July 7, 1961, p. 2.

36. *NYT*, July 9, 1961, p. 1.

37. Ibid., July 11, 1961, p. 21. The *WSJ*, July 12, 1961, p. 14, editorialized that the BAC never had anything to do with running the government but was only a group of businessmen willing to give time and opinions to any secretary of commerce who wanted help.

38. *NYT*, Sept. 20, 1961, p. 39.

39. *BW*, Oct. 28, 1961, p. 34.

40. Bernard D. Nossiter, *The Mythmakers* (Boston, 1964), p. 6. Nossiter's thesis was that businessmen purposely kept pressure on Kennedy because they believed this was the best way to get what they wanted. See pp. 1–42.

41. Letter, Jan. 10, 1967, Walter W. Heller to the author.

42. *BW*, May 19, 1962, pp. 27–28. Although relations between the council and the president were generally cordial, some animosity was present. In 1963 Kennedy caustically remarked that the BC was the only audience not to rise to its feet upon the appearance of the president. Sorensen, *Kennedy*, p. 564.

43. *Pub. P., 1961*, p. 22.

44. Ibid., p. 73.

45. Hodges, *Business Conscience*, pp. 22–23; Theodore L. Thau, "The Business Ethics Advisory Council: An Organization for the Improvement of Ethical Performance," *The Annals of the American Academy of Political and Social Science*, 343 (Sept., 1962): 129–32.

46. Reverend Raymond C. Baumhart, SJ, "How Ethical Are Businessmen?" *HBR* 39 (July–Aug. 1961): 160, 166.

47. Thau, "Business Ethics," p. 136.

48. *Pub. P.*, 1962, p. 24.
49. Hodges, *Business Conscience*, pp. 27–29.
50. *WSJ*, Jan. 25, 1962, p. 12.
51. Henry Ford II, "Business Ethics in 1961," Apr. 20, 1961, speech pamphlet.
52. Clarence Randall, "For a New Code of Business Ethics," *NYT Magazine*, Apr. 8, 1962, p. 24. J. Irwin Miller, chairman of Cummins Engine Company, warned that if business did not behave responsibly, it would eventually crash. Interview with Miller, *Steel*, Mar. 26, 1962, p. 77.

CHAPTER 3

1. Sorensen, *Kennedy*, p. 244, cited the recession as one of the seven key factors that provided the final margin of victory in the election.
2. *Senate Reports*, 87 Cong., 1 sess., no. 994, part 3, p. 337.
3. *Senate Reports*, 87 Cong., 1 sess., no. 994, part 1, pp. 936, 942.
4. *Senate Reports*, 87 Cong., 1 sess., no. 994, part 3, p. 471.
5. *WSJ*, Oct. 10, 1960, p. 2; Oct. 26, 1960, p. 2; Oct. 28, 1960, p. 4.
6. *Pub. P.*, *1960–1961*, p. 1051.
7. *WSJ*, June 8, 1960, p. 2; June 15, 1960, p. 1; June 28, 1960, p. 7; Sept. 7, 1960, p. 17; Oct. 18, 1960, p. 11; *BW*, survey of executives, Aug. 13, 1960, pp. 25–26; *Fortune*, Sept. 1960, pp. 59 ff.; Oct. 1960, pp. 59 ff. *USNWR*, Oct. 31, 1960, p. 54, reported that the prevailing mood at the autumn meeting of the Business Advisory Council was "cautious." *Newsweek*, Oct. 31, 1960, p. 68, noted that economists at the October meeting of the National Association of Business Economists agreed that the economy was in a downturn and due to get worse. Not all economists were so gloomy. Dr. Jules Bachman of New York University declared that the economy was basically strong and much better than the alarmists were saying. *CFC*, Oct. 27, 1960, p. 7.
8. *BW*, Oct. 15, 1960, pp. 29–30.
9. *Purchasing Magazine*, Dec. 5, 1960, p. 76.
10. Wilfred Lewis, Jr., *Federal Fiscal Policy in the Postwar Recessions* (Washington, 1962), pp. 241–42. Lewis placed heavy, although not exclusive, blame on excessive budget tightening.
11. *Business Statistics, 1965* pp. 6, 15; *Economic Indicators*, Mar. 1961, pp. 9, 14.
12. Joseph A. Pechman, *Federal Tax Policy* (Washington, 1966), pp. 12–13.
13. *Pub. P.*, *1962*, p. 6.
14. Edward S. Flash, Jr., *Economic Advice and Presidential Leadership* (New York, 1965), p. 175.
15. For the text of the report, see *CR*, 87 Cong., 1 sess., pp. 491–94.
16. For the text of the report, see *Senate Hearings*, 87 Cong., 1 sess., Committee on Banking and Currency, *Area Redevelopment, 1961*, pp. 55–63. Also useful is Sar A. Levitan, *Federal Aid to Depressed Areas* (Baltimore, 1964).
17. *Federal Register* 26: 639, Executive Order 10914, Jan. 21, 1961.

18. *Pub. P., 1961*, p. 7. The bill proposed technical assistance, loans for private and public facilities, and job training and retraining. The president's bill generally paralleled the Douglas report, but placed the program under the Department of Commerce. Douglas favored the creation of an independent agency. See Conley H. Dillon, *The Area Redevelopment Administration* (College Park, 1964).

19. *Pub. P., 1961*, pp. 19–20.

20. *WSJ*, Feb. 1, 1961, p. 1. The *Journal* interviewed executives in a dozen major cities. Arthur B. Sinkler of Hamilton Watch Company is the executive quoted. Emerson P. Schmidt of the USCC expressed similar sentiments. See *Joint Hearings*, 87 Cong., 1 sess., Joint Economic Committee, *January 1961 Economic Report of the President*, p. 171.

21. *Pub. P., 1961*, p. 31.

22. Walter W. Heller, *New Dimensions of Political Economy* (Cambridge, 1966), p. 75.

23. Henry C. Wallich and Stephen H. Axilrod, "The Postwar Record of Monetary Policy," in *The Battle Against Unemployment*, ed. Arthur M. Okun (New York, 1965), pp. 189–90.

24. *BW*, Feb. 25, 1961, p. 148; Mar. 4, 1961, p. 96. The economist Seymour Harris wrote that by this action Kennedy served warning that he would allow the Federal Reserve independence only within limits. *Economics of the Kennedy Years* (New York, 1964), p. 120.

25. *Pub. P., 1961*, pp. 41–53.

26. House Minority Leader Charles Halleck (Indiana) and Senate Minority Leader Everett Dirksen (Illinois) attacked the program. *NYT*, Feb. 3, 1961, p. 1.

27. *WSJ*, Feb. 3, 1961, p. 10; *BW*, Feb. 4, 1961, p. 100; *MWS*, Feb. 11, 1961, pp. 535–36; *NAM News*, Feb. 10, 1961, p. 2.

28. Testimony by George Hagedorn, Director of Research, NAM, *Joint Hearings*, 87 Cong., 1 sess., Joint Economic Committee, *January 1961 Economic Report of the President*, pp. 191–207. Also see *Fortune*, Jan. 1961, pp. 75–76.

29. Quoted in Heller, *New Dimensions*, p. 26. Heller noted that Kennedy quickly added, "but always make clear that the recession started *last year*."

30. Schlesinger, *Thousand Days*, pp. 626–28. The fiscalists cited World War II as a prime example of heavy government spending's raising employment sharply. Kennedy recognized that structural unemployment would be difficult to eliminate, even in a substantial recovery, but he maintained that his goal was to reduce the unemployment rate to a 4 percent maximum. *Pub. P., 1961*, pp. 187–88. In the twentieth century no decade has passed without severe unemployment (over 7 percent of the labor force) occurring at least once; and none, except the 1930s, has passed without at least one year of what may be called minimum unemployment (3 percent or less). Stanley Lebergott, "Labor Force Mobility and Unemployment, 1800–1960," in *New Views on American Economic Development*, ed. Ralph Andreano (Cambridge, 1965), p. 372. Extremes of

opinion as to what percentage of unemployed is reasonable have varied sharply. *Fortune,* Jan. 1944, pp. 84 ff., suggested a figure of 7 percent. Lord Beveridge, *Free Employment in a Free Society* (New York, 1945), pp. 127–29, argued for 3 percent.

31. Heller, *New Dimensions,* pp. 30–31.

32. *Economic Indicators,* Mar. 1961, p. 9. The February rate was 8.1 percent (6.8 percent seasonally adjusted).

33. *NYT,* Feb. 11, 1961, p. 1.

34. *Pub. P., 1961* pp. 86–87. Advised by newsmen that some business-men regarded his avoidance of the term "recession" in his speech as an optimistic sign, Kennedy declared, "I think we have been in a recession for some months and that we have not fully recovered from the recession of '58, which is a matter, of course, of great concern." Ibid., p. 94.

35. *NYT,* Feb. 15, 1961, p. 1.

36. *American Banker,* Feb. 16, 1961, p. 4; *Kiplinger Letter,* Feb. 25, 1961, p. 1. A *Dun's Review* presidential panel of nearly two hundred corporate executives reflected no serious misgivings about Kennedy but worry about the cost of his recession program. *Dun's Review,* Mar. 1961, pp. 30–31.

37. *House Hearings,* 87 Cong., 1 sess., Committee on Ways and Means, *Temporary Unemployment Compensation, 1961,* esp. pp. 113–29, 245–54, 409–20.

38. *Senate Hearings,* 87 Cong., 1 sess., Committee on Banking and Currency, *Area Redevelopment, 1961,* esp. pp. 283–92, 323–61, 402–3, 417–19. Also see USCC, *Policy Declarations, 1961* (Washington, 1961), pp. 16–17.

39. *NYT,* Feb. 10, 1961, p. 13; Feb. 16, 1961, p. 1; Feb. 20, 1961, p. 1; Feb. 23, 1961, p. 19.

40. Ibid., Feb. 19, 1961, p. 55.

41. Corporation profits and the gross national product showed a healthy increase in the second quarter. *Business Statistics, 1965,* pp. 1, 6, 9.

42. *BW,* Mar. 11, 1961, p. 144; Mar. 18, 1961, p. 41.

43. Heller, *New Dimensions,* pp. 31–32.

44. *PONS,* Mar. 2, 1961 and Mar. 14, 1961.

45. *Senate Hearings,* 87 Cong., 1 sess., Committee on Labor and Public Welfare, *Amendments to the Fair Labor Standards Act,* esp. pp. 133–36, 142–51, 164–67, 332–40, 559–60, 668–71. Also see *Nation's Business,* Jan. 1961, pp. 29–31. For a colorful account of the behind-the-scenes maneuvering connected with the passage of the bill, see Tom Wicker, *JFK and LBJ* (New York, 1968), pp. 93–116.

46. Sorensen, *Kennedy,* p. 445. Business sources were not enthusiastic. Derogatory descriptions, such as "dole" and "professional reformers," were frequently used in business editorials. For example, see *WSJ,* April 28, 1961, p. 12; May 10, 1961, p. 14.

47. Lewis, *Fiscal Policy,* pp. 273–74.

48. *Pub. P., 1961,* p. 53.

49. Heller, *New Dimensions,* p. 65. For views of the ADA, see *NYT,*

Feb. 13, 1961, p. 27. For samples of business opinions, see *J of C*, Mar. 23, 1961, p. 4; *NAM News*, Mar. 24, 1961, p. 1. For example of AFL-CIO views, see *NYT*, May 21, 1961, p. 28.

50. Sorensen, *Kennedy*, p. 447.

51. Heller, *New Dimensions*, p. 32.

52. *Economic Indicators*, Sept. 1961, p. 9.

53. *Pub. P., 1961*, p. 537. President Kennedy announced his plan to ask Congress for new defense appropriations when he spoke to the nation on radio and television concerning the Berlin crisis.

CHAPTER 4

1. *Pub. P., 1961*, pp. 20–21.

2. *Business Statistics, 1967*, pp. 1, 15, 39. The GNP climbed from $503.6 billion (annual rate) in the first quarter of 1961 to $605.8 billion in the fourth quarter of 1963. The industrial index of production increased from 108.7 in 1960 to 124.3 in 1963 (1957–1959 = 100). The consumers price index (1957–1959 = 100) rose from 93.3 in 1955 to 103.5 in 1960 and to 106.9 in 1963.

3. Harris, *Economics of the Kennedy Years*, p. 5; Heller, *New Dimensions*, pp. 36–37.

4. Burns, *John Kennedy*, pp. 30–31, 47.

5. Sorensen, *Kennedy*, p. 18.

6. Harris, *Economics of the Kennedy Years*, pp. 17–18.

7. Flash, *Economic Advice*, p. 271.

8. Address to the NICB, Feb. 13, 1961, *Pub. P., 1961*, p. 87.

9. Interview with Charles Percy of Bell and Howell, *Iron Age*, Sept. 29, 1960, p. 85; Arthur H. Motley, president of the USCC, "Economic Growth Is Not for Sale," *VS*, Feb. 15, 1961, pp. 262–65.

10. Sorensen, *Kennedy*, pp. 445–46. A *Dun's Review* president's panel of nearly two hundred corporation executives favored balancing the budget. *Dun's Review*, Mar., 1961, p. 31.

11. *Pub. P., 1961*, pp. 21–22.

12. Ibid., p. 221.

13. The *J of C*, Sept. 15, 1961, p. 4, observed that not all deficits in a recession were harmful, except that they promoted inflation. The *WSJ*, Sept. 21, 1961, p. 12, expressed concern because there had seldom been a budget balance over a span of years. One business organization, the CED, accepted the cycle balancing concept as early as the 1940s. See Karl Schriftgiesser, *Business Comes of Age* (New York, 1960), p. 101.

14. Arthur F. Burns, Chairman of the Council of Economic Advisers under Eisenhower, "Progress toward Economic Stability," *American Economic Review*, 50 (Mar. 1960): 1–18.

15. Heller, *New Dimensions*, p. 61.

16. *Senate Reports*, 87 Cong., 1 sess., no. 994, part 1, pp. 415, 560, 825, 948, 1078; *Pub. P., 1961*, pp. 393, 537, 683.

17. *Pub. P., 1962*, pp. 25–39.

18. *WSJ*, Jan. 22, 1962, p. 10. Also see *CFC*, Jan. 25, 1962, p. 1; *J of C*, Jan. 19, 1962, p. 4. The *American Banker*, Jan. 23, 1962, p. 4, urged

a mechanism for enforcing economies and eliminating wasteful departmental programs.

19. See Dillon's speech of June 20, 1961, in which he attempted to assure business that deficits did not necessarily mean inflation. Published in *CFC*, June 29, 1961, pp. 1 ff.

20. *Business Statistics, 1965*, pp. 6, 15; *Economic Indicators*, Mar. 1962, p. 9; Mar 1963, p. 10.

21. Measures to assist the unemployed that were requested by Kennedy in 1962 and passed included welfare revision, expanded public works, and manpower retraining. Requested but not enacted were medical care for the aged, youth employment, and aid for urban areas. In 1963 the president asked for, but Congress did not enact, social security medical care, youth employment, a national service corps, and area redevelopment. *Senate Documents*, 88 Cong., 1 sess., no. 53, *Summary of the Three-Year Kennedy Record and Digest of Major Accomplishments of the 87th Congress and the 88th Congress, 1st Session*, pp. 59–60, 61–66.

22. Department of Commerce, *Long-Term Economic Growth, 1860–1965* (Washington, 1966), pp. 107–8.

23. *Pub. P., 1961*, pp. 481–82.

24. Heller, *New Dimensions*, pp. 62–64.

25. *WSJ*, Dec. 7, 1961, p. 18. The *Journal*, Jan. 3, 1962, p. 12, also charged that much of the argument over growth was political talk.

26. Heller, *New Dimensions*, pp. 64–65.

27. For examples of such charges, see *CFC*, Feb. 16, 1961, p. 1; *MWS*, Oct. 7, 1961, p. 59.

28. Sorensen, *Kennedy*, pp. 464–65.

29. Heller, *New Dimensions*, p. 37. Heller noted that Kennedy wrote much of the speech himself.

30. *Pub. P., 1962*, pp. 471–73. Trust fund transactions are included in the Consolidated Cash Statement. The National Income Account records government transactions on the accrual basis. For fiscal 1963 the National Income Account projected a $4.4 billion surplus; the conventional budget estimated a $.5 billion surplus.

31. *Iron Age*, June 14, 1962, p. 5; *WSJ*, June 12, 1962, p. 18; *BW*, June 23, 1962, pp. 43–44, 134; *USNWR*, June 25, 1962, p. 108.

32. Interview with Emerson E. Mead, president of Smith-Corona Marchant, Inc., in *Nation's Business*, Aug. 1962, pp. 34–35.

33. *NYT*, June 30, 1962, p. 1.

34. The Business Council called for reduced government spending. *NYT*, Oct. 20, 1962, p. 1. The NFIB *Mandate*, no. 286, reported that 90 percent of the NFIB members responding to a recent poll favored federal spending's not exceeding revenues except in time of war or national emergency declared by Congress. Also see NAM, *The Federal Budget in 1963* (New York, 1963); Edwin P. Neilan, president of the USCC, "A Program for Tax and Spending Reductions," July 15, 1962, speech pamphlet.

35. Heller, *New Dimensions*, p. 33.

36. *Pub. P., 1962*, pp. 575, 611–17; *Pub. P., 1963*, pp. 26–27, 307–8, 566–67.

37. Ibid., pp. 210–11, 258–60, 383–88, 403–4, 710–12, 813–14, 863–66.
38. Ibid., p. 43.
39. Ibid., pp. 68–69.
40. Heller, *New Dimensions*, pp. 33–35.
41. *WSJ*, July 10, 1963, p. 10. The president estimated an $11.9 billion deficit. *Pub. P., 1963,* p. 28.
42. A survey of over 1,400 executives, mainly from large corporations, revealed that only 39 per cent favored a tax cut if it clearly would increase deficits. Leo Cherne, "1,588 Opinions on National Goals," *The General Electric Forum* 6 (July–Sept. 1963): 37. Small businessmen members of the NFIB overwhelmingly (83 percent) urged Congress to match tax cuts with spending reductions. NIFB *Mandate,* no. 282.
43. Alvin H. Hansen, "Comments of a Keynesian," *New Republic*, Oct. 20, 1962, pp. 28–29.
44. *New Republic*, Sept. 10, 1962, p. 2; May 18, 1963, p. 2; *The Progressive*, July 1963, p. 3.
45. Schlesinger, *Thousand Days*, pp. 1009–14. Schlesinger recalled the president's telling Heller, "First we'll have your tax cut; then we'll have my expenditures program."
46. Albert T. Sommers, "A Primer on the New Economics," *Conference Board Record*, Aug. 1968, p. 33; First National City Bank of New York, *Monthly Economic Letter*, Mar. 1965, pp. 30–32; *BW*, Feb. 5, 1966, p. 125; Rudolph A. Peterson, president of the Bank of America, "The Paradox of Prosperity," *VS*, May 15, 1968, pp. 477–78. Karl Schriftgiesser placed the CED in the vanguard of business groups promoting the new economics. *Business and Public Policy: The Role of the Committee for Economic Development: 1942–1967* (Englewood Cliffs, 1967), p. 203.
47. James Tobin, "The Intellectual Revolution in U.S. Economic Policy Planning," Noel Buxton Lecture, University of Essex, England, Jan. 18, 1966 (mimeographed). Other economists have expressed similar views. See Walter W. Heller, excerpts from speech, "Prosperity, Inflation, and Gold: What Next?" May 3, 1968 (mimeographed).
48. Numerous writers have commented on the difference in style between Kennedy and Johnson. For example, see David Bazelon, *Power in America: The Politics of the New Class* (New York, 1967), p. 107.
49. Sommers, "A Primer," p. 33.
50. Interview with Stans, *USNWR*, Dec. 13, 1965, pp. 82–86. George W. Coleman, a bank economist, speculated that the new economics had succeeded because of conditions conducive to success. But he warned that there was no guarantee that the success would continue. "The New Economics," *Bankers Monthly*, Aug. 1965, p. 22.
51. Gilbert Burck, "Must Full Employment Mean Inflation?" *Fortune*, Oct. 1966, p. 120; Orson H. Hart, "Some Observations of a Financial Economist on National Economic Policy," *Financial Analysts Journal* 23 (Nov.–Dec. 1967): 101–2; *CFC*, Dec. 29, 1966, p. 31.
52. Milton Friedman, "Has the New Economics Failed?" *Dun's Review*, Feb. 1968, pp. 38–39; *BW*, May 13, 1967, p. 96.
53. Byrl W. Sprinkel, vice-president, Harris Trust & Savings Bank, testi-

mony, *Joint Hearings*, 90 Cong., 1 sess., Joint Economic Committee, *January 1967 Economic Report of the President*, pp. 665; William F. Butler, vice-president, Chase Manhattan Bank, "The Flaw in the New Economics," *Dun's Review*, Oct. 1966, p. 41.

54. *WSJ*, Jan. 4, 1967, p. 12; Feb. 16, 1966, p. 16; Feb. 23, 1966, p. 18; *USNWR*, Feb. 28, 1966, pp. 99–101.

55. Douglas C. North, *Growth and Welfare in the American Past* (Englewood Cliffs, 1966), p. 184.

56. Henry C. Wallich, "Cooperation to Solve the Gold Problem," *HBR* 39 (May–June 1961): 47–49.

57. Ibid., pp. 50–54; Henry C. Aubrey, *The Dollar in World Affairs* (New York, 1964), esp. pp. 248–63. For valuable suggestions to improve the international monetary system, see Robert Triffin, *Gold and the Dollar Crisis* (New Haven, 1961), esp. pp. 10–14, 145–47. Also see Walter S. Salant, *The United States Balance of Payments in 1968* (Washington, 1963), esp. pp. 241–62.

58. *J of C*, Feb. 7, 1961, p. 4; L. F. McCollum, president of Continental Oil Company, "The Changing Role of U.S. World Trade," *Journal of Marketing* 26 (Jan. 1962): 3–5; speech by David Rockefeller, president, Chase Manhattan Bank, Mar. 7, 1961, published in *CR*, 87 Cong., 1 sess., pp. A3156–57.

59. *WSJ*, Mar. 14, 1961, p. 16; Nov. 14, 1962, p. 20; *American Banker*, Jan. 16, 1962, p. 4; Sept 20, 1963, p. 4.

60. *Pub. P., 1961*, pp. 57–66.

61. For examples of Kennedy's declarations not to devaluate, see *Pub. P., 1961*, p. 21; *Pub. P., 1962*, p. 547. For business views on devaluation, see *Financial World*, Sept. 5, 1962, p. 3; McCollum, "The Changing Role," p. 3; David Rockefeller, "Letter to the President: What to Do about the Economy," *Life*, July 6, 1962, p. 31.

62. *House Hearings*, 87 Cong., 1 sess., Committee on Ways and Means, *President's 1961 Tax Recommendations*, esp. pp. 3578–90. Also see *Senate Hearings*, 87 Cong., 2 sess., Committee on Finance, *Revenue Act of 1962*.

63. *Pub. P.*, 1963, pp. 574–84.

64. *Federal Reserve Bulletin*, Oct. 1963, p. 1354.

65. *BW*, July 27, 1963, p. 104; *Fortune*, Oct. 1963, pp. 81–82; Aug. 1963, p. 92; *WSJ*, July 23, 1963, p. 14; *House Hearings,* 88 Cong., 1 sess., Committee on Ways and Means, *Interest Equalization Tax Act*, esp. pp. 157–75, 217–19, 355–58, 423–32.

66. For example, see Kennedy's comments at the American Bankers Association Symposium on Economic Growth, *Pub. P., 1963*, pp. 214–15.

67. Ibid., p. 580.

CHAPTER 5

1. *Pub. P., 1961*, p. 51.

2. During his first two years as president, Eisenhower did have a Republican-controlled Congress, but the margin was tenuous.

3. Heller, *New Dimensions*, p. 80. Business planned to spend less for

total capital investment in 1961 than it had in 1960. McGraw-Hill Department of Economics, *Business' Plans for New Plants and Equipment, 1961–1964* (New York, 1961), p. 1.

4. *Pub. P., 1961*, pp. 290–303.

5. Joseph A. Pechman, tax expert, estimated that at 1966 profit and investment levels, the revenue cost of the credit was about $2 billion per year. *Federal Tax Policy*, p. 121.

6. *Pub. P., 1961*, pp. 293–94. Kennedy justified his decision to urge a tax credit instead of accelerated depreciation on the grounds that (1) increased depreciation tends to raise current costs and deter price reductions; (2) the proper determination of the length of an asset's life has a normal function wholly apart from any consideration of incentive; and (3) the entire amount of the credit would be available for investment without increasing a company's tax liability.

7. *BW*, Apr. 29, 1961, pp. 30–31; *WSJ*, May 19, 1961, p. 12; *Steel*, May 1, 1961, pp. 23–25; *House Hearings*, 87 Cong., 1 sess., Committee on Ways and Means, *President's 1961 Tax Recommendations*, esp. pp. 983–1006, 1127, 1175–78, 1345–56, 1488.

8. Ibid., esp. pp. 973–77, 1059–61, 1065–66.

9. Ibid., esp. pp. 1435–62, 1484–87. A survey of NFIB members revealed that a majority favored the president's incentive tax plan. *Results of National Survey of Small Business on President Kennedy's 1961 Tax Revision Program* (Burlingame, Calif., 1961).

10. *House Hearings, 1961 Tax Recommendations*, pp. 1006–11, 1140–51.

11. Interview with Stanley S. Surrey, *Challenge*, June 1961, pp. 20–21.

12. *Pub. P., 1961*, p. 346; *Pub. P., 1962*, pp. 553–54.

13. *WSJ*, July 13, 1962, p. 2; Sept. 26, 1962, p. 1.

14. *Senate Hearings*, 87 Cong., 2 sess., Committee on Finance, *Revenue Act of 1962*, esp. pp. 467–541, 653–740, 803–23.

15. A poll of 30,000 businessmen, taken in June 1962 by the Research Institute of America, reported that over 65 per cent favored the tax credit. *NYT*, June 27, 1962, p. 11. Also see speech, May 17, 1962, by G. L. Phillippe, president of General Electric, "Taxes and Economic Growth," in *Executive Speeches and Reports to the Shareholders, 1961–1962, General Electric Co.*, collected papers (n.p.).

16. *BW*, Oct. 6, 1962, pp. 28–29, reported that the business community appeared to be taking the tax credit with a surprising "ho-hum" shrug. The final version of the law allowed a firm to deduct from its income tax an amount equal to 7 percent of new investments having service lives of eight years or more.

17. *WSJ*, Nov. 15, 1962, p. 30; *BW*, Apr. 27, 1963, pp. 72–74.

18. Ibid., p. 132.

19. *Business Statistics, 1965*, p. 9.

20. *House Hearings, 1961 Tax Recommendations*, esp. pp. 1610–24, 1657–74; *Senate Hearings, Revenue Act of 1962*, esp. pp. 469, 507, 1154. NFIB *Mandate*, no. 288, reported that 65 percent of its members responding to a poll favored management's having more freedom in taking deductions for customer entertaining and business travel costs.

21. *J of C,* May 25, 1961, p. 4. Clarence Randall, retired chairman of Inland Steel Company, chided business for not wanting to put its house in order. *The Folklore of Management* (Boston, 1961), pp. 107–17.

22. *BW,* Jan. 5, 1963, p. 92; *WSJ,* Apr. 8, 1963, p. 16.

23. *BW,* Jan. 5, 1963, p. 22; *Steel,* Dec. 10, 1962, pp. 28–29; *WSJ,* Apr. 8, 1963, p. 16.

24. *WSJ,* Oct. 11, 1962, p. 1; *BW,* Mar. 30, 1963, p. 29.

25. *House Hearings, 1961 Tax Recommendations,* esp. pp. 823–34. 845–84, 2309–42, 2539–89. Also see *Senate Hearings, Revenue Act of 1962,* esp. pp. 472, 509–11, 543–44. For a detailed argument against the proposed reform, see article by George E. Barnes, past chairman of the Midwest Stock Exchange, in *Investment Dealers Digest,* May 21, 1962, pp. 29–30.

26. James Deakin, *The Lobbyists* (Washington, 1966), pp. 195–201. For reproductions of Savings and Loan advertisements used, see Ibid., pp. 288–91. The United States Savings and Loan League listed expenditures of $113,013 during 1962. Only four other lobbying organizations acknowledged larger expenditures during the year, according to records filed. *Congressional Quarterly Almanac, 1963* (Washington, 1964), p. 1036.

27. *Pub. P., 1962,* p. 375.

28. Interview with Surrey, *Challenge,* pp. 21–22.

29. The revenue code of 1954 provided for an exclusion from income of the first $50 of dividends received from domestic corporations and for a 4 percent credit against tax of such dividend income in excess of $50. The argument for these provisions was that they stimulated equity investment and helped to offset the so-called double taxation of dividend income. Kennedy maintained that neither purpose was served well. *Pub. P., 1961,* pp. 297–98.

30. Public Law 87–834 (76 Stat. 960).

31. *Pub. P., 1962,* pp. 711–12.

32. While the Senate was debating the bill, Secretary of the Treasury Dillon wrote Majority Leader Mike Mansfield (Democrat, Montana) to endorse the bill even without the withholding or dividend credit and exclusion reforms. *CR,* 87 Cong., 2 sess., pp. 18736–37. Senator John Carroll (Democrat, Colorado) questioned why the president made no greater effort to obtain support for the reforms at the grass-roots level. Ibid., p. 18111.

33. Kennedy signed the bill on October 16, 1962. *Pub. P., 1962,* pp. 787–88.

CHAPTER 6

1. For an extreme small-business view of the evils of monopoly, see C. Wilson Harder, president of the NFIB, "Monopoly Breeds World-Wide Communism," NFIB pamphlet (San Mateo, California, 1966).

2. Richard Hofstadter, "What Happened to the Antitrust Movement?" in Earl F. Cheit, ed., *The Business Establishment* (New York, 1964), p. 150.

3. *WSJ,* Jan. 8, 1962, p. 18; *Dun's Review* president's panel of corporation executives, *Dun's Review,* July 1961, p. 30; Robert H. Bork and

Ward S. Bowman, Jr., "The Crisis in Antitrust," *Fortune,* Dec. 1963, pp. 138–40 ff.; Crawford H. Greenewalt, chairman of the du Pont Corporation, "A Businessman Looks at Antitrust Laws," Aug. 13, 1963, speech pamphlet; John E. Swearingen, president of Standard Oil of Indiana, "Government and American Business," *VS,* Nov. 1, 1961, pp. 40–41.

4. NFIB *Mandate,* nos. 272, 274, 277, 279, 280, 284, 286, 288, contained results of polls on various issues which indicated the support of small businessmen for changes to strengthen antitrust laws and enforcement.

5. *Fortune,* Nov. 1962, pp. 104, 106.

6. A. D. H. Kaplan, *Big Enterprise in a Competitive System* (Washington, 1964), pp. 73–91, 107–53, 212–24; Richard J. Barber, "Merger: Threat to Free Enterprise," *Challenge,* Mar. 1963, pp. 6–10.

7. Gabriel Kolko, *Wealth and Power in America* (New York, 1962), pp. 56–65; NICB, *Corporate Directorship Practices* (New York, 1959), pp. 15, 22.

8. According to a poll taken by the Opinion Research Corporation for seventy big corporations, a majority of the public favored regulation to prevent excessive concentration of business, *but* seemed generally unconcerned about the threat of monopoly. *WSJ,* Aug. 2, 1962, p. 1.

9. Walter Adams and Horace M. Gray, *Monopoly in America* (New York, 1955), p. 176.

10. Ibid., p. 177; Hofstedter, "Antitrust Movement?" p. 133.

11. Sumner Slichter, "The Growth of Competition," *Atlantic,* Nov. 1953, p. 66.

12. Richard J. Barber, *The Politics of Research* (Washington, 1966), pp. 71–84.

13. Richard J. Barber, "The New Partnership, Big Government and Big Business," *New Republic,* Aug. 13, 1966, p. 17.

14. For an enlightening narrative of the price-fixing conspiracy, see John Herling, *The Great Price Conspiracy* (Washington, 1962).

15. *Senate Hearings,* 87 Cong., 1 sess., Subcommittee on Antitrust and Monopoly of the Committee on the Judiciary, *Administered Prices,* parts 27–28.

16. *Federal Register* 26: 3555–56, Executive Order 10936, Apr. 24, 1961.

17. *WSJ,* Mar. 30, 1961, p. 1; Apr. 4, 1961, p. 12.

18. *Senate Hearings,* 87 Cong., 1 sess., Committee on Interstate and Foreign Commerce, *Sundry Nominations—1961,* pp. 11–48.

19. George Bookman, "Loevinger vs. Big Business," *Fortune,* Jan. 1962, p. 93. Throughout 1961 and 1962, big-business spokesmen repeatedly expressed worry that Kennedy would unleash a vicious attack on big business. For examples, see *MWS,* May 6, 1961, p. 175; *WSJ,* Apr. 13, 1961, p. 1; *BW,* Oct. 28, 1961, pp. 41–42; Charls E. Walker, executive vice-president, American Bankers Association, "Does Antitrust Mean Antibusiness?" *Banking,* Feb. 1962, p. 40; Bert C. Goss, president of Hill and Knowlton, Inc., "Trial outside the Courtroom," *VS,* Dec. 15, 1962, pp. 137–41.

20. NICB, *The Climate of Antitrust* (New York, 1963), pp. 23–39. For a useful, brief summary of important cases initiated and handled by the Antitrust Division, see Department of Justice, *Annual Report of the Attorney General of the United States for Fiscal Year Ended June 30, 1961*, pp. 107–12; and ibid., *1962*, pp. 89–98.

21. *Dun's Review*, Dec., 1961, p. 34.

22. Lee Loevinger, "Recent Developments in Antitrust Enforcement," *Antitrust Bulletin* 6 (Jan.–Feb. 1961): 5–6.

23. Robert F. Kennedy, "Vigorous Enforcement Assists Business," *VS*, Dec. 15, 1961, pp. 134–36.

24. *BW*, Oct. 13, 1962, pp. 56, 58.

25. Lee Loevinger, "Antitrust Developments in 1961 and 1962," *Antitrust Bulletin* 8 (May–June 1963): 353–56.

26. *BW*, May 18, 1963, p. 28; *WSJ*, June 4, 1963, p. 18.

27. *BW*, Aug. 10, p. 40; *Iron Age*, July 4, 1963, pp. 58–59; Nov. 14, 1963, p. 252; *WSJ*, Nov. 12, 1963, p. 18; USCC, *Policy Declarations, 1961*, pp. 13–15; *1962*, pp. 9–13; *1963*, pp. 9–12.

28. The White House Committee on Small Business was appointed in April 1961. See the committee's reports: *Small Business in the American Economy* (Washington, 1962); *Progress Report to the President* (Washington, 1962).

29. *Pub. P., 1961*, pp. 93, 182–83, 346; *Pub. P., 1962*, pp. 192–93, 722. In particular, the president hoped to increase the share of defense contracts awarded to small business.

30. *WSJ*, May 14, 1962, p. 14; July 2, 1962, p. 10; *Barron's* Oct. 23, 1961, p. 1; *J of C*, Sept. 12, 1961, p. 4; Aug. 12, 1963, p. 4; *Senate Hearings*, 87 Cong., 1 sess., Committee on Banking and Currency, *Small Business Act Amendments of 1961*, esp. pp. 178–88, 212–18.

31. *Pub. P., 1961*, pp. 182, 582–83; *Pub. P., 1962*, pp. 192–93; *Pub. P., 1963*, pp. 895–96; Small Business Administration, *Semi-Annual Report*, 1957–1961, and *Annual Report*, 1962–1964.

32. Loevinger, "Antitrust Developments," p. 356.

33. George J. Stigler, "Administered Prices and Oligopolistic Inflation," *Journal of Business* 35 (Jan. 1962): 1. The basis of the theory of administered prices is that firms with a significant share of their respective markets will normally "administer" their prices, based on the calculation of long-term prospects and costs, and announce them to the trade. Kaplan, *Big Enterprise*, p. 156.

34. Stigler, "Administered Prices," p. 9.

35. *Senate Hearings*, 87 Cong., 2 sess., Committee on the Judiciary, *Refusal of Certain Steel Companies to Respond to Subpoenas*, esp. pp. 1–10, 31, 205, 219–29; *CR*, 87 Cong., 2 sess., Daily Digest, p. D574.

36. Thalidomide, a sedative which apparently caused deformities in babies when taken by pregnant women, was sold in Europe, but not in the United States, thanks to the delay in marketing approval caused by a suspicious researcher in the Food and Drug Department. For a detailed narrative of the events surrounding the passage of the drug bill, see Richard Harris, *The Real Voice* (New York, 1964).

37. *CR,* 87 Cong., 2 sess., p. 10105. Also see Estes Kefauver, with the assistance of Irene Till, *In a Few Hands, Monopoly Power in America* (New York, 1965), pp. 8–79.

38. *Senate Hearings,* 87 Cong., 1 and 2 sess., Subcommittee on Antitrust and Monopoly of the Committee on the Judiciary, *Drug Industry Antitrust Act,* esp. pp. 1301–17, 1993–2041, 2736–66, 2854–55.

39. *Pub. P., 1962,* pp. 239–41, 313–14.

40. *CR,* 87 Cong., 2 sess., pp. 10105–7.

41. Public Law 87–781 (76 Stat. 780).

42. *Pub. P., 1962,* p. 751. Kennedy signed the Drug Act on October 10, 1962.

43. Remarks by John T. Connor of Merck and Company, *NYT,* Oct. 5, 1962, p. 24.

44. *Pub. P., 1961,* pp. 582–83; *Pub. P., 1962,* pp. 241–42.

45. *House Hearings,* 87 Cong., 1 sess., Antitrust Subcommittee of the Committee on the Judiciary, *Premerger Notification,* esp. pp. 50–52, 57–58, 87–88. For the president's views, see *Pub. P., 1962,* pp. 241–42.

46. For business testimony opposing premerger notification, see *House Hearings, Premerger Notification,* pp. 117–54, 169–95, 264–71. For business testimony in favor of the bill, see pp. 154–62, 251–56, 266, 271–72, 275–77.

47. *Senate Hearings,* 87 Cong., 1 sess., Subcommittee on Antitrust and Monopoly of the Committee on the Judiciary, *Authorization for Department of Justice to Make Demand for Evidence in Civil Antitrust Investigations,* esp. pp. 17–98, 144–49.

48. Presidential Press Conference, Nov. 9, 1961, *Pub. P., 1961,* p. 708.

49. Adolf A. Berle, Jr., *The American Economic Republic* (New York, 1963), p. 153. The companies involved were Brown Shoe Company, primarily a manufacturer, and G. R. Kinney Company, a large retailer.

CHAPTER 7

1. *Senate Reports,* 87 Cong., 1 sess., no. 994, part 1, pp. 557–58, 663, 1061, 1110.

2. *Pub. P., 1961,* p. 52.

3. The Labor-Management Committee was appointed by Executive Order 10918, February 16, 1961. It was composed of seven members each from business and labor, plus five from the public and the two cabinet secretaries. *Federal Register* 26: 1427.

4. Jack Stieber, "The President's Committee on Labor-Management Policy," *Industrial Relations* 5 (Feb. 1966): 1–19.

5. See chapter 3 for details of the minimum wage bill of 1961.

6. For a useful examination of the purchasing power argument as a weapon against unemployment, see J. M. Culbertson, *Full Employment or Stagnation* (New York, 1964).

7. *Pub. P., 1962,* p. 778.

8. *Pub. P., 1961,* p. 185; *Pub. P., 1962,* p. 65; *Pub. P., 1963,* p. 205.

9. President's Advisory Committee on Labor-Management Policy, *Automation* (Washington, 1962), p. 6.

10. *Senate Documents,* 88 Cong., 1 sess., no. 53, pp. 55–66. Structural unemployment is persistent unemployment caused by technological change, shifts in composition of demand, import competition, and changes in the structure of wages relative to the pattern of labor demand.

11. The President's Labor-Management Advisory Committee recommended policies to promote retraining, education, job placement, aid to relocation of workers, and protection of worker equity and security. *Automation,* pp. 3–5. Henry Ford II of the Ford Motor Company dissented from the report, criticizing tying technical advances and unemployment so closely together. Ibid., pp. 8–9.

12. *Senate Hearings,* 87 Cong., 1 sess., Committee on Banking and Currency, *Area Redevelopment, 1961,* esp. pp. 306–17, 323–73, 402–3, 417–19; *House Hearings, 87* Cong., 2 sess., Committee on Public Works, *Standby Capital Improvements Act of 1962,* esp. pp. 338–52, 702–14; *Senate Hearings,* 88 Cong., 1 sess., Committee on Banking and Currency, *Area Redevelopment Act Amendments, 1963,* esp. pp. 270–306, 350–53; *House Hearings,* 87 Cong., 1 sess., Subcommittee on Labor of the Committee on Education and Labor, *Youth Employment Opportunities Act of 1961,* esp. pp. 400–1. For the NAM's plan to create more jobs, see *NAM News,* Mar. 24, 1961, p. 3.

13. *Senate Hearings, Area Redevelopment, 1963,* esp. pp. 200–3, 263–70.

14. *Economic Indicators,* Mar. 1962, p. 9; Mar. 1963, p. 10; Mar. 1964, p. 10.

15. Joseph M. Becker, William Haber, and Sar A. Levitan, *Programs to Aid the Unemployed in the 1960's* (Kalamazoo, Michigan, 1965), pp. 27–28.

16. For examples of organized labor's displeasure with the efforts of Kennedy, see *NYT,* Feb. 25, 1962, p. 1; Feb. 23, 1963, p. 1; May 16, 1963, p. 21.

17. For a comparison of consumer and wholesale prices in the Kennedy and Eisenhower years, see *Statistical Abstract, 1966,* pp. 351, 356.

18. John Kenneth Galbraith, *The Affluent Society* (Boston, 1958), pp. 220–24, 248–49.

19. Sorensen, *Kennedy,* p. 489.

20. *Economic Report of the President, Transmitted to the Congress January 1962, Together with the Annual Report of the Council of Economic Advisers* (Washington, 1962), pp. 37–38. John Sheahan in *The Wage-Price Guideposts* (Washington, 1967), pp. 16–17, described the general idea of guideposts as not original with the Kennedy CEA; what was somewhat new was the official presentation of a more specific set of principles.

21. Heller, *New Dimensions,* p. 43.

22. *Annual Report of the Council of Economic Advisers, 1962,* pp. 185–90.

23. *BW,* Mar. 17, 1962, p. 132; *WSJ,* May 24, 1962, p. 1; July 10, 1962, p. 1; W. Barnard Thulin, "Productivity Guidelines Won't Work," *HBR* 40 (Nov.–Dec., 1962): 70–78; Jules Bachman, "No Guideposts for Wage

Settlements," *Challenge,* June 1962, pp. 24–27; public letter from Joseph Curran, president of the National Maritime Union, to labor members on the President's Labor-Management Advisory Committee, published in *Labor Today,* 1 (Fall 1962): 3–5.

24. Lloyd Ulman, "The Labor Policy of the Kennedy Administration," *Proceedings of the Fifteenth Annual Meeting of the Industrial Relations Research Association, 1962* (Madison, 1963), pp. 250–53, 260; *Fortune,* Apr. 1962, p. 94; *Dun's Review,* Nov. 1962, pp. 121–25; *CFC,* Mar. 1, 1962, p. 1; R. Heath Larry, vice-president of United States Steel, "Guidelines and the National Interest," *U.S. Steel Quarterly* 16 (Nov. 1962): 5.

25. *Senate Hearings,* 87 Cong., 2 sess., Communications Subcommittee of the Committee on Commerce, *Communications Satellite Legislation,* p. 245.

26. CED, *The Public Interest in National Labor Policy* (New York, 1961), p. 138; USCC, *Policy Declarations, 1961,* pp. 92–93; NAM, *Industry Believes, 1963,* pp. 1–10; NFIB, *Mandate,* nos. 273, 279. Also see *WSJ,* Jan. 4, 1963, p. 12; *Nation's Business,* Dec. 1961, pp. 31–33 ff.

27. "Will the Guideposts Stick?" *Dun's Review,* July 1964, pp. 42–43. The article featured comments on the guideposts by corporate executives.

28. *Steel,* Dec. 10, 1962, p. 25; *J of C,* Jan. 17, 1963, p. 4; *USNWR,* Dec. 24, 1962, p. 84.

29. James Stern, "The Kennedy Policy: A Favorable View," *Industrial Relations* 3 (Feb. 1964): 24–25.

30. For a detailed examination of the wage-price guideposts, see Sheahan, *Wage-Price Guideposts.* Briefer, but also valuable, is Marvin J. Levine, "The Economic Guidelines," *Labor Law Journal* 18 (Aug. 1967): 478–504.

31. George Meany in Meany, Roger M. Blough, and Neil H. Jacoby, *Government Wage-Price Guideposts in the American Economy* (New York, 1967), pp. 1–18. Also see Sheahan, *Wage–Price Guideposts,* pp. 47–48; *Joint Hearings,* 90 Cong., 2 sess., Joint Economic Committee, *1968 Economic Report of the President,* testimony by Nathaniel Goldfinger of the AFL-CIO, pp. 721–32.

32. Ibid., esp. pp. 745–49, 754–55; *Joint Hearings,* 90 Cong., 1 sess., Joint Economic Committee, *1967 Economic Report of the President,* esp. pp. 688–89, 793, 1016. Also see Martin Bronfenbrenner, "A Guidepost-Mortem," *Industrial and Labor Relations Review* 20 (July 1967): 646; Blough in *Government Wage-Price Guideposts,* pp. 21–49.

33. Sheahan, *Wage-Price Guideposts,* p. 181.

34. Levine, "Guidelines," p. 488; Arthur A. Thompson, "The Case of the Wage-Price Guideposts," *Banking,* Oct. 1967, p. 42. Also see *House Hearings,* 89 Cong., 2 sess., Government Operations Committee, *Congressional Review of Price-Wage Guideposts.* For a valuable and varied discussion of the strengths and weaknesses of the guideposts, see American Bankers Association, *A Symposium on Business-Government Relations* (New York, 1966), esp. pp. 36–47, 80–105.

35. Sheahan, *Wage-Price Guideposts,* p. 204.

36. Ibid., p. 196; George L. Perry, "Wages and the Guideposts," *American Economic Review* 57 (Sept. 1967): 903.

37. For examples, see *Iron Age,* July 21, 1966, pp. 25–26 ("Wage Guidelines Almost Frayed Out"); *Financial World,* Sept. 14, 1966, pp. 3–4 ("After Guideposts, What?"); *Engineering News-Record,* Aug. 4, 1966, p. 56 ("Wage Guidelines Now Called a Shambles").

38. Roderick M. Hills, "A Close Look at Three Administration Policies," *Industrial Relations* 3 (Feb. 1964): 6; Sorensen, *Kennedy,* p. 494. The President's Labor-Management Advisory Committee recommended improvement in fact-finding procedures, in the public mediation process, and in methods of handling emergency disputes. *Collective Bargaining* (Washington, 1962), pp. 1–6.

39. Sorensen, *Kennedy,* p. 494.

40. Hills, "A Close Look," p. 7.

41. Stern, "The Kennedy Policy," p. 26; *Missiles and Rockets,* Oct. 8, 1962, p. 46; Dec. 3, 1962, p. 46; *Fortune,* Jan. 1963, p. 68; *Pub. P., 1962,* pp. 680, 713–14.

42. Ibid., pp. 489–90.

43. *Pub. P., 1963,* pp. 586–94, 646. Also see John L. Blackman, Jr., *Presidential Seizure in Labor Disputes* (Cambridge, 1967), pp. 242–46.

44. *WSJ,* Jan. 23, 1962, p. 14; M. R. Lefkoe, "The NLRB's New, Rough Line," *Fortune,* Nov. 1963, pp. 164, 178; Kenneth C. McGuiness, *The New Frontier NLRB* (Washington, 1963), pp. 6–7, 9, 240–41; Joseph Grodin, "The Kennedy Labor Board," *Industrial Relations* 3 (Feb., 1964): 34–35.

45. McGuiness, *New Frontier NLRB,* p. 246.

46. Hills, "A Close Look," p. 16.

47. Grodin, "Kennedy Labor Board," pp. 43–45.

48. David B. Johnson wrote that the Kennedy NLRB's liberal interpretations added proof to the charge that the board was a partisan agency. "The New Frontier Collective Bargaining Policy," *Labor Law Journal* 13 (July 1962): 596. Joseph Stern disagreed, arguing that the partisan reputation of the NLRB more realistically depended upon "whose ox is being gored." "The Kennedy Policy," p. 28.

49. Speaking to labor groups, the president frequently compared the friendly response he received from labor with the cool reception he sometimes got from business audiences. *Pub. P., 1961,* p. 786; *Pub. P. 1962,* p. 364.

50. According to Sorensen, the president did favor amendments to the Taft-Hartley Act. *Kennedy,* p. 494.

51. *Statistical Abstract, 1966,* pp. 218, 220.

52. *Federal Register* 26: 1977–79, Executive Order 10925, Mar. 6, 1961.

53. Ibid., pp. 1978–79.

54. *Pub. P., 1961,* p. 396; President's Committee on Equal Employment Opportunity, *Report to the President, November 26, 1963* (Washington, 1963), pp. 108–9.

55. Ibid., p. 118.

56. *BW,* June 3, 1961, p. 23.

57. *NYT,* Jan. 26, 1962, p. 14.

58. Ibid., Feb. 23, 1961, p. 19; Feb. 27, 1961, p. 20; Dec. 15, 1961, p. 1.

59. Ibid., Jan. 16, 1962, p. 15.
60. Ibid., Apr. 17, 1963, p. 21.
61. President's Committee on Equal Employment Opportunity, *The American Dream—Equal Opportunity* (Washington, 1962), p. 12.
62. Officials responsible for administering the program reported about a dozen firms on a blacklist. But the officials noted that no contracts had been canceled for violation of the executive order. *BW*, Aug. 17, 1963, pp. 53–54.
63. *Report to the President*, p. 115.
64. Jack Gourlay, *The Negro Salaried Worker*, American Management Association Study no. 70 (New York, 1965), pp. 8–15, 25–27; Georges F. Doriot et al., *The Management of Racial Integration in Business* (New York, 1964), pp. 6–7. Also see Dale Hiestand, *Economic Growth and Employment Opportunities for Minorities* (New York, 1964); John Perry, "Business—Next Target for Integration," *HBR* 41 (Mar.–Apr. 1963): 104–15; Robert B. McKersie, "The Civil Rights Movement and Employment," *Industrial Relations* 3 (May 1964): 1–22.

CHAPTER 8

1. The examples of growing disfavor for Kennedy among business spokesmen are legion. For examples, see *J of C*, July 24, 1961, p. 1; *WSJ*, Aug. 17, 1961, p. 12; *Kiplinger Letter*, Sept. 2, 1961, p. 1; *BW*, Sept. 16, 1961, pp. 41–42; interviews with executives of a number of major corporations, published in *USNWR*, Dec. 25, 1961, pp. 54–59; *Fortune*, Jan. 1962, pp. 59–60.
2. *Pub. P., 1961*, pp. 86–87, 708, 773–75.
3. For examples of business concern with profits, see Augustus C. Long, chairman of Texaco Corporation, "What's Wrong—and Right with Profits?" *Dun's Review*, Sept. 1961, pp. 34–36; G. Keith Funston, president of the New York Stock Exchange, "Are Profits Going out of Style?" June 10, 1961, speech pamphlet; E. J. Hanley, president of Allegheny Ludlum Steel Corporation, "Who Speaks for Profit?" June 12, 1961, speech pamphlet; *Dun's Review* president's panel of three hundred executives, "A New Philosophy of Profit," *Dun's Review*, July 1962, pp. 34–35.
4. Profits in the steel industry in 1955, 1956, and 1957 were excellent. They slumped badly in 1958, increased strongly in 1959, slipped again in 1960, and fell sharply in 1961 and 1962. *Business Statistics, 1965*, p. 102.
5. *J of C*, May 25, 1961, p. 1; *NAM News*, Sept. 1, 1961, p. 2.
6. *Pub. P., 1961*, pp. 576–77.
7. Ibid., pp. 592–94.
8. For examples, see *J of C*, Sept. 11, 1961, p. 4; *WSJ*, Sept. 15, 1961, p. 10; editorial by David Lawrence, *USNWR*, Sept. 18, 1961, p. 140.
9. Letter, September 8, 1961, from David J. McDonald to President Kennedy, Press Releases of the President, Sept. 14, 1961 (mimeographed).
10. The answers of the steel executives to the president's letter were released by the White House. Ibid., Sept. 22, 1961 (mimeographed).
11. Blough's performance as a spokesman for business on issues such as

inflation, wages, and prices impressed fellow executives. *Dun's Review* president's panel of top executives voted Blough "Executive of the Year" for 1961. *Dun's Review*, Jan. 1962, pp. 31–35.

12. Letter, Blough to Kennedy, Sept. 6, 1961, published in *CR*, 87 Cong., 1 sess., pp. 19700–701. The trend of profits in the steel industry as measured by "profit per dollar of sales" was detailed for the years 1940 to 1963 in American Iron and Steel Institute, *Charting Steel's Progress in 1963* (New York, 1964), p. 55. It may be seriously questioned if 1940 was a valid year to use as a standard for fair earnings, since the industry was already benefiting from sharply increased defense spending in that year.

13. *Pub. P., 1962*, pp. 18, 201.

14. Ibid., p. 284.

15. Grant McConnell, *Steel and the Presidency, 1962* (New York, 1963), p. 75.

16. For detailed narratives of the steel crisis, see ibid., and Roy Hoopes, *The Steel Crisis* (New York, 1963).

17. For comments supporting the action of the steel companies, see *WSJ*, Apr. 12, 1962, p. 12; *Barron's*, Apr. 16, 1962, p. 1. For views questioning the wisdom of the price increase, see *American Banker*, Apr. 13, 1962, p. 4; *BW*, Apr. 14, 1962, p. 184.

18. *Pub. P., 1962*, p. 315.

19. *BW*, Apr. 21, 1962, pp. 29–30; *Printers' Ink*, Apr. 20, 1962, p. 16; *NAM News*, Apr. 20, 1962, p. 2; *Iron Age*, Apr. 19, 1962, p. 5; *MWS*, Apr. 21, 1962, pp. 63–64; *WSJ*, Apr. 13, 1962, p. 1; *American Banker*, Apr. 17, 1962, p. 4; *J of C*, Apr. 16, 1962, p. 1; *Forbes*, May 1, 1962, pp. 11–12; *Fortune*, May 1962, pp. 97 ff.

20. *Business Statistics, 1965*, p. 102. Production of steel fell steadily during May, June, and July, then gradually increased during the remainder of 1962.

21. See *WSJ* for comments by Arthur B. Homer, chairman of Bethlehem Steel, and Avery C. Adams, chairman of Jones and Laughlin Steel, Apr. 27, 1962, pp. 4–5. Also see speeches by Allison R. Maxwell, Jr., president of Pittsburgh Steel, and Thomas F. Patton, president of Republic Steel, at the annual meeting of the American Iron and Steel Institute, published in *Yearbook of the American Iron and Steel Institute, 1962* (New York, 1962), pp. 235–42, 251–71.

22. Roger M. Blough, "In the Public Interest," May 7, 1962, speech pamphlet. Blough, "Chairman's Letter," *U.S. Steel Quarterly* 16 (May 1962): 1–2; Blough, "My Side of the Steel Story," *Look*, Jan. 29, 1963, pp. 19–23.

23. Schlesinger, *Thousand Days*, pp. 634–40; Sorensen, *Kennedy*, pp. 503–9.

24. McConnell, *Steel*, p. 115.

25. *Pub. P., 1962*, pp. 331–33, 336.

26. *NYT*, Apr. 23, 1962, p. 25.

27. *Pub. P., 1962*, pp. 379–80.

28. President Eisenhower is alleged to have made the same remark in December 1959 in reference to businessmen involved in the electrical sup-

ply company price-fixing scandal. Quoted in Herling, *The Great Price Conspiracy,* p. 80.

29. According to Theodore C. Sorensen, the FBI was instructed to confine investigative efforts to business hours and not to call individuals at home. *Kennedy,* p. 510. Contrary to the reaction of businessmen, 58 percent of the general public approved the president's action in the steel affair. *PONS,* May 19, 1962.

30. *Newsweek,* July 16, 1962, pp. 15–19.

31. Malcolm Forbes writing in *Forbes,* May 1, 1962, p. 12.

32. Ray A. Dinsmore of Goodyear Tire and Rubber Company, speaking to the Commercial Chemical Development Association, May 24, 1962. Quoted in *J of C,* May 25, 1962, p. 1.

33. Quoted in ibid. Also see Charls E. Walker, executive vice-president of the American Bankers Association, "Our Domestic Position," *VS,* June 15, 1962, pp. 530–33. Business publications carried numerous stories reflecting criticism of the administration.

34. *Pub. P., 1962,* pp. 348–49. Chamber of Commerce members, queried after the president's speech expressed pleasure with his conciliatory tone. But most indicated that they were still skeptical about his intentions toward business. *NYT,* May 1, 1962, p. 1.

35. *NYT,* May 6, 1962, p. 1; May 19, 1962, p. 1; Ladd Plumley, "The Businessman's Role on the New Frontier," May 29, 1962, speech pamphlet.

36. *NYT,* May 14, 1962, p. 25.

37. Gerald Phillippe, president of General Electric, "Energizing Economic Growth," May 18, 1962, *Executive Speeches and Reports to Shareholders, 1961–1962, General Electric Company,* collected papers (n.p.); Raymond C. Firestone of Firestone Rubber Company, "National Aims and Business Responsibility," June 20, 1962, speech pamphlet.

38. In the two months following the steel crisis, Kennedy spoke to a number of business groups: USCC, CED, the White House Conference on National Economic Issues, and the Brookings Institution's Public Policy Conference for Business Executives. See *Pub. P., 1962,* pp. 348–52, 397–98, 420–23, 464–65.

39. See the following weekly investment news letters for April, May, and June, 1962: *Investograph Stock Survey, The Outlook, Moody's Stock Survey, United Business Service.*

40. *Pub. P., 1962,* p. 405.

41. Ibid., pp. 433–34, 456–57.

42. *The Value Line,* Apr. 30, 1962, p. 1; Merrill, Lynch, Pierce, Fenner, and Smith, Inc., *Security and Industry Survey,* Spring 1962, p. 2; *Moody's Stock Survey,* May 7, 1962, p. 601.

43. *WSJ,* May 29, 1962, p. 14; May 31, 1962, p. 10; *Barron's,* June 4, 1962, p. 1.

44. *Pub. P., 1963,* p. 675. Only 20 percent of the general public pointed to Kennedy's action in the steel crisis as the chief cause for the slump in the stock market; 78 percent of the public did not believe that a serious recession would follow. *PONS,* June 16, 1962 and June 19, 1962.

45. *House Documents,* 88 Cong., 1 sess., no. 95, *Securities and Ex-*

change Commission, Report of Special Study of Securities Markets, especially part 4, chap. 13, "Market Break of May 1962." For daily averages of the New York Stock Exchange, see *Index to the Wall Street Journal* for 1962 and 1963, appendix.

46. James Reston wrote that not since the days of Franklin D. Roosevelt had there been so much anti–White House talk in the business community. *NYT,* June 3, 1962, ed. 4, p. 12. Also see *Iron Age,* June 14, 1962, p. 5; *BW,* June 23, 1962, pp. 43–44; July 7, 1962, pp. 92–93.

47. Dun and Bradstreet survey of over 1,500 businesses. *Dun's Review,* June, 1962, pp. 32–33.

48. The poll was taken by the Research Institute of America. *NYT,* June 27, 1962, p. 11. *Purchasing Magazine's* Business Confidence Index, based on a survey of 1,000 purchasing agents, declined in May, June, and July but rallied strongly in August. *Purchasing Magazine,* selected issues, Apr. through Sept. 1962.

49. *Pub. P., 1962,* p. 515.

50. Ibid., pp. 473–75.

51. For examples of efforts by administration officials to placate business in private meetings, speeches, and conferences, see *NYT,* May 18, 1962, p. 8; May 23, 1962, p. 1; May 30, 1962, p. 1; June 5, 1962, p. 1; June 6, 1962, p. 55; June 14, 1962, p. 27. On June 11, 1962, within hours after the president delivered his speech on economic myths at Yale, he met privately with five business leaders, including Roger M. Blough. Officially, the purpose of the meeting was explained as being to discuss the balance of payments deficit. Ibid., June 12, 1962, p. 1.

52. *Pub. P., 1963,* pp. 321–22, 330–31. United States Steel had emphasized its low earnings by cutting quarterly dividends by one-third on October 30, 1962. *U.S. Steel Quarterly* 16 (Nov. 1962): 1.

CHAPTER 9

1. Interviews with manufacturing executives, *Iron Age,* Nov. 17, 1960, pp. 107–8; *Dun's Review* president's panel of nearly two hundred executives from major corporations, "What Business Wants from Kennedy," *Dun's Review,* Mar. 1961, p. 30.

2. John J. Corson of McKinsey and Company, "More Government in Business," *HBR* 39 (May–June): 82–84; interview with Dan A. Kimball, president of Aerojet-General Corporation, *Iron Age,* Nov. 17, 1960, p. 108.

3. Corson, "More Government," pp. 84–88; *WSJ,* Feb. 13, 1961, p. 1.

4. USCC, *Policy Declarations, 1961,* pp. 1–25; NFIB, *Mandate,* nos. 263, 270, 280; John S. Sinclair, "President's Report," *The 45th Annual Report of the National Industrial Conference Board, Inc.* (New York, 1961), pp. 6–7; NAM, *Industry Believes, 1963,* pp. 61–62; Frederick R. Kappel, chairman of American Telephone and Telegraph, "Realism in Economic Life," Dec. 1, 1961, speech pamphlet.

5. James Tobin, "How Planned Is Our Economy?" in *National Economic Policy* (New Haven, 1966), pp. 5–6.

6. Sorensen, *Kennedy,* pp. 263–67.

7. *WSJ,* June 5, 1961, p. 12; *Nation's Business,* Apr. 1962, pp. 42–43 ff.;

speech by Donald Hardenbrook, president of the NAM, Dec. 7, 1962, published in *NAM News,* Dec. 14, 1962, p. 15; E. J. Hanley, president of Allegheny Ludlum Steel, "Who Speaks for Profit?" June 12, 1961, speech pamphlet.

8. *Dun's Review* president's panel of nearly three hundred executives of major corporations, "Can Free Enterprise Come Back?" *Dun's Review,* July 1961, pp. 29–30; L. du Pont Copeland, president of the du Pont Company, "It Takes Two to Make a Partnership Work," Feb. 10, 1964, speech pamphlet; Elliott V. Bell of *Business Week,* "The Way to Make Our Economy Grow," Feb. 19, 1963, speech pamphlet; speech by L. F. Mc-Collum, president of Continental Oil Company, Nov. 14, 1962, *Proceedings, American Petroleum Institute, Section I, General, 1962* (New York, 1962), pp. 22–23.

9. *Pub. P., 1961,* pp. 267–76, 324–26, 348–49, 371–72, 392–93. For the text of the Landis Report, see *Senate Reports,* 86 Cong., 2 sess., Submitted by the Chairman of the Subcommittee on Administrative Practices to the Committee on the Judiciary, *Report on Regulatory Agencies to the President-Elect,* esp. pp. 83–87.

10. *House Hearings,* 87 Cong., 1 sess., Committee on Government Operations, *Reorganization Plans No's 1, 2, 3, and 4 of 1961,* esp. pp. 186–88, and *Reorganization Plan No. 5 of 1961,* esp. pp. 19–22, 33–36, 82–84; *Senate Hearings,* 87 Cong., 1 sess., Committee on Government Operations, *Reorganization Plans of 1961,* esp. pp. 91–94, 114–16, and *Reorganization Plan No. 5 of 1961—National Labor Relations Board,* esp. pp. 79–125, 233–46; *Senate Hearings,* 87 Cong., 1 sess., Communications Subcommittee of the Committee on Commerce, *Reorganization of the FCC,* esp. pp. 77–82.

11. Robert G. Dunlop, president of Sun Oil Company, expressed management's belief that day-to-day actions by regulatory agencies were a serious reason for confusion and uncertainty in business. "Profits and a Free Society," Oct. 10, 1962, speech pamphlet.

12. Newton Minow, "Program Control," *VS,* June 15, 1961, pp. 533–37; *WSJ,* May 11, 1961, p. 14.

13. *Senate Hearings, Reorganization of the FCC,* esp. pp. 77–82; *Reorganization Plans of 1961,* esp. pp. 91–98.

14. *Electrical World,* June 19, 1961, p. 47; *Nation's Business,* Sept. 1961, pp. 48–50; *Public Utilities Fortnightly,* Jan. 4, 1962, pp. 1–12; *Barron's,* Sept. 10, 1962, p. 1.

15. *NYT,* Feb. 24, 1961, p. 13; June 9, 1961, p. 24; June 29, 1961, p. 6; Aug. 19, 1961, p. 18.

16. *Barron's,* June 5, 1961, p. 1; *Financial World,* Jan. 10, 1962, p. 3; *Electrical World,* May 8, 1961, p. 3; *WSJ,* May 22, 1962, p. 14.

17. *Pub. P., 1962,* pp. 248–49; *Pub. P., 1963,* p. 388.

18. *Pub. P., 1961,* p. 118; *Pub. P., 1962,* p. 183; Joseph C. Swidler, "The Federal Power Commission—A Program for the Future," *Antitrust Bulletin* 7 (July–Aug. 1962): 567–81.

19. Interview with Charles F. Avila of the Boston Edison Company, *Challenge,* Jan. 1963, pp. 19–20.

20. *NYT,* Jan. 26, 1963, p. 1. Morgan's letter to the president was made public. Chairman Swidler defended the FPC, charging that personality differences had influenced Morgan's complaints. Ibid., Jan. 31, 1963, p. 9. For liberal dissatisfaction with the New Frontier power policies, see *The Progressive,* June 1962, pp. 19–21.

21. *Pub. P., 1962,* pp. 235–43.

22. Ibid., pp. 240–42.

23. *American Banker,* June 4, 1963, p. 4; *WSJ,* Mar. 7, 1963, p. 14; *Senate Hearings,* 87 Cong., 1 sess., Committee on Banking and Currency, *Truth in Lending Bill,* esp. pp. 393–407, 526–65, 616–52, 787–93,1010–34.

24. *Senate Hearings,* 88 Cong., 1 sess., Subcommittee on Antitrust and Monopoly of the Committee on the Judiciary, *Packaging and Labeling Legislation,* esp. pp. 62–69, 83–88, 229–71, 333–45, 552–83, 596–603, 710–27.

25. For a comprehensive account of the writing of the Employment Act of 1946, see Stephen Kemp Bailey, *Congress Makes a Law* (New York, 1950).

26. Flash, *Economic Advice,* pp. 209–14.

27. *Nation's Business,* Feb. 1961, p. 35, predicted "Ahead is the greatest attempt at peacetime regimentation since the 1930's."

28. Heller, *New Dimensions,* pp. 61–63; *BW,* Oct. 14, 1961, pp. 34, 36. In Western European nations, especially France, business, government, and labor have cooperated to project economic trends for four to five years ahead. Walter F. Blass, "Economic Planning, European Style," *HBR* 41 (Sept.–Oct. 1963): 109–20. James Tobin wrote in 1963 that perhaps someday business, labor, and government in the United States will trust one another enough to permit similar joint efforts. "How Planned," pp. 11–12.

29. Heller, *New Dimensions,* pp. 32–37.

30. *Senate Reports,* 87 Cong., 1 sess., no. 994, part 1, pp. 140, 150, 781, 826.

31. *WSJ,* Apr. 17, 1961, p. 1; June 20, 1961, p. 1.

32. Heller, *New Dimensions,* p. 56; *Pub. P., 1963,* p. 148.

33. Harris, *Economics of the Kennedy Years,* pp. 120–21; M. J. Rossant, "Mr. Martin and the Winds of Change," *Challenge,* Jan. 1964, pp. 11–13. Martin agreed to the president's desire for low interest rates on long-term loans and high interest rates for short-term loans, despite business complaints that this strategy went against the law of supply and demand. See testimony by David Rockefeller, president of the Chase Manhattan Bank, *Joint Hearings,* 87 Cong., 1 sess., Subcommittee on International Exchange and Payments of the Joint Economic Committee, *International Payments Imbalances and the Need for Strengthening International Financial Arrangements,* p. 154.

34. *Nation's Business,* Feb. 1961, pp. 35–37; *WSJ,* Feb. 13, 1961, p. 1; *USNWR,* May 15, 1961, p. 124; *MWS,* July 15, 1961, pp. 456–57.

35. *USNWR,* Apr. 30, 1962, p. 42.

36. *American Banker,* Apr. 17, 1962, p. 4.

37. *CFC,* Apr. 19, 1962, p. 1; *WSJ,* May 1, 1962, p. 1; May 7, 1962, p. 12; *NAM News,* May 11, 1962, p. 2; *Kiplinger Letter,* Apr. 28, 1962, p. 1;

Sales Management, May 4, 1962, p. 19. In the midst of efforts by administration officials to calm business feeling that the New Frontier was anti-business, Solicitor General Archibald Cox declared in a speech on June 13, 1962, that some new procedural arrangement would likely be required for general price stability. Cox later denied that he was calling for more government regulation, but his remarks added to the apprehension of the business community. *WSJ,* June 14, 1962, p. 3; June 21, 1962, p. 12.

38. The President's Special News Conference with Business Editors and Publishers, Sept. 26, 1962, *Pub. P., 1962,* pp. 710–11.

39. *Pub. P., 1963,* pp. 258, 330–31.

40. See, NAM, *Industry Believes, 1963,* p. 61; USCC, *Policy Declarations, 1961,* pp. 1–25; NFIB, *Mandate,* Nos. 272, 280, 285.

41. *Pub. P., 1961,* pp. 246, 355.

42. In 1961, the president asked Budget Director David E. Bell to review the government policy of contracting with private enterprise for scientific and technical work. *Pub. P., 1961,* pp. 550–51. Bell's report concluded that it was in the national interest to continue heavy reliance on contracts with nonfederal institutions. *Senate Documents,* 87 Cong., 2 sess., no. 94, *Report to the President on Government Contracting for Research and Development,* p. vii. Also see *Senate Staff Report,* 88 Cong., 1 sess., Committee on Government Operations, *Government Competition with Free Enterprise,* esp. pp. 1–7. For Budget Bulletin 60–2, which specified government policy toward commercial or industrial activities, see ibid., pp. 47–51.

43. Edwin P. Neilan, "Our Own Public Scandal," *VS,* Sept. 15, 1963, pp. 730–32.

44. *J of C,* Sept. 12, 1961, p. 4; *WSJ,* Feb. 15, 1962, p. 10; May 14, 1962, p. 14; *Senate Hearings,* 87 Cong., 1 sess., Committee on Banking and Currency, *Small Business Act Amendments of 1961.* For testimony by business groups in favor of the amendments, see esp. pp. 94–97, 121–26, 211–12. For statements of business witnesses opposed, see esp. pp. 178–88, 212–25.

45. *Pub. P., 1961,* pp. 529–31; *Pub. P., 1962,* pp. 118–20. Kennedy's plan included two classes of stock ownership: a voting stock, eligible for dividends, to be purchased by the general public; and a nonvoting, non–dividend-earning stock to be owned by commercial communications companies. The companies would benefit by having the amount they invested in the satellite corporation included in determining their rate base for other international communications services provided.

46. *Senate Hearings,* 87 Cong., 2 sess., Committee on Aeronautical and Space Sciences, *Communications Satellite Legislation,* esp. pp. 213–55, 283–306, 469–70. Some companies warmly supported the bill. See pp. 77–143, 220.

47. Ibid., pp. 465–68. Both the USCC and the NAM backed the private ownership concept. Also see *WSJ,* Aug. 1, 1961, p. 10; Mar. 19, 1962, p. 14.

48. Kennedy termed the legislation "a step of historic importance." *Pub. P., 1962,* pp. 657–58.

49. H. L. Nieburg, *In the Name of Science* (Chicago, 1966), p. 306.

50. See *Senate Hearings*, 88 Cong., 1 sess., Select Committee on Small Business, *Patent Policies*, esp. pp. 2–21.

51. *Federal Register* 18: 10943, Memorandum: Government Patent Policy, Oct. 10, 1963.

52. NFIB, *Mandate*, no. 262; *Senate Hearing, Patent Policy*, pp. 379–86; *Steel*, Oct. 21, 1963, p. 44. Samuel Lenher, a du Pont Company executive, declared that patents protected society, induced investment, and produced progress. "Patents and Progress," Nov. 14, 1961, speech pamphlet.

53. *Pub. P., 1962*, pp. 292–94; *Pub. P., 1963*, pp. 234–35.

54. *WSJ*, Mar. 19, 1963, p. 18.

55. *House Hearings*, 88 Cong., 1 sess., Committee on Interstate and Foreign Commerce, *Transportation Act, 1963*, esp. pp. 42–58, 352–65, 799–820, 873; *Transport Topics*, July 16, 1962, p. 14; Daniel P. Loomis, president of the Association of American Railroads, "Why Not Let Competition Go to Work in Transportation," Jan. 14, 1963, speech (mimeographed).

56. *House Hearings, Transportation Act, 1963*, pp. 968–72, 985–86, 1055–57.

CHAPTER 10

1. According to an opinion poll taken in the spring of 1962, only 13 percent of the public was conversant with the specifics of Kennedy's trade proposals. Among those who were familiar with the plan, the majority approved. *PONS*, Apr. 7, 1962.

2. Bauer, de Sola, and Dexter, *American Business*, pp. 224–29.

3. The House approved the bill by a vote of 299–125 (Republicans, 80–90; Democrats, 219–35). The vote in the Senate was 78–8 (Republicans, 22–7; Democrats, 56–1). *CR*, 87 Cong., 2 sess., pp. 12090, 19876.

4. *Pub. P., 1961*, pp. 12, 64, 707, 776–81, 790–91.

5. *Statistical Abstract, 1966*, p. 859. Exports over imports averaged from $4.5 billion to over $6 billion annually.

6. David Thompson, *Europe since Napoleon* (New York, 1962), pp. 842–43.

7. *Pub. P., 1961*, pp. 212–13, 279–80.

8. Ibid., p. 763.

9. Ibid., p. 701.

10. Sorensen, *Kennedy*, p. 460.

11. *Pub. P., 1961*, p. 770.

12. Ibid., pp. 685–86; Aubrey, *The Dollar in World Affairs*, pp. 85–86.

13. *Senate Hearings*, 87 Cong., 1 sess., Committee on Interstate and Foreign Commerce, *Problems of the Domestic Textile Industry*.

14. *Pub. P., 1961*, pp. 345–46.

15. Ibid., p. 764.

16. NFIB, *Mandate*, no. 268.

17. *Dun's Review* president's panel, "Can Free Enterprise Come Back?" *Dun's Review*, July, 1961, p. 31. Reflecting the diversity of their members, the NAM and the USCC maintained very general policies on trade issues—neither for nor against high or low tariffs. NAM, *Industry Believes, 1963*

(trade policy adopted in 1957), pp. 77–78; USCC, *Policy Declarations, 1962*, pp. 65–66.

18. Schlesinger, *Thousand Days*, pp. 724–25. Schlesinger added that later he came to believe that Kennedy may have chosen to continue the politics of consensus instead of the politics of conflict because he acutely sensed the underground antagonism present in the nation.

19. Sorensen, *Kennedy*, pp. 460–62; Schlesinger, *Thousand Days*, pp. 845–46.

20. Ibid.

21. *WSJ*, Sept. 20, 1961, p. 1; *BW*, Nov. 11, 1961, p. 176; Horace B. McCoy, president of the Trade Relations Council of the United States, "United States Foreign Economic Policy," *VS*, May 1, 1961, pp. 428–30. The Synthetic Organic Chemical Manufacturers Association launched a vigorous campaign late in 1961 to keep the tariff law "as is." *Chemical Week*, Nov. 25, 1961, p. 21; Dec. 16, 1961, p. 23.

22. *Pub. P., 1961*, pp. 773–84, 786–93. NAM president Donald J. Hardenbrook promised careful study of the trade proposal. *NAM News*, Jan. 12, 1962, p. 1. The AFL-CIO supported the president's plan from the first. See George Meany, president of the AFL-CIO, "An American Trade Policy," in *American Trade Policy*, ed. Bower Aly (Columbia, 1962), pp. 207–14.

23. *J of C*, Dec. 8, 1961, p. 4; *WSJ*, Dec. 7, 1961, p. 18.

24. *Pub. P., 1962*, pp. 74–77.

25. Ibid., pp. 68–69. A report of the Joint Economic Committee, issued January 17, 1962, 87 Cong., 2 sess., *Foreign Economic Policy for the 1960's*, agreed that greater authority to negotiate trade agreements was needed.

26. Samplings of business opinion indicated that the majority of executives favored the trade bill. But the minority was strong enough to seriously challenge the measure in Congress. See *Printers' Ink*, Mar. 30, 1962, p. 5; *Dun's Review* president's panel, "Business and the Common Market," *Dun's Review*, Mar. 1962, p. 35.

27. *WSJ*, Jan. 26, 1962, p. 8; Mar. 14, 1962, p. 16; *BW*, Feb. 3, 1962, p. 108; *J of C*, Jan. 29, 1962, p. 4.

28. *House Hearings*, 87 Cong., 2 sess., Committee on Ways and Means, *Trade Expansion Act of 1962*, esp. pp. 1268–70, 1977–86, 2002–4, 2155–70, 2668–78, 2903–14, 3129–33; *Senate Hearings*, 87 Cong., 2 sess., Committee on Finance, *Trade Expansion Act of 1962*, esp. pp. 902–3, 1269–75. Among the various spokesmen supporting freer trade were representatives of the American Bankers Association, the aluminum industry, book publishers, and manufacturers of heavy equipment and hard goods.

29. *House Hearings, Trade Expansion Act of 1962*, pp. 3924–30; *Senate Hearings, Trade Expansion Act of 1962*, pp. 1629–34.

30. Ibid., pp. 691–98; *House Hearings, Trade Expansion Act of 1962*, pp. 2062–91.

31. Ibid., esp. pp. 1224–32, 1312–57, 1389–93, 1470–75, 1626–36, 1724–28, 1969–77, 2148–51, 2175–78, 2279–83, 2373–78, 2741–60, 2808–11, 2964–68, 2998–3009, 3133–52. Among the interest groups ex-

pressing strong opposition were domestic manufacturers of bicycles, pianos, beverage machinery, textiles, mirrors, hats, scissors, optical equipment, millinery, and synthetic chemicals. Small-business members of the NFIB strongly opposed giving the president power to reduce tariffs. NFIB, *Mandate*, Nos. 272, 274, 276.

32. *Pub. P., 1962*, pp. 357–61. Also see pp. 350, 408–12, 614, 703.

33. Ibid., p. 246. *Barron's*, Mar. 26, 1962, p. 1; *Kiplinger Letter*, Mar. 3, 1962, p. 1; *BW*, June 2, 1962, p. 33; *WSJ*, Sept. 20, 1962, p. 14.

34. A poll of 30,000 businessmen, conducted in early summer by the Research Institute of America, reported that 57 percent favored the trade bill, with 25 percent opposed. *NYT*, June 27, 1962, p. 11.

35. *Pub. P., 1962*, pp. 759–60. Kennedy signed the bill on October 11, 1962.

36. The president expressed regret that the trade bill specifically discriminated against Polish goods. Ibid., p. 783. In the Foreign Assistance Act of 1963, Congress restored the president's right to extend most-favored-nation trade privileges to Yugoslavia and Poland. Public Law 88–205 (77 Stat. 390).

37. *Pub. P., 1962*, p. 759.

38. Ibid., pp. 827–28, 858, 881–82.

39. Schlesinger, *Thousand Days*, pp. 845–47.

40. Ibid., pp. 855, 871.

41. *Dun's Review* president's panel, "The Grim Reality of Foreign Trade," *Dun's Review*, May 1963, pp. 73–74; Leo Cherne, "1,588 Opinions on National Goals," *The General Electric Forum* 6 (July–Sept. 1963): 34.

42. *BW*, May 25, 1963, p. 27; June 1, 1963, p. 112; *Steel*, June 3, 1963, p. 15. Also see *Pub. P., 1963*, p. 420.

43. Werner Feld, *The European Common Market and the World* (Englewood Cliffs, 1967), p. 97. Also see *BW*, Aug. 10, 1963, p. 132; *Fortune*, Sept. 1963, pp. 91–92.

44. *Statistical Abstract, 1966*, pp. 869–70.

45. Feld, *Common Market*, pp. 100–102, 109.

46. Economist Seymour Harris in *Economics of the Kennedy Years*, p. 173, observed that the reduction of tariff barriers is a way of increasing productivity, which thus reduces jobs in the short run. In the long cycle, however, expanded trade can stimulate economic growth which will theoretically produce more and more jobs.

CHAPTER 11

1. From a survey of over 1,400 business leaders representing all sizes and types of companies, Cherne, "1,588 Opinions," p. 38. For examples of editorials in business journals urging a tougher foreign policy, see *Barron's*, July 17, 1961, p. 1; Apr. 15, 1963, p. 1; *WSJ* Mar. 25, 1963, p. 14; *Iron Age*, Oct. 24, 1963, p. 5.

2. *NAM News*, Dec. 15, 1961, esp. pp. 4, 7, 10, 11, 14. For similar implications, see *WSJ*, May 24, 1961, p. 18.

3. Allison R. Maxwell, Jr., president of Pittsburg Steel, "Steel's Profit

Problem," *Yearbook of American Iron and Steel Institute, 1962*, pp. 267–69.

4. Ernest G. Swigert, chairman of the Hyster Company, "The Real Role of Government," *Credit and Financial Management*, Sept. 1962, pp. 14, 37.

5. For examples of advertising designed to alert the public about the evils of collectivism, see the periodic advertisements by Warner and Swasey Corporation and the Hyster Company in *Newsweek, 1961–63*. For description of companies telling the free enterprise story in employee publications, see *Management Record*, Oct. 1962, pp. 14–17.

6. Donald I. Rogers, "Advertising of Enemies," *VS*, Aug. 15, 1962, pp. 653–56.

7. *Dun's Review* president's panel, "Are Businessmen Speaking Out?" *Dun's Review*, Nov. 1963, p. 33. A similar reaction was reported a decade earlier. William Whyte, *Is Anybody Listening?* (New York, 1952), pp. 1–20.

8. For useful examinations of business interest in foreign affairs, see Charles C. Campbell, Jr., *Special Business Interests and the Open Door Policy* (New Haven, 1951); Herbert Feis, *The Diplomacy of the Dollar: First Era, 1919–1932* (Baltimore, 1950); James W. Prothro, *The Dollar Decade* (Baton Rogue, 1954). A highly controversial and provocative treatment of the subject is provided by William A. Williams, *The Tragedy of American Diplomacy* (Cleveland, 1959).

9. *CR*, 87 Cong., 1 sess., pp. 3147, 6946–50, 7961–63. Among the titans of free enterprise sending messages of support for Wiley's plan were IBM, Goodyear Rubber, Remington Rand, and the New York Stock Exchange.

10. *Pub. P., 1961*, pp. 180–81; *Pub. P., 1962*, pp. 481, 710.

11. Ibid., pp. 584–85.

12. *Pub. P., 1961*, pp. 87, 773–75; *Pub. P., 1962*, pp. 194, 348–52, 421; *Pub. P., 1963*, pp. 210–11, 403, 862–63, 875.

13. *Barron's*, July 17, 1961, p. 1; *WSJ*, June 26, 1961, p. 10; *CFC*, July 13, 1961, p. 27; *Iron Age*, Oct. 24, 1963, p. 45; NFIB, *Mandate*, various numbers, 1961–63.

14. In particular, Kennedy hoped to use trade ties with Poland and Yugoslavia to woo these nations from Soviet domination.

15. *CR*, 87 Cong., 1 sess., pp. 2527–28, 2659, 3155, 8272–73, 9360–61.

16. *Pub. P., 1961*, p. 158.

17. *House Hearings*, 87 Cong., 1 sess., Select Committee on Export Control, *Investigation and Study of the Administration's Operation and Enforcement of the Export Control Act of 1949, and Related Acts*, pp. 61–104.

18. Cherne, "1,588 Opinions," p. 34; *J of C*, Sept. 26, 1963, p. 4; *BW*, Oct. 5, 1963, p. 29.

19. *House Hearings, Export Control Act of 1949*, pp. 477–511.

20. *Pub. P., 1963*, pp. 767–68, 776–79.

21. *WSJ*, Oct. 11, 1963, p. 12; *J of C*, Oct. 9, 1963, p. 4; Oct. 14, 1963, p. 4; *BW*, Oct. 5, 1963, p. 144; *CFC*, Oct. 17, 1963, p. 1. A majority of the public favored more trade with Russia, and an even larger percentage

approved the proposed wheat sale, according to opinion polls. *PONS,* Oct. 24, 1963.

22. *BW,* Oct. 5, 1963, pp. 29–30.

23. William Schulz, "Trading with the Enemy," *National Review,* Aug. 26, 1961, p. 116.

24. Secretary of Commerce to the President, the Senate, and the House of Representatives, *Export Control,* 41st quarterly report, third quarter, 1957, p. 7; 74th quarterly report, fourth quarter, 1965, p. 6.

25. *Pub. P., 1962,* pp. 872–73.

26. In Los Angeles, Bullock's Department Store secured an injunction against anti-Communists placing cards in the store protesting the sale of Communist-made merchandise. *NYT,* Jan. 11, 1963, p. 9; Feb. 20, 1963, p. 4. The more widespread "Buy America" movement pressured local and state governments to buy no materials from any foreign country, communist or otherwise. *WSJ,* Oct. 2, 1962, p. 1.

27. *Pub. P., 1961,* p. 393; *CR,* 87 Cong., 1 sess., 9522–23, 11220–21; *NYT,* May 18, 1961, p. 8; May 21, 1961, p. 1; May 23, 1961, p. 1. Sixty-seven percent of the public opposed the trade, according to a sample poll. *PONS,* July 6, 1961.

28. See detailed narrative of the prisoner exchange, *NYT,* Dec. 26, 1962, p. 1.

29. *BW,* Dec. 22, 1962, p. 21.

30. *Fortune,* Apr. 1963, p. 84. General Mills Corporation, in its *Annual Report,* May 31, 1963, p. 9, explained that the net cost of its contribution to the prisoner ransom fund would be sharply reduced by allowable tax deductions.

31. For speculation about government pressure on business, see *Fortune,* Feb. 1963, pp. 81–82.

32. *Pub. P., 1961,* pp. 533–40.

33. *Statistical Abstract, 1966,* pp. 391–92.

34. Two useful studies on the economic, political, and ethical questions involved in the government-defense industry relationship are Nieburg, *In the Name of Science,* and Barber, *The Politics of Research.*

35. Irven Travis and Charles L. Register, "Research Relationships between Industry and Government," in *Technical Planning in the Defense Industry,* American Management Association, Management Bulletin no. 25 (New York, 1963), pp. 10–11.

36. *Pub. P., 1961,* pp. 550–51.

37. *Senate Documents,* 87 Cong., 2 sess., No. 94, esp. pp. vii-ix, 4, 16, 20.

38. *Joint Hearings,* 88 Cong., 1 sess., Subcommittee on Defense Procurement of the Joint Economic Committee, *Impact of Military Supply and Service Activities on the Economy,* esp. pp. 15, 21–25. H. V. Hannum, "The Need for Profit," in *Research and Defense Contracting* (Washington, 1963), pp. 156–57, noted that according to Renegotiation Board reports, defense industry profits as a percentage of sales had declined from an average of 6.3 percent in fiscal 1956 to 3.1 percent in fiscal 1962.

39. National Science Foundation, *Reviews of Data on Science Resources* 1 (May 1965): 8.

40. Max Tishler, president of Merck, Sharp, & Dohme Research Laboratories, "The Government's Role and the Future of Discovery," Sept. 26, 1963, speech pamphlet.

41. *House Hearings,* 88 Cong., 1 and 2 sess., Select Committee on Government Research, *Federal Research and Development Programs,* esp. pp. 777–80, 1032–34; *Joint Hearings, Impact of Military Supply,* pp. 162–65; Donald W. Collier, vice-president of research for Borg-Warner Corporation, "Are Our R & D Dollars Paying Off?" *Steel,* Aug. 26, 1963, pp. 25–27; James Tobin, "On the Economic Burdens of Defense," in *National Economic Policy,* p. 74.

42. *Pub. P., 1962,* pp. 192–93; *Pub. P., 1963,* pp. 895–96.

43. Small Business Administration, *Semi-Annual Report,* 1957–61; *Annual Report,* 1962–64. The small business share of total prime government contracts during the New Frontier reached a high of 19.3 percent in fiscal 1962, compared with 26.8 percent in fiscal 1954.

44. In one survey of businessmen, only 1 percent rated the government's direction and supervision of defense contracts as excellent. Thirty percent classed the government's performance as good; 51 percent, fair; and 18 percent, poor. Cherne, "1,588 Opinions," p. 36.

45. General Dynamics was selected over Boeing Aircraft to build the TFX (Tactical Fighter Experimental). Congressional critics, led by congressmen from states where Boeing's operations heavily influenced the economy, charged that civilian authorities in the Defense Department overruled military officers who preferred the Boeing design. McNamara justified the choice on the grounds that in the long run the General Dynamics model would mean a sizeable savings in costs. See *Senate Hearings,* 88 Cong., 1 sess., Permanent Subcommittee on Investigations of the Committee on Government Operations, *TFX Contract Investigation.* For the president's comments, see *Pub. P., 1963,* pp. 274–75, 306, 833.

46. *Senate Hearings,* 87 Cong., 2 sess., National Stockpile and Naval Petroleum Reserves Subcommittee of the Committee on Armed Services, *Inquiry into the Strategic and Critical Material Stockpiles of the United States.*

47. *Pub. P., 1962,* p. 91.

48. *Senate Hearings, Inquiry into Stockpiles,* pp. 2106–2218.

49. Glenn H. Snyder, *Stockpiling Strategic Materials* (San Francisco, 1966), pp. 238–52, 292–94.

50. *BW,* Feb. 10, 1962, pp. 30–31.

51. The *WSJ,* Feb. 2, 1962, p. 8, agreed that it was time for a spotlight on stockpiling.

52. Sorensen, *Kennedy,* pp. 467–69. For a description of the effect on communities where military bases were closed, see *WSJ,* Apr. 18, 1961, p. 1. The *Journal* gibed at Kennedy when the Boston Naval Shipyard, scheduled to be closed, got a reprieve, ostensibly because of the Berlin crisis. Aug. 24, 1961, p. 8.

53. United States Arms Control and Disarmament Agency, *Economic*

Impacts of Disarmament (Washington, 1962), esp. pp. 3, 8–9, 23–25, and *The Economic and Social Consequences of Disarmament* (Washington, 1962), esp. pp. 3–5, 37–39; Roger E. Bolton, *Defense Purchases and Regional Growth* (Washington, 1966), esp. pp. 83–85, 97–98.

54. *Pub. P., 1963*, pp. 599–606.
55. *Pub. P., 1963–1964, Book 1*, pp. 78–79.
56. Cherne, "1,588 Opinions," pp. 35–36.
57. *BW*, Aug. 3, 1963, pp. 21–22.
58. See *NYT*, Aug. 16, 1963, p. 31, for a survey of the attitudes of the twenty-five largest prime defense contractors concerning disarmament. Also see *Western Aerospace*, Oct. 1963, p. 9, for a survey of the missile industry on the same subject.
59. Testimony at *Senate Hearings*, 88 Cong., 1 sess., Committee on Labor and Public Welfare, *The Nation's Manpower Revolution*, pp. 3049–54; Lockheed Aircraft Corporation, *32nd Lockheed Report, 1963* (Burbank, 1963), pp. 1–3.
60. *Morgan Guaranty Survey*, published by the Morgan Guaranty Trust Company of New York, Aug. 1963, pp. 8–15.

CHAPTER 12

1. *Statistical Abstract, 1966*, p. 852.
2. Quoted in Robert C. Good, "National Interest and Moral Theory: The 'Debate' among Contemporary Political Realists," in *Foreign Policy in the Sixties* ed. Roger Hilsman and Robert C. Good (Baltimore, 1965), p. 274.
3. There are many valuable examinations of American foreign aid. Especially helpful to me were John D. Montgomery, *The Politics of Foreign Aid* (New York, 1962); Herbert Feis, *Foreign Aid and Foreign Policy* (New York, 1964); David A. Baldwin, *Economic Development and American Foreign Policy, 1943–1962* (Chicago, 1966).
4. Thomas V. DiBacco, "Return to Dollar Diplomacy? American Business Reaction to the Eisenhower Foreign Aid Program, 1953–1961" (Ph.D. diss., The American University, 1965), pp. 235–39.
5. John Kenneth Galbraith, "A Positive Approach to Economic Aid," *Foreign Affairs* 39 (Apr. 1961): 444–57; Edward S. Mason, *Foreign Aid and Foreign Policy* (New York, 1964), pp. 95–96.
6. Feis, *Foreign Aid*, pp. 128–29.
7. Schlesinger, *Thousand Days*, pp. 591–92; Sorensen, *Kennedy*, p. 596.
8. *Pub. P., 1961*, pp. 204–5.
9. *Statistical Abstract, 1966*, p. 852. Approximately 60 percent of aid spending between fiscal 1961 and fiscal 1964 was for economic assistance, either grants or loans.
10. *Pub. P., 1961*, pp. 207, 409–10. Approved by Congress, the reorganization of the foreign aid agency took place under Executive Order 10973, Nov. 3, 1961. See *Federal Register* 26: 10469–70.
11. Schlesinger, *Thousand Days*, pp. 604–9; Sorensen, *Kennedy*, pp. 598–99. Business spokesmen were generally quiet regarding the Peace Corps, although the *WSJ*, Mar. 6, 1961, p. 10, expressed skepticism that

an army of young people could be of very great consequence in solving complex problems.

12. *Pub. P., 1961,* p. 1. Also see Schlesinger, *Thousand Days,* pp. 186–97.

13. Ibid., pp. 201–3.

14. *Pub. P., 1961,* pp. 170–75. The president's message was broadcast in multiple languages to Latin America by the Voice of America.

15. Ibid., pp. 565–66. The text of the Punta del Este agreement was published in the *Department of State Bulletin* 45 (1961): 463–69.

16. See especially Sorensen, *Kennedy,* pp. 601–4.

17. *Joint Hearings,* 87 Cong., 2 sess., Subcommittee on Inter-American Economic Relationships of the Joint Economic Committee, *Economic Development in South America,* pp. 44–95. Executives from the Chase Manhattan Bank, Whirlpool Corporation, International Basic Economy Corporation, W. R. Grace & Co., and Sears, Roebuck testified. Also see *BW,* July 5, 1961, pp. 67–69, 128; *Barron's,* July 3, 1961, p. 1.

18. *Pub. P., 1961,* pp. 209, 407–8.

19. *Senate Hearings,* 87 Cong., 1 sess., Committee on Foreign Relations, *International Development and Security,* pp. 940–41. The NFIB reported that only 15 percent of its members responding to a poll favored the president's proposal. *Mandate,* no. 268. Also see *WSJ,* May 22, 1961, p. 12. The advantages of the plan for certain types of business did not go unnoticed. For example, *Engineering News-Record,* Mar. 30, 1961, p. 59, suggested that the long-term program would greatly stimulate overseas work for American contractors and engineers.

20. *Pub. P., 1961,* p. 572.

21. *CR,* 87 Cong., 2 sess., pp. 7893, 9940–44.

22. *Senate Hearings,* 87 Cong., 2 sess., Committee on Foreign Relations, *Foreign Assistance Act of 1962,* pp. 26–27, 30, 557–58. For Kennedy's comments, see *Pub. P., 1962,* pp. 203, 882.

23. Ibid., p. 459.

24. *Senate Documents,* 87 Cong., 1 sess., No. 48, *Appropriations, Budget Estimates, Etc.,* p. 709; *Senate Documents,* 87 Cong., 2 sess., no. 162, *Appropriations, Budget Estimates, Etc.,* pp. 734–35.

25. *Pub. P., 1962,* pp. 689–90.

26. The White House announced the formation of the Committee to Strengthen the Security of the Free World—the Clay committee—on December 10, 1962. Members of the nine-man committee with close or direct ties to the business world were Clay, Robert B. Anderson, Eugene Black, Robert A. Lovett, L. F. McCollum, and Herman Phleger. *Pub. P., 1962,* p. 935. Sorensen wrote that Kennedy privately acknowledged that the Clay committee was a "calculated risk." *Kennedy,* p. 393. Schlesinger named AID Director David Bell, Ralph Dungan, and Kenneth O'Donnell as presidential advisers opposed to the use of the committee to examine foreign aid. *Thousand Days,* pp. 597–98. President Eisenhower appointed comparable groups under Clarence Randall in 1954, Benjamin Fairless in 1956–57, and William H. Draper, Jr., in 1959.

27. Department of State, Report to the President of the United States

from the Committee to Strengthen the Security of the Free World, *The Scope and Distribution of United States Military Aid and Economic Assistance Programs* (Washington, 1963), esp. pp. 1, 20–21. Hereafter cited as the Clay Report. Committee member George Meany, president of the AFL-CIO, dissented from the report, charging that the report would encourage unwise reductions of funds for the AID program and complaining that the committee failed to give the labor movement just credit for its role in the fight against communism. Ibid., pp. 22–25. The *WSJ*, Mar. 26, 1963, p. 18, commended the Clay Report, noting that "too much money, too little thought," about summed up American foreign aid.

28. *Pub. P., 1963*, p. 302. Also see Sorensen, *Kennedy*, p. 393; Schlesinger, *Thousand Days*, pp. 595–96, 598–99; Otto Passman, "The Report of the Clay Committee on Foreign Aid: A Symposium," *Political Science Quarterly* 78 (Sept. 1963): 350–51.

29. *House Hearings*, 88 Cong., 1 sess., Committee on Foreign Affairs, *Foreign Assistance Act of 1963*, pp. 160–61.

30. For comments by Clay warning against further cuts, see *NYT*, July 12, 1963, p. 1; Aug. 20, 1963, p. 1; Aug. 23, 1963, p. 1; Aug. 25, 1963, p. 1; Oct. 11, 1963, p. 1. Clay also appeared with Kennedy at a special news conference to defend the aid request. *Pub. P., 1963*, pp. 646–48.

31. *Senate Documents*, 88 Cong., 1 sess., no. 49, *Appropriations, Budget Estimates, Etc.*, p. 511. For examples of strong presidential appeals for his aid request, see *Pub. P., 1963*, pp. 629–30, 641–42, 840–42, 846–47.

32. *New Republic*, May 18, 1963, p. 2.

33. Eighty-eight percent of NFIB members responding to a poll favored Congress's setting a definite time limit on foreign aid and notifying the President to start cutting back on the assistance program. *Mandate*, no. 289.

34. USCC, *Policy Declarations, 1963–1964* (Washington, 1963), p. 88. The NAM adopted a standing policy on Feb. 15, 1962, affirming support of the principles and purposes of the AID Act of 1961. *Industry Believes, 1963*, pp. 73–74. Also see Baldwin, *Economic Development*, p. 263.

35. *House Hearings*, 87 Cong., 1 sess., Committee on Foreign Affairs, *The International Development and Security Act*, pp. 1163–82; *House Hearings*, 87 Cong., 2 sess., Committee on Foreign Affairs, *Foreign Assistance Act of 1962*, pp. 899–922; *House Hearings, Foreign Assistance Act of 1963*, pp. 1602–31.

36. Besides dominating membership of the Clay committee, big business leaders also figured prominently in the Commerce Committee for the Alliance for Progress and the Citizens Committee for International Development, a volunteer group which fostered support for the president's foreign aid bill in 1961.

37. Cherne, "1,588 Opinions," p. 33.

38. *Statistical Abstract, 1966*, p. 846.

39. McGraw-Hill Department of Economics, *Overseas Operations of U.S. Industrial Companies, 1962–1964* (New York, 1964), p. 1.

40. McKinsey & Company, Inc., *International Enterprise: A New Dimension of American Business* (New York, 1962), pp. 7, 16. Conclusions were drawn from a survey of 100 American companies operating abroad.

41. Clay Report, pp. 3, 6, 19; Department of Commerce, Commerce Committee for the Alliance for Progress, _Proposals to Improve the Flow of U.S. Private Investment to Latin America_ (Washington, 1963), pp. 6, 12–23, 35–40. For a persuasively reasoned argument for the advantages of private enterprise over public investment in the development of backward countries, see Emilio G. Collado, vice-president of Standard Oil of New Jersey, "Economic Development through Private Enterprise," _Foreign Affairs_ 41 (July 1963): 708–20.

42. Cherne, "1,588 Opinions," p. 33. The Commerce Committee for the Alliance for Progress stressed the critical need for low-cost housing in Latin America. _Proposals to Improve_, pp. 35–40.

43. _Pub. P., 1963_, pp. 299–300.

44. Ibid., p. 377; _CR_, 88 Cong., 1 sess., pp. 15594–600.

45. Cherne, "1,588 Opinions," p. 33; NFIB, _Mandate_, no. 279; _WSJ_, June 8, 1962, p. 10; Aug. 2, 1963, p. 6; _Forbes_, July 1, 1963, pp. 11–12; _J of C_, Sept. 3, 1963, p. 4.

46. _CFC_, Aug. 24, 1961, p. 1; _BW_, July 15, 1961, p. 128; Cherne, "1,588 Opinions," p. 33.

47. _BW_, Sept. 29, 1962, p. 148; _J of C_, Sept. 3, 1963, p. 4; NFIB, _Mandate_, no. 263.

48. George Champion, Chairman of the Chase Manhattan Bank, "Foreign Aid—A New Approach," _Advanced Management-Office Executive_, June 1963, p. 22.

49. Clay Report, pp. 14–16.

50. _Pub. P., 1961_, p. 64. Also see _Pub. P., 1962_, pp. 547–48.

51. _Pub. P., 1963_, pp. 214–15.

52. L. F. McCollum, president of Continental Oil Company, "The Changing Role of U.S. World Trade," _Journal of Marketing_ 26 (Jan. 1962): 3; M. Monroe Kimbrel, president of the American Bankers Assocation, "Our International Financial Position," _VS_, Mar. 1, 1963, pp. 303–5; Clay Report, pp. 2–3.

53. _Senate Hearings, International Development and Security_, pp. 51–53, 138; _Senate Hearings, Foreign Assistance Act of 1963_, p. 25. Some critics of foreign aid maintained that the large sums expended overseas for payrolls, transportation, and construction represented a major cause of the dollar drain despite efforts to channel aid funds into the domestic market. See Lewis E. Lloyd of Dow Chemical Company, "Big Factor in the Dollar Drain," _Challenge_, Feb. 1964, pp. 34–37.

54. _Pub. P., 1963_, p. 840. Also see ibid., pp. 684–85; _Pub. P., 1962_, pp. 36, 50; _Pub. P., 1961_, pp. 63–64, 210.

CHAPTER 13

1. Heller, _New Dimensions_, pp. 29–30, 33, 39–40, 64–70; Sorensen, _Kennedy_, p. 481.

2. _Pub. P., 1962_, p. 457. The president listed his intention to seek tax reduction and reform along with several other actions taken or planned to make certain that recovery was not cut short by recession.

3. Ibid., p. 458. At subsequent press conference during June, July, and

early August, Kennedy stressed that the administration was watching the economic situation closely and reserving judgment on whether to seek tax reduction in 1962. Ibid., pp. 516, 540, 544–45, 593.

4. For examples of statements by business groups urging lower tax rates, see *Joint Hearings,* 87 Cong., 1 sess., Joint Economic Committee, *January 1961 Economic Report of the President,* (NAM), p. 200; *Joint Hearings,* 87 Cong., 2 sess., Joint Economic Committee, *January 1962 Economic Report of the President,* (USCC), p. 682.

5. The USCC, consistent with its testimony before the Joint Economic Committee, promptly issued a statement supporting an immediate tax cut, even at the risk of a budget deficit. *NYT,* June 30, 1962, p. 1.

6. *Forbes,* July 1, 1962, p. 10.

7. *BW,* Aug. 11, 1962, p. 32. The small business NFIB reported in its *Mandate,* no. 278, that 50 percent of its members responding to a poll favored an across-the-board tax cut in 1962. The *WSJ,* July 9, 1962, p. 8, stressed that tax cuts should be geared to lower federal spending. *BW,* June 16, 1962, p. 152, and *Fortune,* Aug. 1962, pp. 63–64, editorially favored tax cuts to stimulate investment growth.

8. *PONS,* July 31, 1962.

9. Speech by Dillon, Nov. 14, 1962, published in Proceedings of a Conference Sponsored by the President's Advisory Committee on Labor-Management Policy, *Fiscal and Monetary Policy* (Washington, 1962), p. 35. Also see Sorensen, *Kennedy,* pp. 481–82.

10. Speech by Heller, Nov. 14, 1962, published in *Fiscal and Monetary Policy,* p. 10.

11. Interview with Mills, *Iron Age,* June 21, 1962, pp. 136–39. The congressman expressed similar views when interviewed later in the year. *USNWR,* Dec. 17, 1962, pp. 42–44.

12. Heller, *New Dimensions,* p. 33.

13. *Pub. P., 1962,* pp. 611–17.

14. Ibid., pp. 736–37, 764.

15. Heller cited three specific causes for the president's doubts: (1) congressional questioning of the need for a tax increase; (2) calls by John Kenneth Galbraith and others for additional federal expenditures to meet unfulfilled public needs; (3) the desire of administration departments for bigger expenditure programs. *New Dimensions,* pp. 33–35.

16. *Pub. P., 1962,* pp. 876–77.

17. Ibid., p. 877. Heller remembered that the president telephoned after his speech to say, "I gave them straight Keynes and Heller, and they loved it." *New Dimensions,* p. 35. Edward S. Flash, Jr., praised the CEA for developing and gaining acceptance for the economic philosophy of a tax cut. But Flash credited the Treasury Department with developing the bulk of the tax reforms. *Economic Advice,* pp. 269–70.

18. *Pub. P., 1962,* pp. 884–85.

19. Roger M. Blough, speech of Oct. 2, 1962, published in *U.S. Steel Quarterly* 16 (Nov. 1962): 6.

20. *BW,* Jan. 19, 1963, p. 26.

21. *WSJ,* Jan. 15, 1963, p. 18.

22. *Fortune,* Jan. 1963, p. 68. The *J of C,* Dec. 12, 1962, p. 4, urged businessmen not to shoot too fast at Kennedy's trial balloon on tax cuts.

23. *Pub. P., 1963,* pp. 74–75.

24. See Philip M. Stern, *The Great Treasury Raid* (New York, 1964). For details on how the use of personal deductions has increased, see *Pub. P., 1963,* p. 85.

25. Joseph A. Pechman, "Individual Income Tax Provisions of the Revenue Act of 1964," The Brookings Institution, Studies of Government Finance Reprints, no. 96 (Washington, 1965), p. 248.

26. Ibid., pp. 248–51.

27. *House Hearings,* 88 Cong., 1 sess., Committee on Ways and Means, *President's 1963 Tax Message,* esp. pp. 1904–7, 2090–2139, 2307–2424, 2431–57, 2640–77. For similar views expressed by business journals, see *Financial World,* Feb. 6, 1963, p. 3; *J of C,* Feb. 22, 1963, p. 4; *BW,* Jan. 26, 1963, p. 144; *WSJ,* Feb. 15, 1963, p. 14; *Steel,* Mar. 25, 1963, p. 27; *Barron's,* Apr. 22, 1963, p. 1.

28. *Pub. P., 1963,* p. 206.

29. *Joint Hearings,* 88 Cong., 1 sess., Joint Economic Committee, *January 1963 Economic Report of the President,* p. 45.

30. *Pub. P., 1963,* pp. 172–73.

31. Heller, *New Dimensions,* p. 35.

32. *Pub. P., 1963,* pp. 173–74, 216–17, 236–37.

33. Ibid., p. 350.

34. Ibid., pp. 351, 377, 393.

35. Representative Thomas Curtis (Republican, Missouri) declared that the Business Committee for Tax Reduction in 1963 was not independent of the executive branch. He charged that the committee, aided by the news media, was attempting to pass over the heads of congressmen with a propaganda campaign directed at the public. *CR,* 88 Cong., 1 sess., p. 19299.

36. *Senate Hearings,* 88 Cong., 1 sess., Senate Finance Committee, *Revenue Act of 1963,* p. 1220. A membership list of the Business Committee for Tax Reduction was published in the *CR,* 88 Cong., 1 sess., pp. 16707–24.

37. *BW,* June 22, 1963, p. 112. Also see *Fortune,* June 1963, pp. 91–92; Henry Ford II, "Taxes and Prosperity," *VS,* Sept. 15, 1963, pp. 717–19.

38. *WSJ,* May 3, 1963, p. 10; *J of C,* July 19, 1963, p. 4. A summer survey of over 1,400 national business leaders indicated that 85 percent favored a tax cut—but coupled with a spending cut. Only 39 percent of those favoring tax reduction said they would do so if a cut clearly increased the budget deficit. Cherne, "1,588 Opinions," p. 37.

39. *Pub. P., 1963,* pp. 637–39. The president wrote Mills on Aug. 21, 1963. Kennedy expressed similar views to the Business Committee for Tax Reduction. Ibid., p. 665.

40. Sorensen, *Kennedy,* p. 486.

41. *Pub. P., 1963,* pp. 687–91.

42. *PONS,* Sept. 28, 1963. Sixty percent favored and 29 percent opposed a tax reduction.

43. *Senate Hearings, Revenue Act of 1963*, pp. 119–21. There was speculation that Byrd hoped to delay the bill at least until the presentation of the fiscal 1965 budget. *BW*, Nov. 9, 1963, p. 42.

44. *Senate Hearings, Revenue Act of 1963*, esp. pp. 461–75, 893–911, 935–42, 965–1006, 1030–36, 1767–68.

45. Ibid., pp. 1219–25.

46. The Business Committee for Tax Reduction was the third largest lobbying spender in 1963 ($141,785). *Congressional Quarterly Almanac, 1964* (Washington, 1965), pp. 902–3.

47. *Senate Hearings, Revenue Act of 1963*, testimony of Treasury Secretary Dillon regarding expected budget deficits, p. 227. Dillon's forecast was on an administrative budget basis. On the National Income Accounts basis, which includes most federal trust fund transactions and uses the accrual system of accounting, government officials projected a surplus for fiscal 1965.

48. *Pub. P., 1963*, pp. 80–81.

49. Despite the lower tax rates, federal receipts from both individual and corporate income taxes increased in the fiscal years after the tax reduction, just as Kennedy's economic advisers had predicted. *Statistical Abstract, 1966*, p. 392.

50. Pechman, "Individual Income Tax," p. 256, table 2.

51. *Statistical Abstract, 1966*, pp. 218, 322–23, 496.

CHAPTER 14

1. Only a relatively few of the president's requests had been signed into law at the time of his death. They included the extension of corporation and excise taxes, federal aid to medical schools and mental health, ratification of the nuclear test ban treaty, extension of the feed grain program, and a joint resolution providing for the settlement of serious railroad labor disputes. Unpassed and in various stages of congressional action were important measures concerning aid for college education, Area Redevelopment Act amendments, civil defense shelters, civil rights, conservation, credits for the wheat sale to the Soviet Union, foreign aid, tax revision, an Urban Affairs Department, urban mass transportation, a wilderness system, and youth employment.

2. *Senate Documents*, 88 Cong., 1 sess., no. 53, pp. 55–57, 59–66. The historian Thomas A. Bailey has warned that emphasis on the "Box Score"— the percentage of presidential requests approved by Congress—can be misleading and possibly harmful. It could lead a president to recommend only sure things. *Presidential Greatness* (New York, 1966), p. 329.

3. For examples, see *The Progressive*, Nov. 1961, pp. 3–4; *New Republic*, Sept. 10, 1962, p. 2; May 18, 1963, p. 2. AFL-CIO official Walter Reuther charged in February 1963, that the Kennedy program was too conservative. *NYT*, Feb. 16, 1963, p. 1.

4. *Pub. P., 1963*, pp. 397–98, 468–71, 601–6, 641–42, 646–48, 687–91.

5. *PONS*, various releases. See chart 1.

6. Elmer E. Cornwell, Jr., *Presidential Leadership and Public Opinion* (Bloomington, 1965), p. 303.

7. Among the major pieces of legislation passed within months of Kennedy's death were tax revision, foreign aid, wheat sale credits, civil rights, and federal aid to college education. Further in the future were the enactment of Medicare, an Urban Affairs Department, and a Poverty Corps.

8. See Richard Wilson, "What Happened to the Kennedy Program," *Look,* Nov. 17, 1964, pp. 117 ff. Wilson interviewed congressional leaders in both parties.

9. Secretary of Commerce Luther Hodges, Secretary of Labor Arthur Goldberg, and Attorney General Robert Kennedy joined with the president during the fall of 1961 to specifically deny that the administration was antibusiness. See *NYT,* Oct. 3, 1961, p. 25; Oct. 21, 1961, p. 8; Nov. 14, 1961, p. 30; *Pub. P., 1961,* pp. 708, 773–74.

10. From an article by Sylvia Porter, reprinted in *CR,* 88 Cong., 1 sess., pp. 20536–37.

11. *Nation's Business,* Feb. 1963, pp. 34–35 ff.

12. *NYT,* May 1, 1963, p. 1.

13. *BW,* May 18, 1963, p. 204. While acknowledging the improved relations between business and the New Frontier, the magazine predicted that the situation would not last. In 1964 Kennedy was expected to stress new welfare bills and be more responsive to the election-year demands of organized labor. Ibid., May 4, 1963, p. 41.

14. *Fortune,* May, 1963, pp. 103–4.

15. *Pub. P., 1963,* pp. 863–64.

16. *WSJ,* Nov. 19, 1963, p. 18.

17. See especially the columns by Washington correspondent James Reston, *NYT,* Oct. 25, 1963, p. 30; Nov. 15, 1963, p. 34. The widely-respected Reston predicted in November that Kennedy would be reelected, but, the journalist wrote, the people "really don't believe in him."

18. In 1962 the Small Business Administration used the following guidelines to determine which businesses were "small": manufacturing concerns with less than 250 employees; wholesale and construction firms with less than $5 million in annual sales or receipts; retail and service companies with less than $1 million in annual sales or receipts. White House Committee on Small Business, *Small Business in the American Economy* (Washington, 1962), pp. 1–2.

19. For general studies on small business, see Bunzel, *American Small Businessman* and Harmon Zeigler, *The Politics of Small Business* (Washington, 1961). Many commentators have cited small businessmen as sources of support for the Radical Right. See Seymour Martin Lipset, "Three Decades of the Radical Right: Coughlinites, McCarthyites, and Birchers," in *Radical Right,* ed. Bell, pp. 341–42; Bunzel, pp. 256–59; Zeigler, pp. 61–62.

20. NFIB membership in the early 1960s was approximately 220,000.

21. For discussions of social responsibility in business, see H. I. Ansoff of Lockheed Electronics Company, "Company Objectives: Blueprint or Blue Sky?" *Management Review,* Sept. 1962, pp. 41–46; Earl F. Cheit, "The New Place of Business: Why Managers Cultivate Social Responsibility," in *Business Establishment,* ed. Cheit, pp. 152–92; Peter F. Drucker,

"Big Business and Public Policy," *Business and Society* 3 (Autumn 1962) : 4–13.

22. For a sampling of calls by influential corporate leaders for cooperation between business and government, see Raymond Firestone of Firestone Rubber Company, "National Aims and Business Responsibility," June 20, 1962, speech pamphlet; Roger M. Blough of United States Steel, "The Real Revolutionaries," Sept. 25, 1963, speech pamphlet; Frederick R. Kappel of American Telephone and Telegraph, "Realism in Economic Life," Dec. 1, 1961, speech pamphlet; L. du Pont Copeland of the du Pont Company, "It Takes Two to Make a Partnership Work," Feb. 10, 1964, speech pamphlet; Elliott V. Bell of *Business Week,* "The Way to Make Our Economy Grow," Feb. 19, 1963, speech pamphlet.

23. Business executives and government officials held strikingly similar views on national issues, according to a survey of over 1,400 business leaders and over 100 government officials taken in 1963. Cherne, "1,588 Opinions," p. 31.

24. Arthur M. Schlesinger, Jr., has pithily observed that "In spite of liberal streotypes to the contrary, Wall Street in recent years appears more enlightened on questions of public policy than Main Street." Letter, Dec. 6, 1966, Schlesinger to the author.

25. Bazelon, *Power in America,* p. 107.

26. White, *President, 1964,* p. 86.

27. Heller, *New Dimensions,* p. 33.

28. *Pub. P., 1962,* p. 473.

29. Ibid., pp. 226, 370, 392, 442–43; *Pub. P., 1963,* pp. 719, 800, 807, 859. The exact wording of the story varied slightly.

Selected Bibliography

I originally planned to provide an itemized bibliography. Two reasons, however, prompted me to include only a select bibliographical essay focusing on the most valuable sources. First, since extensive source notes are used to document the text, a complete bibliography seemed unnecessary. Second, most, though not all, of the sources used in the book were cited in the detailed bibliography in my Ph.D. dissertation which is on file at Stanford University and is available on microfilm. I hope that serious students of the subject will consult the notes and the dissertation.

GOVERNMENT DOCUMENTS

Publications by the federal government are a logical starting point for any examination of a presidential administration. Essential to my study were the *Public Papers of the Presidents, John F. Kennedy,* three volumes, one for each year, 1961–63. These volumes contain the bulk of the significant speeches and public writings of President Kennedy. Executive orders and memorandums were conveniently collected in the *Federal Register.* Also important were the various reports of committees appointed by the chief executive, especially those by the Advisory Committee on Labor-Management Policy, the Commission on Equal Employment Opportunity, and the White House Committee on Small

Business. The *Economic Reports of the President, Transmitted to the Congress Together with the Annual Report of the Council of Economic Advisers* were of special value. Issued each January, these reports provide a blueprint for economic policies recommended by the president's chief ecomonic advisers. The Council of Economic Advisers also makes available useful statistical measurements of the economy in its monthly *Economic Indicators*.

Publications by federal departments and agencies offered a treasure of information. *Annual Reports* by the Department of Justice were helpful in appraising antitrust policy. A number of publications of the Department of Commerce proved useful, including the *Statistical Abstract of the United States* and *Business Statistics,* both issued annually; *Long Term Economic Growth, 1860–1965* (Washington, 1966); and quarterly reports on *Export Controls.* The *Department of State Bulletin* provided data regarding foreign relations as they interrelated with economic policy. The State Department also published special reports, such as the 1963 Clay Report on foreign aid. For valuable information concerning research spending, see publications by the National Science Foundation. The economic impacts of armament spending were described in various reports by the United States Arms Control and Disarmament Agency. The *Federal Reserve Bulletin* presented pertinent material about the policies and activities of the Federal Reserve System, while the Small Business Administration's *Annual Reports* furnished data on government efforts to assist small entrepreneurs.

Congressional publications were a rich source for the views of legislators, the public, and interest groups. The *Congressional Record* provided not only opinions and voting records of senators and representatives, but also a wide variety of letters, speeches, articles, and editorials which were inserted into the record by the legislators.

More useful to my study, however, were hearings held by congressional committees. Testimony given at the hearings by spokesmen for various interest groups offered valuable insight into the attitudes of the nonmonolithic business community on specific issues. Particularly significant among the more than seventy different hearings that I used in my research were those conducted by House Committees on Education and Labor, Foreign Affairs, Interstate and Foreign Commerce, Judiciary, and Ways and Means; by the Joint Economic Committee and several of its subcommittees; and by Senate Committees on Aeronautical and Space Sciences, Banking and Currency, Commerce, Finance, Foreign Relations, Government Operations, Interstate and Foreign

Commerce, Judiciary, Labor and Public Welfare, and Small Business. Reports and Documents issued by the two chambers also provided helpful information.

BUSINESS SOURCES

I drew heavily upon publications by business and business-oriented groups, notably the American Bankers Association, American Iron and Steel Institute, American Management Association, American Marketing Association, American Petroleum Institute, Chamber of Commerce of the United States, Committee for Economic Development, National Association of Manufacturers, National Federation of Independent Business, National Planning Association, and National Industrial Conference Board, plus annual reports and interim publications by specific companies.

Business-oriented and trade and industry periodicals and newspapers provided a lode of material, including speeches and articles by executives, editorial opinion, and general business and economic news. Examined intensively for the period 1960–63 and selectively for the years 1964–68 were *Advanced Management-Office Executive, Advertising Age, American Banker, Bankers Monthly, Banking, Barron's, Bulletin of the National Association of Purchasing Agents, Business Management, Business Week, Challenge, Chemical Week, Commercial and Financial Chronicle, Conference Board Record, The Controller, Credit and Financial Management, Distribution Age, Dun's Review, Electrical World, Engineering News-Record, Factory, Financial Analysts Journal, Financial World,* First National City Bank of New York *Monthly Economic Letter, Forbes, Fortune, The General Electric Forum, Harvard Business Review, Investment Dealers Digest, Investograph Stock Survey, Iron Age, Journal of Commerce, The Kiplinger Letter, Magazine of Wall Street, Management Record, Management Review,* Merrill, Lynch, Pierce, Fenner, and Smith's *Security and Industry Survey, Missiles and Rockets, Moody's Stock Survey, Morgan Guaranty Survey, NAM News, Nation's Business, Printers' Ink, Public Utilities Fortnightly, Purchasing Magazine, Sales Management,* Standard and Poor's *The Outlook, Steel, Taxpayer's Dollar, Transport Topics, United Business Service, The Value Line Investment Summary, Wall Street Journal,* and *Western Aerospace.*

Many significant speeches by company and industry executives do not receive wide circulation, being privately printed or mimeographed. The sizable collection of speech pamphlets held by the Stanford University Graduate School of Business offered a rich supplement to my knowledge of business sentiments. In addition, a number of corporate officials furnished helpful answers to my letters which posed questions on specific topics.

BOOKS BY KENNEDY ADVISERS

Invaluable to my study were books about the New Frontier by three of Kennedy's closest advisers: Walter W. Heller, chairman of the Council of Economic Advisers, *New Dimensions of Political Economy* (Cambridge, 1966); Theodore C. Sorensen, *Kennedy* (New York, 1965); and Arthur M. Schlesinger, Jr., *A Thousand Days* (Boston, 1965). A collection of essays by another member of Kennedy's Council of Economic Advisers, James Tobin, *National Economic Policy* (New Haven, 1966), was also useful. Less important, but still helpful, was Secretary of Commerce Luther H. Hodges's *The Business Conscience* (Englewood Cliffs, 1963).

OTHER SOURCES

The *New York Times,* polls on a variety of issues by the American Institute of Public Opinion (*Public Opinion News Service*), and a host of news and opinion periodicals were perused for additional information. Also adding to my understanding of the subject were books and articles by scholars and specialists in specific areas. Although less significant for my purpose than government documents, business sources, and accounts by administration insiders, a select number of these special studies deserve mention even in this abbreviated essay.

For a lively, often annecdotal narrative of Kennedy's relationship with the business community, see Hobart Rowen, *The Free Enterprisers: Kennedy, Johnson, and the Business Establishment* (New York, 1964). An overview of the economic policies of the New Frontier is provided by Seymour Harris, *Economics of the Kennedy Years* (New York, 1964) and *The Economics of Political Parties* (New York, 1962). Helpful for an understanding of the role of the Council of Economic Advisers is Edward S. Flash, Jr., *Economic Advice and Presidential Leadership* (New York, 1965). An admirable résumé of federal fiscal policy since 1945 is given in Wilfred Lewis, Jr., *Federal Fiscal Policy in the Postwar Recessions* (Washington, 1962).

Among the many studies about the ideology of business in modern America, I found the following to be particularly valuable: Raymond A. Bauer, Ithiel de Sola Pool, and Lewis A. Dexter, *American Busi-*

ness and Public Policy: The Politics of Foreign Trade (New York, 1963); Earl F. Cheit, ed., *The Business Establishment* (New York, 1964); John H. Bunzel, *The American Small Businessman* (New York, 1962); R. Joseph Monsen, Jr., *Modern American Capitalism: Ideologies and Issues* (Boston, 1963); and Frances X. Sutton, et al., *The American Business Creed* (Cambridge, 1956).

Informative on the subject of ethics in business are Raymond C. Baumhart, "How Ethical Are Businessmen?" *Harvard Business Review* 39 (July–Aug. 1961): 6–19; Theodore L. Thau, "The Business Ethics Advisory Council: An Organization for the Improvement of Ethical Performance," *The Annals of the American Academy of Political and Social Science* 343 (Sept. 1962): 128–41; and Hodges, *The Business Conscience.*

Useful on the role of business in political and lobbying activities are Paul W. Cherington and Ralph L. Gillen, *The Business Representative in Washington* (Washington, 1962); James Deakin, *The Lobbyists* (Washington, 1966); David J. Galligan, *Politics and the Businessman* (New York, 1964); and J. J. Wuerthner, Jr., *The Businessman's Guide to Practical Politics* (Chicago, 1961).

For commentaries on the power structure in America, see David Bazelon, *Power in America: The Politics of the New Class* (New York, 1967); C. Wright Mills, *The Power Elite* (New York, 1956); John Kenneth Galbraith, *The New Industrial State* (New York, 1967); Grant McConnell, *Private Power and American Democracy* (New York, 1966); Bernard Nossiter, *The Mythmakers* (Boston, 1964); Michael Reagan, *The Managed Economy* (New York, 1963); and Arnold Rose, *The Power Structure* (New York, 1967).

Antitrust problems are examined in A. D. H. Kaplan, *Big Enterprise in a Competitive System* (Washington, 1964); Richard J. Barber, "Mergers: Threat to Free Enterprise," *Challenge,* Mar. 1963, pp. 6–10, and "The New Partnership, Big Government and Big Business," *New Republic,* Aug. 13, 1966, pp. 17–22; Lee Loevinger, Kennedy's first antitrust chief, "Recent Developments in Antitrust Enforcement," *Antitrust Bulletin* 6 (Jan.–Feb. 1961): 3–7, and "Antitrust in 1961 and 1962," *Antitrust Bulletin* 8 (May–June 1963): 349–79; Adolf A. Berle, Jr., *The American Economic Republic* (New York, 1963); and Estes Kefauver, with the assistance of Irene Till, *In a Few Hands, Monopoly Power in America* (New York, 1965). For a colorful description of the passage of the drug bill in 1962, see Richard Harris, *The Real Voice* (New York, 1964).

The Kennedy administration's efforts to alleviate unemployment and aid depressed areas are described in Arthur M. Okun, ed., *The Battle against Unemployment* (New York, 1965); Conley H. Dillon, *The Area Redevelopment Administration* (College Park, 1964); Sar A. Levitan, *Federal Aid to Depressed Areas* (Baltimore, 1964), and *Federal Manpower Policies and Programs to Combat Unemployment* (Kalamazoo, 1964); and Joseph M. Becker, William Haber, and Sar A. Levitan, *Programs to Aid the Unemployed in the 1960's* (Kalamazoo, 1965). An engaging account of the attempt to amend the wage and hour law in 1961 is found in Tom Wicker, *JFK and LBJ* (New York, 1968).

On the New Frontier labor policy, see Kenneth C. McGuiness, *The New Frontier NLRB* (Washington, 1963); John L. Blackman, Jr., *Presidential Seizure in Labor Disputes* (Cambridge, 1967); Jack Stieber, "The President's Committee on Labor-Management Policy," *Industrial Relations* 5 (Feb. 1966): 1–19; Roderick M. Hills, James Stern, and Joseph Grodin, "A Symposium: Labor Relations and the Kennedy Administration," *Industrial Relations* 3 (Feb. 1964): 5–45; Lloyd Ulman, "The Labor Policy of the Kennedy Administration," *Proceedings of the Fifteenth Annual Meeting of the Industrial Relations Research Association, 1962* (Madison, 1963), pp. 248–62; and David B. Johnson, "The New Frontier Collective Bargaining Policy," *Labor Law Journal* 13 (July 1962): 591–98.

The controversial wage-price guideposts are analyzed in John Sheahan, *The Wage-Price Guideposts* (Washington, 1967); Marvin J. Levine, "The Economic Guidelines," *Labor Law Journal* 18 (Aug. 1967): 478–504; Martin Bronfenbrenner, "A Guidepost-Mortem," *Industrial and Labor Relations Review* 20 (July 1967): 637–49; George Meany, Roger M. Blough, and Neil H. Jacoby, *Government Wage-Price Guideposts in the American Economy* (New York, 1967); and George L. Perry, "Wages and the Guideposts," *American Economic Review* 57 (Sept. 1967): 897–904.

The exciting 1962 steel crisis is detailed in Grant McConnell, *Steel and the Presidency—1962* (New York, 1963), and Roy Hoopes, *The Steel Crisis* (New York, 1963). On the relationship between government and the defense industry, see Richard J. Barber, *The Politics of Research* (Washington, 1966); H. L. Nieburg, *In the Name of Science* (Chicago, 1966); Roger E. Bolton, *Defense Purchases and Regional Growth* (Washington, 1966); and Emile Benoit and Kenneth Boulding, eds., *Disarmament and the Economy* (New York, 1963).

Among the imposing array of books and articles pertaining to foreign aid and foreign trade, those that give particular attention to the Kennedy administration include Bower Aly, ed., *American Trade Policy* (Columbus, 1962); Werner Feld, *The European Common Market and the World* (Englewood Cliffs, 1967); Frank M. Coffin, *Witness for Aid* (Boston, 1964); Stanley D. Metzger, *Trade Agreements and the Kennedy Round* (Fairfax, 1964); and Herbert Feis, *Foreign Aid and Foreign Policy* (New York, 1964). Also useful is David A. Baldwin, *Economic Development and American Foreign Policy, 1943–1962* (Chicago, 1966). For a valuable commentary on the Clay Committee report, see Jacob Viner, George Meany, Fowler Hamilton, Otto Passman, and Paul Hoffman, "The Report of the Clay Committee on Foreign Aid: A Symposium," *Political Science Quarterly* 78 (Sept. 1963): 321–61.

On the knotty balance of payments problem, especially good are studies by Henry C. Aubrey, *The Dollar in World Affairs* (New York, 1964); Walter S. Salant, *The United States Balance of Payments in 1968* (Washington, 1963), and *Does the International Monetary System Need Reform?* (Washington, 1964); and Robert Triffin, *Gold and the Dollar Crisis* (New Haven, 1961).

A concise and cogent examination of tax policy is provided by Joseph Pechman, *Federal Tax Policy* (Washington, 1966). Also see the same author's "Individual Income Tax Provisions of the Revenue Act of 1964," Brookings Institution Government Finance Reprint no. 96 (Washington, 1965). For a colorful description of how tax loopholes are used and abused, see Philip M. Stern, *The Great Treasury Raid* (New York, 1964).

Had I desired a subtitle for this book, I would have chosen "The New Economics and the New Frontier," for the story of the acceptance and use of the new economics by Kennedy and by important segments of the business community is a major theme of this study. Among the important sources which focus on the new economics are the previously cited works by Kennedy's advisers, especially Heller and Tobin, and the two cited books by Seymour Harris. I hope that readers will find the response of business to the new economics chronicled in these pages and convincingly documented by a multitude of source notes.

Index